The Logic of History

New Babylon

Studies in the Social Sciences

11

Mouton · The Hague · Paris

The Logic of History

CHARLES MORAZÉ

Translated and Annotated by
WILSON O. CLOUGH

Mouton · The Hague · Paris

ISBN: 90 279 7781 X

© Original edition: *La Logique de l'Histoire*
   Editions Gallimard, 1967.

Translated from the French by Wilson O. Clough, Litt. D.

© English edition: 1976, Mouton and Co.

Jacket design by Helmut Salden

Printed in The Netherlands

To Monique

Contents

PART I: THE FUNCTION OF HISTORICITY

1. Humanity as the problem 53

I. Collective violences may have been only the fact of a transitory
period in human evolution. They would be the price of the passage
from a natural prehistoric condition to a post-historic scientific state. —
II. The biological condition of humanity appears to destine it for an
organic unity. — III. On the other hand, it appears no less that
humanity perceives itself only through its conflicts. These latter, nevertheless, do not have their origin in the collectivity, but in a natural and
complex function: namely, historicity, the creator of events.

2. The event as datum 68

I. Before being human, the event is a natural event, and as such sketches
the models on which cultural evolution is inscribed. — II. The human
event is specifically cerebral, and is an effectual interpretation of an
apprenticeship in logic, realized by virtue of the historic experience. —
III. This apprenticeship obligates the noting of a distinction between causality and chance.

PART II: THE EXPLORATION OF THE POSSIBILE

I. Events are defined in relation to institutions. Events, as revealers of the disruption of the collective group, one part of which continues while the other accepts the risks of change, are manifested as chance. Institutions, on the other hand, express the average of laws, arranged in evolutive cycles. − II. Whatever is held to be worthy of commemoration is relative to the needs to commemorate before it is relative to what is commemorated. − III. This transfer of an actual event dreamed up into an artificial original or source event is the effect of a logical deepening, and is the cause of an acceleration in history. This transference has its seat in the imaginative faculty.

The imaginative act is a transfiguration of concrete experiences and a chemistry of the future. − I. The imaginative act at first collectively sums up the emotions which are given a living reality by pain and hope, death and regeneration. This content takes the form of a model fixed by institutions. The container transcends in supernatural evocations the conditions of logic. − II. Beginning with the 18th century the cerebral begins to prevail over the emotive in the realm of the imaginative. Nationalistic sentiment serves as a mediator between the emotive ecumenism and the rational humanism.

Works, which constitute events insofar as they are completed, give expression to the imaginative element which events modify. − I. As testimony, they imply that their authors are set apart by what they represent. This process of distinction defines styles. The style of a language is a combination of all the representations. The most effective works have language as their medium of expression, the lightest, more rapid and complete of all acts. − II. Words are born as symbols. When put to the test by sentences, certain words become the abstract signs of operative articulations, others tend to develop algorisms, the use of numbers. As substitutes for realities held to be irreducible, the two unite for a scientific pertinency. But science does not interrupt the process of symbolization.

PART III: ENCOUNTERS WITH THE CERTAIN

Birth, death, and pain are the enduring certitudes. — I. The ways by which generations manage their growths define all social and cultural evolutions, where the relations between men and women are indicative of the degrees of stability and security within human groupings. — II. The agricultural soil, the first factor in production, gives rise to the solidarity of mass. Exchange, a factor of differentiation, leads to the discovery of the articulations of space, and involves technological rivalry. — III. When this process of exchange is imposed from outside, as is the case with all acculturation and particularly of all colonization, the collective regulations of collectivities brought face to face are transformed thereby: enrichment is then a process of aging, pauperization is a swarming.

I. The collective universe conditions the desires and representations of individuals, whose choices are aleatory, matters of chance, insofar as circumstances do not favor certain desires or representations, of which the circumstances then become the causes. — II. Collectivities are excessively attached to options made sacred by a first success. The individual does not challenge this tendency except within a group that is enfeebled, at the risk of his own equilibrium, and as a consequence of physiological laws which are the substratum of sound reasonings, introducing the articulations of reflection into the emotive mass of experiences lived through. — III. The invention of a pertinent innovation is the unconscious product of a voluntary being-in-a-situation. — IV. The unconscious products of a spontaneous logic are ordered according to the necessity of things.

Every element of reality which man's reason masters to make a tool of it becomes a factor in production, which, in turn, masters man. — I. The invention of numbers called natural was inspired by the orders of parental relations; their acquisition was also correlative with the explication of the notion of mass through that of space. The extreme pertinence of realizing these processes inspired the demonstrative spirit. — II. The syllogism, however, is not operative until it can be applied to notions pertinently named as a consequence of concrete experience. — III. Since logical structures are correlative to social structures, abstract analysis does not reach its full development until the moment when man conceives a coherent system of universal law. — IV. When an absolutely dominant society, such as that of bourgeois Europe, has at its disposal a sufficient number of brains which have mastered the processes of the intellect, the rise of science involves the rise of technologies; this science aggravates conflicts before they are made internal.

PART IV: ESSENTIAL HISTORY

I. Human evolutions present four branchings, of which the three first have not conquered the art of demonstration. Savage culture holds to an implicit logic, the Amerindian to an arithmetic sterilized by its too exclusively cosmological ambitions. The Asiatic cultures have not gathered into a system the infinite procedures of their immense experience. — II. More profoundly disturbed than the others by the event, whose power leads to an extreme every process of the replacement of cultures and social classes, the Occident discovered within the tragic of the human condition the most rapid path to the scientific age.

I. The century of enlightenments introduces an era of sciences and technologies without abolishing the need for collective myths. The bourgeois ideology becomes nationalistic. — II. Marxism fails to replace the bourgeois capitalism which is supported by a colonial imperialism. Marxism becomes effective in countries of communitarian traditions which the expansion of an emerging economy destines for a subversion. — III. In the meantime, man has put nature to work and since then depends not only on nature, but on the progress of his own knowledge of it. The play of events, therefore, is found less in the passion of crowds than in the individual situation, and more in scientific operations than in the decisions of States, from which history begins to escape by becoming humanitarian.

Translator's foreword

Professor Charles Morazé had undertaken no simple task in his *The Logic of History*, for his primary goal is no less than the search for some consistency within the record of human history, some clue to cause and effect, that might enable man in his present dilemmas to proceed less dangerously. The product of some fifteen years of concentration on his topic, this book proposes a more adequate synthesis of the so-called 'sciences of man', both for the under-standing of past and present, and as a help for the future. As the great age of technological advances, unprecedented in previous history, begins to reveal its limitations and its threats, his answer is not sought in a moratorium on science, but in an extension of its best methodology to all that concerns man as man, his physiology, psychology, socio-biology, his origins and his collective representations. The obstacles to such an intellectual ecumenism are many, not the least being the inertia of habit; but the attempt must be made.

Mr. Morazé comes to his task from an impressive range of activities. Lecturer at the Ecole Pratique des Hautes Etudes, an editor and director of *Annales*, author of various books, delegate to international conferences and member of international committees of Unesco, one-time member of Mendès-France's cabinet, placed by De Gaulle over all communication media during the Algerian crisis, he has shared from the inside the history of France over the past four decades.

Mr. Morazé began his career with a special interest in economic and social history. Beginning with his second book, *La France Bourgeoise* (1946), his attention was drawn to the importance of systems of representation, and the possibility that somewhere within them lay some logical clue. This interest persisted in his *Les Bourgeois Con-*

quérants (translated in 1966 as *The Triumph of the Middle Classes,* and well received). Participating on an international commission to attempt *A History of the Scientific and Cultural Development of Humanity,* he found his problem enlarging beyond further postponement.

An earlier work, *The French and the Republic,* had viewed the return of De Gaulle to power as a consequence of the failure of French capitalism to find a solution in Algeria, and had led Morazé to articles demanding a reform of French education. Invited by De Gaulle in 1958 to act as an adviser, Morazé eventually withdrew from the post in protest at the lack of a genuine interest in the problems of education and information. He succeeded only in helping create an Institute of Interethnic Studies, and a National Commission on the same, which he served as president. Mr. Morazé has also been a founding member of the National Foundation of Political Sciences and the National Foundation of the House of the Sciences of Man, positions which have facilitated his studies. He serves also on the directive Council of the Ecole Polytechnique.

The interventions of chance brought the present work to this translator's attention: a brief acquaintance with Mr. Morazé in 1947 when he participated in an Institute on International Affairs at the University of Wyoming, and, incidentally, proved to be an enthusiastic mountain climber; the more recent kindness of the gift of this present work; and the temptation on my part to undertake to render the book into English, no simple item, though I have been generously assisted by letters from Mr. Morazé.

The emphasis on *logic* in the title is Gallic in its insistence on intellect as a tool for the attack upon the problems to be surveyed. The major problem, as Mr. Morazé's Preface admits, has been that of a synthesis of divergent fields. Abstracting from already abstract sciences, the author has had to keep the general reader in mind. The book, therefore, is not easy reading; and the reader is advised to persevere, for after the Preface and Chapter 1, the language becomes somewhat more concrete. This work is not historical narrative as such; nor is it a plea for any one science — anthropology, biology, physiology, political science, sociology, economics, linguistics — but a review of man's emotive, imaginative, and intellectual history, as experienced over millenia of time, and as embodied in his institutions, his science, and his representative arts.

The definition of history shifts with the centuries. Early man viewed all through seasonal, vegetative, and anthropomorphic symbols. Thucydides in the fifth century B.C. first insisted on verifiable fact and ignored supernatural interpretations. Aristotle attempted to bring order into politics, and Polybius in the second century B.C., seeking an explanation for Rome's sudden rise to power and her challenge to the fatal cycle of nations, found it in Rome's representative government. The Middle Ages, far from objective, nevertheless added a universal system of dating and a teleological system which brought its measure of order. Analogies with geometry and celestial mathematics appealed to the Age of Enlightenment; but only after Darwin could an evolutionary view make its appearance. French positivism, then, especially Auguste Comte, taught that social phenomena might be reduced to laws, and that the scientific view was the third and highest stage of man's advancement.

Mr. Morazé's analogies are primarily biological and evolutionary, though he is too thoroughly twentieth century to justify a search for nineteenth century antecedents. The biological tree which pictures the evolution of life, the genealogy, as it were, of man's physiological and intellectual ancestry, is the favored scheme. The rise and fall of species, for a time adaptive, then failing to forestall replacement, may serve as a pattern and a warning. But man introduces a unique element, the rise of inventiveness, the search for causes, the use of the logic of demonstration and experimentation, the contributions of the imaginative and the reflective, all of which at least warrants the hope of playing some part in his own destiny.

To the obvious element of determinism — man, too, began his long story as an object in nature — Mr. Morazé applies the term *historicity*, those actualities within the nature of man and his environment that must, willy-nilly, be confronted, the part imposed on man by the nature of things, the compelling hand of *necessity*, a necessity which in the afterthought may appear to have decided more of his fate than his boasted deeds or his deepest desires could accomplish. In fact, man's deeds themselves become an element in historicity, imposing and entailing consequences both factual and imaginative such as he, in his ignorance, could neither see nor forestall. It is this combination of man's contribution and the implacable power of things and events that constitutes the complex logic of history. The argument, then, is that if man can more clearly comprehend his own past and present, he may in some degree enter into the determination of his future.

We may say that man's history has been a perpetual search for an equilibrium among forces. Yet his environment includes himself and his own institutions; and stability itself may be a hazard, precluding a sufficient alertness to change. How much, then, shall be granted to man's will and intent, how much to the force of inertia within a temporary stability, and how much to the pressure of things? Are there any certitudes? At what point may stability harbor senescence? What factors lie behind the immense acceleration of Western civilization in the last four centuries? What has caused its deadly wars? Mr. Morazé observes that however inevitable the events of World War II, there must have been a time when indeterminate forces, if more clearly understood by a sufficient number of minds, might have been open to modification by man. Does history, then, do it all by itself? Or has man some part in his own destiny? If so, why, then, is it so easy to destroy and so difficult to unite against self-destruction? Such are some of the questions raised by this book.

In his Preface, Mr. Morazé mentions three or four names which have modified his thinking. Hoping to find therein some clues to his major thesis, I asked him if he might kindly give me in a sentence or two for each what element had influenced him more specifically. Here are his answers, slightly condensed:

Claude Lévi-Strauss: 'Anthropologists until recently assigned "savage" customs to a pre-logical stage. Lévi-Strauss, on the contrary, in his thesis "The Elementary Structures of Kinship", shows that the relations between relatives as well as marriage customs obey strict rules analogous to very modern mathematical formulations. No less rigorous demands are found in the composition of the narratives studied in the four volumes of his *Mythologies*.'

Jean Piaget: 'Jean Piaget has studied how the child gives evidence of intelligence. Each of the stages through which his personality passes in its growth brings about some new success in the art of locating himself in the midst of things, space, time. At first by gesture, then by reflection, he proceeds to experiences more successful, thereby learning to forecast the result when it is stable and determined. Thus he is finally able to realize objectively a cerebral operation which is reversible; for example, subtract what he has added.'

Kurt Goedel: 'Goedel, Austrian logician of mathematics, has formulated and demonstrated by different methods a basic theorem according to which the universe, as it can be expressed by the most rigorous human language, cannot be the result of pure deduction alone.'

Julian Huxley: 'Julian has often insisted to me on the importance of experimentation in the sciences. It seems to him to have played in the nineteenth century an even more important role than mathematics.'[1]

Now, these four summaries immediately suggest a central thesis of major importance for the understanding of Professor Morazé's argument, which we may condense as follows: Man has emerged over many millenia, evolving in a universe which does exist, and which cannot be a product of his imagination only. In that emergence, he has moved gradually and progressively toward intelligence, by stages recognizable both in history and in the child, from the emotive to the cerebral, toward the utilization of experimentation as a means of participating increasingly in his own destiny.

Having accepted this broad foundation for his meditations, Mr. Morazé wastes no time on certain philosophical speculations of origin or epistemology, but proceeds to examine that evolution in terms of historicity (the nature of things) and history (man's own contribution). In the course of that argument, certain terms recur. These include:

Collectivity: The totality of a social or cultural group as distinct from ethnic or political entities, though the terms overlap.

Representation: The signs, symbols, or images, including art and linguistic symbols, by which a collectivity represents, consciously or unconsciously, its deepest emotive or imaginative concepts of itself, its past and present, its heroic figures, and its destiny. These may take the form of monuments, art objects, institutions, rituals, myths, or beliefs.

Grammar and syntax: These terms may have a special meaning, as the study of the basic elements or principles of any science or art, and syntax as any connected or orderly arrangement of such material.

Diachronic and synchronic: Originating in linguistics, these terms there referred to the study of a given language within a specified period, such as the present (syn-chronic, one time), treated as 'pure' or fixed grammar, and ignoring previous history; or as referring to the study of a language over its known duration, its history and evolution (dia-chronic, across time). Diachronic presupposes synchronic studies, and the latter is said to be the more scientific. As to our present world, the technological present (synchronic) may be contrasted with the effort (humanist) to see how it got that way

1. Letter from Charles Morazé, as translated, January 13, 1971. Translator's note.

during historic time (diachronic). Can the two be synthesized for the salvaging of civilization?

Other terms may be noted in footnotes as required.

For the American reader, Mr. Morazé's illustrations may appear Mediterranean. Yet the roots of Western civilization, for better or for worse, were in the Mediterranean basin; and the result is a book in the Gallic tradition, alert to its own inheritance, somewhat unsparing of its less informed readers. It must be admitted, for example, that Mr. Morazé's Table of Contents makes more sense *after* one has read his book than as an Introduction to his thesis, for an already abstract work is summarized to the point of a genuine obscurity. Hence I have ventured here a resumé, hopefully a little less difficult, and with apologies to the author. I shall not treat here the Preface, since its purpose is to trace in some degree the genesis of this work.

RESUMÉ OF THE ARGUMENT

Part I. *The function of historicity*. Chapter 1: 'History as the problem'. Biology would seem to destine man for unity, as all one species. The Renaissance promise of a universal humanism has not been realized, however. Yet our wars may be transitory, between the pre-historic and the post-scientific. Human evolution has proceeded through conflicts, nor can humanity ever escape the pressures of living, the intervention of *things*. This latter element, which places man in his cosmos, limits his physiology, his liberty, his consciousness and his will, and so directs much of his history, is here labelled *historicity*.

Chapter 2: 'The event as datum'. Since historicity has no specific organ, it must be studied through events, especially the natural events which preceded man's own contribution, the cerebral event. Matter was the first pure event, and man exists by virtue of mineral, vegetable and animal nature. Only after long apprenticeship with natural events did man notice cause and effect, the logic of events. Science had to withdraw the event from the mythical and the emotive to distinguish causality from chance, to proceed to reflection. This progress owed much to the Greeks, and was the cause of tragedy. Millenia had to pass before the discovery of the syllogism and the art of demonstration. A science of chance, the aleatory, had to wait longer still.

Part II. *The exploration of the possible*. Chapter 3: 'Memorable deeds'. The deed fascinates not by ethics but by excess, and is memorable as a collectivity makes it so, in its need to commemorate and to find itself. The event seems chance, whereas institutions evolve and are organized. Yet the great deed is an event challenging some aspect of an order. First commemorated were seasonal events, then family and political events, only later intellectual events, as the deed became dated, less mythological, and provoked reflection. Deeds confronting opposition become 'explorations of possibles'. The imaginative faculty decides what is commemorated, and in time proceeds to reflection, and so to conceptual systems. Thus comes a 'logical deepening', a speeding up of future possibles.

Chapter 4: 'Conquests of the imaginative'. The imaginative is the point where 'man's nature intervenes in its own concerns'. It is first charged with emotivity, and so animates speech, representations, myths, to translate experience. Myths are what is left of pre-history, of man in nature. They record man's earliest awareness of birth, pain, death, hunger. Only in time do they take form in institutions. The imaginative creates pieties, beliefs, to be challenged by history. Greek rationalism returns after the Renaissance, but on a firmer base, as the cerebral begins to prevail over the emotive. Nationalisms lie between the older ecumenism of faith and the newer universality of science, as scholars seek an orderly catalogue of experience in emotive arts as in scientific discoveries.

Chapter 5: 'Successful expressions'. Works of art preserve great deeds. Long labor lies behind style, given the setting of a collectivity, a language, and events to modify the imaginative. The author-artist is agent-carrier of new articulations, shaped by what has preceded, sensitive to emerging differences, yet bound to the signs of his milieu. Language is the most economical tool of expression, both for beauty and exactitude. Words, symbols, relate to complex cultures, yet·question them. To serve as abstract tools for reason, calculation, and logic, they must be drained of the emotive. Thus a long history of language lies behind logic and science, an increase in exact vocabularies, though this does not destroy the emotive language of the arts.

Part III. *Encounters with the certain.* Chapter 6: 'Collective regulations'. Certain basic certitudes are given, from pre-history: as birth, death, the effort to keep alive. These are constants, and, though indirectly, the source of science. The family was the cell, the image of stability and security. Numbers of children were valued when mortality was high; fewer, with better times. Society has wavered between reckless numbers and the risk of too few, as upper classes limited them. Women, too, might weaken or renew energy for resistance. Agricultural production increased family solidarity, and the masses were relied on for renewal. Surplus introduced privilege, finally permitting some to claim transcendental authority, the disposal of lands, even of marriages, and the use of palaces and temples. Exchange brought merchant challengers, rivals in technology. Industry came to depend on colonization, transfiguring those invaded. As individual ownership grew, the poor were thrust into cities and poverty, though revolt was staved off by rising standards of living. Science joined with industry for progress, but without an aging process, not foreseen by its agents.

Chapter 7: 'Determinations'. Man is less free than he appears, subject to physical and genetic laws, born in a culture not his making. Yet the illusion of freedom plays its part in evolution. Earliest discoveries, fire, metals, were by-products of natural activities, but each success in nature seduces us to new trials. The imaginative world was first vast and confusing, and reflection small. Collectivities dislike excess, and are attached to what has worked in the past. Thus innovation depends on exceptional persons. Yet the individual challenges the collectivity at his own risk, and when it is enfeebled. Like society, he begins with the emotive, and education is necessary to teach historic sequences, and to reduce self-reference for the reflective and the objective. Yet pure objectivity frightens. But history is less great deeds than the evolution of innovations. The imaginative, however mysterious in origin, is tested by reason. Inventions arise from a situation demanding solution, and threaten some previous order. Cerebral labor demands a setting, and, in seeking order, finds the order of things. The inventor is less author than agent.

Chapter 8: 'The order of things'. Each advance is a maturation in a milieu prepared for it, in a sequence of collective readjustments. Science extrapolates its findings as durable in time, yet open to refinement. Each certitude weakens the link between emotive and reason. Results create new needs, so innovations may become masters. Numbers originated in the duality of family. Other factors entered, as weight and distance. Evaluating quantities for exchange, man discovered mass in space, and numbers, each such item leading to reflection and demonstration. The syllogism in the ancient world halted short of experiment. Only later in Europe did it operate with guide-marks, maps, voyages, new names, a vocabulary for physics and chemistry. Commerce led to calculation on risks, the relations between causality and chance, and so to mathematicians and analysis. Thus enters a quantitative era, equipped with physical and verbal tools. Man is encouraged to think that, given sufficient good brains, he can conquer all. Yet nature dictates still, and new progress arouses an uneasiness, a new submissiveness, a new wish for unity.

Part IV. *Essential history.* Chapter 9: 'Inspired societies'. Four types of society emerge: (1) Savage, with no history except simple skills, and a search for culprits instead of causes; (2) Amerindian, with castles and temples, an arithmetic of addition, and calendars, but sterilized in sacred rituals; (3) The Orient, especially China, immensely ingenious and with many workshops, but handicapped by ideographic writing and ancestor worship, and not organized into a body of science and logic; and (4) That between the Indus and the Atlantic, a crossroads, disturbed by violence, yet pushed to monotheism, the syllogism, demonstration, the vocabulary of science, inheritor of the Ionian alphabet, written language, arithmetic and geometry, and abstract concepts. This increase is cerebral, stimulated by commerce, colonization, technology, directed by experiment and reflection. Yet all is at the price of relativity within knowledge, and conflicts external and internal.

Chapter 10: 'Humanity considered'. A rising awareness of changes in the human condition centers on the rise of the bourgeois, of nationalism, and freedom of enterprise, with Great Britain setting the pace. Exaltation of the individual is accompanied by a nostalgia for the past, as romanticism returns to legends, epics, and mythologies of national histories, with warlike results. Marx failed to perceive Russia's future or the advance in worker status. Old representations linger, and a recourse to feudal standards of heroism. The historic event has still its mysterious power. Man has advanced from physical labor as power to fossil energy, and to the technological. Having put nature to· work, man cannot turn back. Science is too much attached to physics still, neglecting the biological, psychological and sociological. Society becomes a single organism, with replacement from within, not by conquests among nations. Great deeds are devalued as man becomes more reflective, and as science prevails over decisions of States. Events still flow from historicity, and nature still decides results; but mankind may be on the verge of a humanitarian morality, a challenge and a hope.

Professor Morazé views this work as introductory in nature, and, despite the pressures of many activities, hopes to pursue the thesis further. In the meantime, so he writes,[2] he has in mind a book on *General de Gaulle and the Republic,* a study of the logical processes behind a rise to power and its consequences; an investigation into how the logic of science originates and is inscribed in the myths, institutions, and religious representations of people; a study of the logical reasons for ethnic groupings in the world; possible articles investigating Islamic property laws, the logical necessities behind the hagiographies of certain Saints of the Roman Church, or the Egyptian myth of Horus as explaining certain aspects of Egyptian mathematics.

It is but natural that Professor Morazé's approach should find its antagonists, notably Mr. Henri Marrou, himself a historian of civilization, writing in *Le Monde* for July 12, 1967. Though Mr. Marrou urges a reading of *The Logic of History* as a stimulating, even scintillating, work, and salutes the author for his hardihood and daring, he asserts at the outset his almost total disagreement with it.

It is not merely that the book is difficult reading, because of the 'distortions of obviously excessive condensations' (Mr. Morazé's own phrase). For Mr. Morazé appears to be rebuked first for having changed his vocation from that of historian to philosopher, in search of a 'universal' history, and a 'logic of development'. Though Mr. Marrou sees the work correctly as of a quite different order from the 'comparative morphology of cultures' such as Spengler and Toynbee undertook, he strangely links Morazé with Teilhard de Chardin, but as a 'materialist Teilhard'. (The gap between them would seem obvious: Morazé, from the outset a student of economic and political history, Teilhard a theologian persuaded that evolution may be incorporated within an ancient faith.)

Mr. Marrou next accuses Morazé of 'neo-scientism', in 'the good old tradition of French positivism', writing what is actually a history of man's scientific development and the genesis and fruition of modern technology. This understood, says Marrou, all becomes clear: History is Greece, geometry and the syllogism, then the Renaissance, and modern science. The rest lies outside this major trajectory. Thus we come to the final charge of 'anti-humanism', and a quotation from Dostoievski that 'all the science in the world is not worth the tears of children'. Mr. Morazé therefore, it appears, 'puts in danger what the Christian heritage has passed on to us, to know . . . the absolute value of the human person'.

2. Letter to translator, April 2, 1971.

It seems hardly necessary to indicate that this critique is scarcely an evaluation of Morazé's actual thesis, but the expression of another aspect of the European inheritance, to be assessed as the reader may prefer.

For Mr. Morazé in his work has surrendered neither to pessimism nor mysticism. Far from being anti-humanist, he opens his Preface with profound concern over the turn European history has taken in the twentieth century. His scientism is less technological in essence than a plea to make use of the best tools of the methodology of dispassionate and accurate examination of all the data available on man as individual and within his collectivities. Again and again, he returns to the power of things; but no less does he emphasize man's slow maturation toward a fruitful cerebral participation in his own destiny. He sternly reminds us that to believe man without resources in time of crisis is to believe him no longer human. Yet his future can no longer be entrusted solely to mythologies, crowd passions, or charismatic leaders aspiring to 'great deeds' of the impulsive sort. Deeds of the mind must take their place among the elements at work; for the logic of history is not yet a closed volume. There is still a possibility of a reassertion of humanity, in its fullest of definitions. Such are some of the challenges of this book, one demanding close attention, yet rewarding in its analysis and its insights.

WILSON O. CLOUGH

Author's preface to the English edition
A new link between biology and history

Several years have passed since a French editor asked permission to publish in a collection of 'Essays' a manuscript which I had written chiefly for myself; namely, *The Logic of History*. Thanks to Mr. Wilson O. Clough and his faithful translation, I find myself now, perhaps paradoxically, urged to acquaint my new readers more clearly than I could do earlier with the reasons for this book, a collection of reflections written, as it were, on the verge of another work — completed but still not released — which might bestow on this present one its truer significance.

The fact is that in 1967 I felt neither prepared nor entitled to reveal the nature of an engrossing undertaking of which I can speak today, at least in brief summation. Thus the pages which follow will not be offered as a simple literary or philosophic exercise based on what everyone already knows; rather, they will touch upon a new scientific insight in order to test certain immediate consequences.

My concern as a historian has for a long time been the effort to comprehend what the knowledge of facts and what any purely quantitative research, however far they may be pushed, are not able to tell us: namely, how the beliefs and scientific knowledge on which great cultural traditions have built their more or less durable certitudes are manifested, are developed, are replaced, or are made more secure one with another. Could the failures be compensated for by treating cultures as if they were living entities whose genetic messages are transmitted, and in their case, transformed when their particular existences have dissolved? To write a history of mankind on the biological model would not be a novelty; nor would such a work at this time compete with illustrious predecessors if it did not rest on a datum which they had overlooked.

No culture would have lasted or even existed if the essence of what constituted its beliefs and out of which it made its religion, its arts and sciences had not that minimum of coherence which would permit one to speak of a *system*. This affirmation, which owes so much to linguists and anthropologists, will strengthen in France the vogue of structuralism. Could one attempt to proceed farther: does not every system and every structure obey universal rules of composition? Numerous examples borrowed from all sorts of historical epochs and domains permit us to establish *de facto* a sort of internal code whose mathematical theory is of the most complex, but whose formal aspect is of the simplest. Ignoring objects as such — that is, when they relate to concrete and external experience — such a code would treat solely of the relations which objects bear one to another; relationships which, considered in their reciprocal status, are capable of eventually establishing or forming notions which are in their turn comparable, as were the original objects. Furthermore, the code will retain from this relationship their positive or negative qualities. For example, in the category of procreation, we may note a *minus* of relationship between persons of the same sex and a *plus* of bisexuality. Further, the relationship of Father-Mother will be positive, but that of Brother-Sister negative, and negative also the relationship of consanguinity-conjugality. This survey concentrating at the minimum on three objects will be translated into a scheme in which six variables will take the value of either a plus or a minus.

More than twenty years of research with a faithful corps of workers, protected from all publicity, has progressed to broad inventories and refined the principles and methods of this analogic analysis. Before we evoke some pertinent examples, let us point out first what adds to their interest: The code thus established is in form identical with the genetic code. But let us state clearly that this mental code was not thought up *to imitate* the biological code; the mental code was set up more than ten years before I had heard of the other, which in itself would not have sufficed, not will it suffice, to justify the extrapolation of biologic findings in the area of mental facts.

What the genetic achieves concretely for the historian is only an abstract model for systematic analysis. This mental code requires itself no less than sixty-four types of elementary combinations, among which twenty have a specific significance. These sixty-four or twenty types, as is true also for biological genes, may be written out by means of an alphabet of four complementary letters, two by two.

These constitutive types or logical 'words' permit the construction of more elaborate structures. The first degree of such constructions does not constitute a closed system unless at least four such 'words' of the codes are caused to intervene, that is to say, four of what the linguists call actants.[1] These are specifically the four persons who constitute the nucleus of consanguinity in primitive societies; and the same model applies to the myths within the same cultures.

History, furthermore, bears witness to the fact that the reproduction of beliefs obeys, at least in certain cases, the same principles as those of the genetic-mental code; that is to say, the reproduction passes through a phase during which a system of meaning or signification is transformed into its contrary. A double transformation thus illustrates specifically the course of the Christian faith as opposed to ancient beliefs. A mythological representation will serve to summarize: The Saint George famed since the time of Constantine is, like Perseus, represented as victorious over the Dragon; but St. George, the martyr, is brought to his death by the anger of the false gods. The City of his triumph is that of the true God as opposed to the city of men; the Woman who witnesses his exploit is the authentic Faith of the faithful Church, not chained to be delivered over to the monster which she, on the contrary, holds in chains. All carnal link is besides excluded between such a man and such a woman. The archaic image of Roman Christianity, and even later, the icons, thus reproduced in negative form the ancient system which made Perseus the spouse of Andromeda, returned to her terrestrial city. In the course of time, and to the degree that medieval Europe prepares the renaissance, hagiographies and painting forget the original significance of the enchained Dragon, and by stages and finally integrally reconstitute the ancient myth. When Delacroix gave the name of Saint George to a warrior cavalier on a small island where the woman is bound, and which Pegasus is permitted to approach, he re-attaches the episode to a cycle become now entirely pagan.

In the same manner modern ideologies are likewise systems in evolution, such as makes each the contrary of another. Marxism is better understood by the negations it introduced into the heart of the mental structures of liberalism. Similarly, the separation of the three powers demanded by democracy of the parliamentarian type

---

1. The term *actants,* borrowed from linguistic usage, does not signify only a person as actor, but may, according to the setting, stand for an object, a social unit, a group, an idea, a number.

has taken the reverse form of the monarchical certitudes. The more detailed the analysis of the vocabulary the clearer the proofs. The King, Elect of God, was the opposite of the popular sovereignty which named its own elect; the manners by which costumes were sanctioned and laws promulgated as well as the content of certain notions as a nation, such as legitimacy, legality, providence or chance, show between them, according to the two examples, now certain relationships, now their contraries. The word to *deliberate*, for example, meant for a king that he meditates alone, confronting his conscience; in a democracy, it demands a public discussion, decided by a majority vote. And when the twentieth century returns to the political scene "El Mando de Uno," the command of one, of providential men, it represents again a return of the political structures which democracy had assumed to be contradicted.

The mental code which with all necessary precautions for precision describes such interlockings of concepts as well as the contradictory life of their vocabularies, gives rise also to certain geometric arithmetic aspects no less precise. Thus the code is involved in its way in the future of the sciences, or at least permits a clarification of the history of their progress. Geometry is not pure space nor is time pure number; but the development and unfolding of the operative reason is that of a continuing dialectic between intuition and analysis, for which the mental code supplies the twofold image.

This code, or mental image, however, as applied to any epoch or any culture, is not capable of offering by itself alone a rational explanation of the modifications that occur in a given milieu as they are affected by time. The code but allows one to authenticate more clearly what has happened, but without the determinations that followed on that fact. The history of cultural entities or units, as is true of genetic psychology in the individual, asserts that in certain moments — for example, as occurred on the brink of the industrial civilization, or as occurs at the different ages in which a child masters a particular form of reasoning — a sudden surge takes place and brings to maturation all of a sudden the part played on the sensitive intuition by arithmetic or calculation. From such occurences arise — or may not arise as yet — the account and description of some mathematical function or of some perfectly lucid logic. Or, if one needs a clearer example, the same part is played by the critical reason at work upon the logic of myths. The biologist, to be frank, is no better situated; for to know the code by which the message of life is conserved, or is changed in the course of reproduction, is far from warranting a complete account of the nature of things or of life. Consider, for example, primarily the interactions between the organism and its millieu, or better yet its environments, physical, organic and social, as a prelude, along with instinct, to a predication of a future mental progress. Perhaps the historian may even have an advantage here — as was hinted in the original Preface — to treat of phenomena infinitely more deliberate and on the macroscopic scale.

But why, if such be the case, was nothing said of such a code in *The Logic of History?* Because the matter was too important to be approached without due precautions. It was necessary to invoke a rule of silence before one could test the consequences of propositions not without their risks.

Today such consequences appear to us to be beyond risk; for if the mental code simplifies and brings order after the event within the recitals of history, it appears — when reduced to what may now be authorized for statement — incapable of replacement by some arbitrary fabrication of beliefs or ideologies. It is nothing other than an analogic commentary, important for the historian, but powerless in the hands of the authors of deeds or inventions.

I was in 1967 neither so certain nor so assured. Furthermore, the present statement responds solely to the question which follows: What becomes of the historical narrative so conceived on an evolutionary model whose deepest structures and their movements would remain beyond prejudice or harm unless there were to be very long detours and the thousands of hypostases (that is, comparable to the failure of genes to reproduce with non-appropriate genes) such as the trials and collective labors of peoples cause to intervene between the messages of life at the reproductive stage and the ultimate expressions of thought?

The reader kind enough to read these pages will discover here less a quest for absolutes than a series of interrogations. If and when finally there may appear more precise proofs of a Mental Code, [2] and

2. For the reader who may wish to know more of the theoretical part before the publication of *L'Œil d'Haurus ou le Code Mental* [The Eye of Horus or the Mental Code], the following by the author may be of interest:
'Pensée sauvage et logique géometrique', in *Echanges et Communications: Mélanges offerts à Claude Lévi-Strauss,* Paris — La Haye, Mouton, 1970, Vol. II, Part III, pp. 964—980.
'St. George: The evolution of a legend', *Réalités* (and *Réalités in America*), Feb.

of how the historian may make use of it, the same reader will judge, as do we, that history is capable of arriving at a still more scientific status, but that the mysteries of human destiny remain essentially untouched.

Paris 1975   *CHARLES MORAZÉ*

1972, pp. 58—66.
Le Général de Gaulle et la République, Paris, Flammarion, 1972. See Chap. I: 'Légitimité et légalité'.
'L'Histoire, science naturelle', *Annales* ESC 29, Jan.-Feb., 1974, pp. 107—137. In part, a review of François Jacob's *La Logique du Vivant* [The logic of life], Paris, 1970. References to studies by Ch. Morazé.
Article coming in *Annales* in 1975.

Author's preface to the original edition

This book is a work of pure theory; it is also the expression of a question of conscience. How shall we teach social evolution or political science unless we ask ourselves the meaning of this power to exterminate which our age has called into being in a world half dying of hunger? There is, nevertheless, a measure of justice in the history which has summoned up this monstrous iniquity: China has the atomic weapon, and now promises it to poorer peoples. To what transgressions do we owe this accumulation of threats and menaces?

Things had not reached this stage when I entered upon the researches whose first results are here made public; but we had already been warned of the threat. For it was at that time that it was thought necessary to sacrifice dozens of millions of men before we could bring action against a few accomplices of a paranoiac who assumed that arms were made for use, since everything was attainable by their use. We know how difficult it was to establish responsibility for this genocide among those who entrenched themselves behind the duty to obey. Would it be any easier today to identify those guilty for the waste now upon us, or for the crime now being prepared? Warriors would argue that true bravery was more appropriate to swords and shells than to the arsenal of buttons now waiting to be pressed. Scholars and technicians would hide behind science and technology not in themselves warlike. Roosevelt would not long be held to blame for having listened to Einstein in the midst of a merciless war; and the precedent would be found useful for imitators. And since one cannot punish economic, social and national structures, this kind of lawless procedure would also be held blameless.

The first result, in our present state of affairs, of this impossibility of setting up a tribunal competent to deal with so serious a matter is its challenge to the cult of great men. How shall we hail them as history-makers when the limits of their responsibilities are so imprecise? Would the explanation be that history does it all by itself?

That was what I first believed at the time I left a French lycée of the Army of the Rhine[1] and came to Paris to test myself in mathematics, philosophy, history and economics. I was especially attracted by history, perhaps because, despite Hitler's reassuring affirmations that he was making every effort to please, I had no doubt that his rise would end in collective murder. When the event surpassed all predictions, I convinced myself and tried to convince others that anyone at all might have been chosen by circumstances to assume the form and shape of the hero, though at the cost of widespread bloodshed. Perhaps I was driven to this reflection by an obscure wish to spare the generation of my parents and teachers the accusation of having permitted the conditions for such a catastrophe to develop.

I have since changed my opinion. For when a collective destiny reaches the point of depending on the decision of a single person, that decision, even if it appears spontaneous, nevertheless at that moment obeys forces beyond all human power. And even so, such forces were brought into play often at a moment long antecedent, when their indeterminate state was still open to modifications, if only those involved had been properly informed. What they needed to know was contained within the totality of actions and deeds constituting that moment and that condition, but in a transfigured form, with necessity as the key to its interpretation.

The discovery of keys to such interpretations was until recently beyond our reach. Only today may a proper scientific research hope to succeed in such a task, by establishing a general method for the study of the past, a study controlled by experimentation in the present, toward which such study would progressively extend. Such an effort could lead the human adventure, if not beyond trials and tribulations, at least toward a haven from irreparable catastrophes.

More than a quarter of a century has slipped by since the sciences of man first authorized such a hope; since Lucien Febvre and Fernand

---

1. Ch. Morazé's father was a member of the French General Staff of the Army of the Rhine following on World War I, and stationed on the left bank. Hence the youth attended a French lycée set up in Mainz in the late 1920s.

Braudel, for example, endeavored to unite the humane sciences, since Henri Wallon uncovered history in psychology, or Saussure and Durkheim were found to be in agreement; since, indeed, a free French people recovered their place in the international task. Here, the cybernetic equations of Norbert Wiener appeared to promise indefinite perspectives within the movement of logical researches, leading from Frege to Hilbert, and illustrated by that apostle of peace, Bertrand Russell, and his followers. In this chorus of innovations, I myself participated within the role played by international and national institutes. I even founded some myself. Thus I arrived at the age of balance sheets and revisions at a time when it was not yet clear that so many trials and labors had changed the face of the world.

Nevertheless, the sciences of man will not deserve the name until humanity is able to prove itself less powerless to know itself, and less incapable of mastering the technological disciplines which have brought mankind to where it is. Before we can comprehend how our societies can so easily secrete the power to destroy all, yet find it so difficult to summon the will to unite in a common effort, the sciences of psychology, sociology, anthropology, and history must pool their offerings. Admirable studies have been written. Without them, we could not even envisage as possible the central task for whose success all must work together. Yet after more than twenty post-war years, during which Jean-Paul Sartre in France proposed the most widely accepted philosophic and literary recommendations, it must be admitted that no certain body of knowledge is yet able to reply satisfactorily to the summons which he launched, or heal the anxiety to which he so forcefully testified.

Of all our studies on man, there is no one specialized branch which has not been marked by important discoveries. But the most advanced of such, those which have most surely established their postulates and sharpened their logic, are locked in vocabularies as specialized as their systems. The evidences of their vitality might be a sufficient guarantee of a better future if necessity did not so press upon us. Furthermore, however new and positive the results achieved by ethnology, linguistics, sociologies, and psychologies, it must be admitted that economists and especially historians − from whom numerous economists have taken their inspiration − still appear to be entirely dependent on the factual, and would very soon be embarrassed to state what basic principles guarantee the legitimacy of their reasonings. In fact, we may assert that in these areas, and aside from

Marxism, we find mostly those who, however they deny it, have become little more than imitators or counterfeits.

It is a commonplace rumor that intellectuals and especially academicians are the accomplices of Marxism. Properly speaking, this is in fact an imprecise assumption. There is, however, a reason for so widespread an opinion. Marxism is much more than a body of propositions set forth in almost unreadable books: for Marx added action to propositions, and offered points of purchase and levers by which the world might be moved. It is this combination of lessons and examples, greatly expanded by successors who believed in him, that casts a compelling prestige over this man's school, though less by clear statement than by implicit models. It was he who first discovered the secret of promising men amid their anguish and distress a science of the future and certain laws of action. There is therefore no reason for astonishment if so many of those who seek and hope find themselves linked with Marx, even while they maintain that they have found the means to refute him.

Today, however, we shall discover in the realm of psychology and in the study of myths and linguistic data the greatest number of innovations that may explicate what Marx called superstructures; for his age, being imbued with idealism, could not push such studies to their limit. Unable to analyze in time the maleficent powers of the imagination and the forms that expression takes, Europe became the first victim of its wars. The same sort of reasoning can explain the stupefaction, the numbness, which overwhelmed the Russian Bolsheviks and rendered them powerless to resist Stalin when he inaugurated his personal cult. It is hardly worth our while today to bring judgments of value to bear on Marxism, but it is tremendously important to understand by what means the contributions of the new sciences may modify it.

To restrict the angle of man's vision solely to the facts of production or distribution, whatever the liberal or spiritual intentions of the economists or historians who practice such, is to put the emphasis precisely on an order of reality whose importance Marx already recognized perfectly. Political economy remaining what it is, history become economics cannot insist that it is non-Marxist except by divesting itself of all theoretical foundation — at least, when it does invoke the intervention of non-materialist forces, by investigating what it is that links them to mythical realities. One may well make use of the economic state of Germany to explain the conditions which created Nazism and gained a hearing for the irrational and incendiary speechs of its promoter. But his power and the system of production which he imposed on his bewitched country depended on the affects of the representation, and on the exciting power of myths like that of transfiguration by death. This same power can aid us to understand the consent which Stalin won from his victims. That power is the overt or secret justification for every murderous heroism. How much weight, then, shall we give to these myths, and what is the significance of these representations which the present-day world erects around its avatars?

Among all the sciences of man, anthropology and linguistics have the advantage of being the most capable of clearly formulating their postulates, and thus of deceiving the least. However, this advantage is won only if they strip our age of the ambiguities of the moral conscience. The age of pure linguistics, like the age of mythics, becomes rational only by ceasing to be the author of what happens to man. These sciences are not loaded with vices like the long duration of history, which Marx called the cruel goddess. What factor, what entity, will unite the era of these new sciences to the duration of history? To accomplish such an identification would be to discover the methodological base common to all the sciences of man, to construct the theoretical corpus indispensable for a truly collective morality and a truly scientific intellectual status, which is to say, capable of compensating for what the technologies have done to aggravate the wars of mankind.

Before proceeding further, it seems advisable to remind ourselves of the difficulties which our French university society opposes to this task, and of the inconveniences which follow therefrom. While, thanks to a broad theoretic body of information as a prelude to practical applications, the exact and natural sciences have been developing in a way to surprise the very intellects which fostered them, the sciences of man have all too often progressed in reverse. Many of our psychologists and sociologists today plan on following active careers. There is, for example, the appeal of the business world or of medical institutions, with the result that these scientists have been considered somewhat more favorably by the ever-cautious public authorities. Obviously, we must give this short-range ambition credit for the successes won in the study of markets, the organization of enterprises, the prediction of election returns, or the remedies for errors of adjustment and adaptation. Yet for all this, involvement in such successes must not allow us to lose sight of the central issue around which the theoretical was originally conceived.

History is not exposed to the same temptations to the market-place. Public taste for the reports submitted by history has not, either among publishers or in the lecture-halls, contributed to promoting an interest in difficult abstractions. As for the teaching of law, a discipline almost wholly devoted to applications, it has not eased the task of the economists assigned to established institutions where the methods of selection attach more value to the virtues of the lecture than to criticism of its claims. The result is a kind of side-tracking of political economy's devotion to the great and praiseworthy effort at theorization. In its most advanced studies, one is well advised to seek the sanction and authority of the concrete, but without surrendering the quality of an elementary instruction less appropriate to practical problematics than to theory.

The French academic organization has not facilitated the integration of the sciences of man into our intellectual world. Its monolithic character causes it to value a rather strongly hierarchical system, which perhaps excessively subordinates research to routine. In the faculty of letters, the thesis, with its long period for maturation, constitutes less an entrance upon a career than a ritual sacred in its own right. The candidate's timidity about premature publication of his more important findings imprisons him in constraint, with a consequent noticeable delay in the diffusion of knowledge. The state of subjection which is his until he is ready encourages neither that creative spontaneity nor that freedom of discussion which are the attraction and the test of maturity. The effects of this weight of inertia are not negligible, and endanger the progress of theoretic adjustments. Leprince-Ringuet could remark recently of young doctors that only after listening to them with the closest attention could he prepare his course at the Collège de France. Why not permit doctors in the human sciences to prove their competence without excessive delays?

It is possible that the disadvantages of our tradition are compensated for by certain important advantages inherent in those disciplines formerly grouped under the name of humanities. This rigorous self-discipline has yielded great and valuable works such as a premature freedom might not have produced. But the sciences of man suffer in consequence; for it is at the outset of a young researcher's work that a wide range of competencies enables us to understand him and to orient him. When finally the great work appears, years have been lost from profiting by whatever excellence or uniqueness is embodied therein, buried in a mass of data more appropriate to some elementary workman's job not requiring genius. It is then too late to correct its errors of principle, which will be absorbed by the young teacher's students along with his most thoroughly grounded documentation.

Thus the sciences of man lag in a mutual acquaintance, evaluation, and appreciation of one another, a lag not without its effect upon education as a whole. Today, though all programs should be rethought in terms of a community of confidence, newly discovered innovations are added to what has already been assumed to be necessary, and instruction as a consequence tends to a kind of overwhelming of pupils and young students with branches of learning treated as if each were irreducible, especially when they are in contradiction among themselves.

Certainly the sciences of man will not replace the humanities: history does not lend itself to being reduced to equations, nor beauty to axioms, nor faith to systems. But they do promise us, or rather permit us, to distinguish what part of our knowledge can be understood from what can be only learned or felt. No amount of reasoning, no calculating machine, will reconstruct the biographies of Napoleon or Racine, nor will they render a better account of the nature of man and their works than of things. But whatever links man with his environment, what produces and transforms him, that, indeed, may be explicated. Our age is not only one in which so much acquired knowledge threatens to submerge us, it must also be an age in which we discover the means to bring it into order.

This is not the first time that education has been called upon to readjust its plans and substitute within itself order for quantity; such revisions have been necessary from age to age. Furthermore, if physiology, psychology, anthropology, linguistics, history and economics will only cease thinking of themselves as so many closed, autonomous disciplines, each sufficient to itself, we shall be allowed to teach beyond the boundaries of classes, nations, cultures, something of what is common to all mankind. Such teaching would then possess the power of conviction such as animates the rigorous logic out of which the exact sciences were born.

It should occasion no surprise that such systematization should appear in our new disciplines at the very moment when it is challenged in the better established sciences. We no longer live in the age of Descartes and Pascal, when every honest man had to accept the power of a geometric demonstration or a well performed experiment. It is not from an understanding of mathematics or physics that common sense believes in science. It is the external evidence of amazing machines such as transform our universe that persuades man that the scientists were right. The sciences of man have not yet arrived at that stage. They are just beginning to approach the point where certain common substructures command intellectual recognition as necessities. They are not to be judged solely by their special applications, but at first by their mutual coherence. After all, the knowledge of man arises from a quite different pattern from that of the knowledge of nature. Since nothing will ever eradicate the living diversity of man, in his thousand centrifugal manifestations, all studies of his behavior which can hope to attract and hold attention must converge on that axial point. The little we are yet able to know of this exact spot gives it the greater importance. This kind of knowledge, like all others, will obviously remain incomplete, provisional, and subject to setbacks. But this is not what we have to fear, provided that the successive systematizations dealing with man first capture, then fittingly accompany, the creative transformations by which science achieves that technological efficiency which our misconceptions about humanity can render so dangerous.

At present, any research toward such a systematization forces its author into breath-taking excursions. The world situation shifts from year to year, along with its sciences and its technologies, even while anthropological researches likewise, in their own rhythm, become more numerous and diversified. Nevertheless, it is a race that must be won.

Let me be specific. It was in 1958 that I resolved to write this book. I had been preparing myself over a long period to present a comprehensive study of practical methods for dealing with history, but I should not have contemplated such a synthesis had I not experienced living through the Algerian drama and the constitutional changes that followed. In July of that same year, General de Gaulle offered me the use of all the resources of radio-broadcasting and television. But if certain words pronounced under certain conditions immediately produce a tremendous effect of resonance, to warn against the future is no reliable guarantee of being heard by those most directly concerned with its threats. Words can fail as fast as they are tossed off, helpless projectiles turned into provocations to the very violences they were meant to quell. The newspapers and books of that period were truthfully reporting the French situation. They were neither understood nor even read by those who should have been most concerned. These great debates were doomed to be cut off by the event, that is, by force. And since the power of the state was that of the army, to withdraw the latter from Africa and to entrust it with an atomic arsenal were the two high points of one process, claiming patriotism as a reason.

Words carry weight only through the energy allotted them by those who hear them. And this it is which truly gives education its great importance. Every public becomes a crowd when it refers the truth not to the inner coherence of what has been said to it, but to the person, that is, the mask, which speaks.

The organization of education and what it must transmit becomes the first of all our problems. And this brings us to the original topic. Faculties may have been labelled letters or law, but they made no pretence of mastering the event. Of course, to require learning of, and to comment on, the deeds of history, the completed activities, the received laws and customs, is obviously to suggest also the attitudes that should be assumed in the face of what will happen. And the academic and intellectual society, here as elsewhere, has played its role of counsel and expectancy. Yet it did not prove to be adapted to the rhythm of events and the developments of force. Now that the same faculties are also labelled human sciences (a misnomer, for what science is not human?), or economic sciences, they promise more, and first of all to introduce into all education what needs to be known of today's world, so that the words may be uttered and heard that can save it from its jeopardy,

We are still very far distant from that goal, and the proof appears in the way reform of our instruction proceeds. Knowledge of our social economy, of the psychological needs of man, and the resources of pedagogy, should have been directing a change by which each might gauge the need for the cultural transformation of this century. Unfortunately, the results here accomplished have not been such as to give the sciences of man a lead over the others. The exact and natural sciences have consequently remained in the ascendent, and perhaps for our common profit, but at the cost of underlining a delay as detrimental to instruction in mathematics as to that in the new humanities.

It is not individuals whom we must hold to blame; their responses on committees and colloquia, their writings on this topic, enable us all too clearly to observe how social situations determine the attitudes of the most liberal, who from then on are dependent on the skepticisms of political authority; unless, that is, some widely shared conviction confers upon the dynamics of expression the compelling power of a communal manifestation.

When, now more than twenty years ago, I entered upon my first abstract studies, hardly then aware where they might lead me, the prevailing academic fashion might have turned me aside from them had it not been for Mario Roque. His immense and insatiable erudition made him impatient of authority, but open to innovations. My project pleased him; and though it was in the role of historian that he opened the doors for me to the School of Advanced Studies, he never faltered in aiding me to discover linguistics.

At that time, however, it was not held suitable for a researcher to range so far from his chosen field. I said as little as possible, therefore, about my theoretical essays, to which I gave only such time as my duties as historian would allow. I benefited no less from the irreplaceable freedom granted me to work at the School, as also from certain American institutions to which I am indebted for permitting me, even though a 'humanist', to profit by contacts with psychologists or mathematicians.

I believed, therefore, that it behooved me to devote myself to theory rather than to completing the editing of a work which I had undertaken ten years earlier with the approval of Marc Bloch, a work dedicated to the industrial evolution of northern France. I had assembled much of the available documentation on this subject, and had even profited by the archives of the Bank of France; but when I tried to give some form to all this, I learned that it did not yield an adequate answer to a problem which eluded me in all its dimensions, for lack of being stated with sufficient breadth.

I was at that time developing a postulate of the greatest simplicity: namely, that the structures of scientific reasoning, of language, and of society, are identical. It became my ambition, starting from there, to establish a kind of general theorem. This led me to consider as a social fact not what the prevailing sociology defined as such, but what it would have to be to bring it into accord with my system; that is to say, a totality dependent on underlying correlations with what could be directly comprised within my inquiry. An unallowable method; and yet I knew that it would become that of the future when Claude Lévi-Strauss brought me the typewritten text of his admirable thesis. What I had assumed, in my observations of modern behavior, to be purely an intellectual exercise, became, from the study of primitive cultures, the opportunity for a marvelous increase in depth.

Similarly, seeking to identify the simple relations between compositions of space, the genesis of numbers, and the logic of propositions, I encountered what Jean Piaget[2] and his school were establishing experimentally. The incompleteness of my own mathematical knowledge would have been an insurmountable obstacle had I not perceived that by holding to very general cases, it would suffice to have recourse to a quite concrete, fairly difficult but elementary mathematics. Nevertheless, I never arrived at a simple, complete theorem, such as I had dreamed of. This failure was the more disappointing because my propositions, at whichever end I took hold of them, and despite my permitting them to make connections almost to their limits, always ended by running into an impossibility.

An examination of Goedel's work enabled me to emerge from this impasse. Assuming the truth of his theorem that no system can contain all the logic and it alone, the incompatibilities against which I was butting my head had to be accepted as raw data, each marking the conclusion of the art of convincing in one age, and thus inaugurating another age, all being recorded under an order derived from chronology alone. Now, this order was revealed as obeying what the psychologists were discovering in the genesis of intellectual operations, even though not all cultures could have completely comprehended the means they were relying on. Furthermore, certain researches in psychoanalysis, psycho-sociology, and social psychology were uncovering a pattern for cerebral activity which I soon discovered to be similar to mine, and which explained the deficiencies that had surprised me. Finally, the incompleted lines of order which I was thinking to find in history now appeared along the pattern of a genealogical tree, comparable to that which the biologists construct for the evolution of life. I came thus to the theory which in this book I shall label as the function of *historicity*. This theory implied a postulate different from the one I had at first announced: namely, structures of reason, language, and society are as closely as possible in contact with a living structure, which disturbs them by introducing into them irreducible innovations. This it does, however, only at the moment when what the innovations replace has become almost perfectly coherent, and at the point of contact where their coherence breaks down.[3]

2. For the specific contributions of Lévi-Strauss, Jean Piaget, and Goedel, see the comment in the Translator's Foreword. Translator's note.
3. This statement is more thoroughly discussed in the chapters below. For 'a living structure', read a collectivity or some phenomenon within such, apparently entrenched as satisfactorily functional, but susceptible to replacement just when it has come to seem static and invulnerable. Translator's note.

This hypothesis seemed to me to take into account the dual nature of the age to which I have referred above, an age defined on the one hand by the disciplines arising from the synchronic (i.e., those in operation at the moment), in which rational effort may reduce the contents of the object studied; and, on the other hand, an age of history as perceived by all disciplines which treat all topics diachronically (i.e., as they have changed and evolved over time), or as appearing as a duration of time within which the organic course of that which resists reduction is recorded.[4] If one considers the ages implied by older cosmologies, those of the Newtonian or Einsteinian principles, there is nothing to prevent a short though different formulation for each, though each may differ from the other (i.e., as viewed synchronically). In the same way, the time of a literary work (that time which includes its statement or submits it for reading) may be reduced to a 'grammar' of episodes or to a syntax of sentences; and this despite the existence of several grammars of representation (i.e., different ways of viewing it at different times or places), as of several grammars of language. For these last especially, the difference may be between those grammars which dispense with the syllogism and those which make us of it.

In the case of historic events, on the contrary, simplification does not intervene in the sense of a reduction. Events are better explained in the degree to which they are placed in cycles of ever longer duration. The longest of all of these is precisely that of the development of scientific thought. Mathematics, viewed in terms of its evolution, becomes the grammar of grammars, that is, logic in its etymologic sense (speech, reason). It is this that forces historicity to condense within its term either a totality of observed articulations or the impossibility of recognizing any such at the point to which, nevertheless, all experiment leads. These two functions of the term are correlative, as are the solutions to the problems which they pose in increasing numbers.[5]

---

4. Again, see Translator's Foreword for a comment on these terms, pp. 14—15. The duality of today consists in the amazing technological and scientific disciplines which we possess, but the lack of understanding on how they arose out of the past and what they may be doing to humanity. Translator's note.

5. In oversimplified terms, are the events of history inexorably linked by discoverable laws? Later chapters will discuss the part of historicity (the nature of things as determining) versus the part played by man's cerebral activity and his experimentation. Translator's note.

One may easily perceive that my second hypothesis is not of the same nature as the first mentioned above. This latter renounces all search for a general axiomatics. Instead, it endeavors to rest all axiomatics on experiment, in terms of what Julian Huxley has led me to value.[6] There remained to be known what basic reality differentiated myth and representation, as also syllogism and logic, subordinating this last to the laws of working on things.[7] Invited to speak on this topic before Soviet colleagues assembled for this purpose by Anatole Zvorikyn, in the setting of the Academy of Moscow, I proposed that this reality was life itself. When I was invited to visit the Pavlov Institute in Leningrad, I was convinced that the study of the brain gave proofs of the inadequacies of axiomatics and their variables. Unfortunately, I am not a biologist. I have had to approach works of biology by first selecting those which specialists have generously written for the use of others; to which I am the more indebted because they have introduced me to certain less elementary studies.

A few months later, at Chicago, at the conclusion of three conferences in which certain economists kindly participated, Kings, Hayek — this latter a liberal if there ever was one — stressed the importance of the non-cerebral. Obviously, I was not forgetting what must be attributed to the factors of material life, nor the role of a certain history of economics of which John Nef, my host, had been one of the restorers. Nevertheless, like him, I thought that statistics did not clarify everything. Having undertaken then to draw up this present synthesis, I had also argued that statistics served more adequately within a historical perspective.

Such reflections, here recalled, have occupied me during more than fifteen years, on the margin of what has remained my main profession.

During this same period, I wrote several books of history, in which in brief passages only did there appear the results of what was nevertheless my major preoccupation. Perhaps the date of these works (before 1958) will suffice to explain the total absence in those

6. Namely, the importance of experimentation. See Translator's Foreword, pp. 14–15.

7. The term *things* (French *choses*) is used in the Lucretian sense, 'the nature of things' (*De Rerum Natura*); that is, as 'implying the existence of social and historical realities such as offer to experience and reflection the same consistence and resistance as those realities which the biologist meets'. Letter from Ch. Morazé to translator, May 15, 1970.

reviews which are one's lot in France of any reference to what had nevertheless become for me the essential thing. The reception abroad, especially later, given my interpretations was somewhat more encouraging. Furthermore, during this same period, I found myself a participant in the labors of the international commission set up by the general assembly of Unesco to write a scientific and cultural history of humanity. Though at first a member of the triumvirate which superintended the drafting of this project, and chairman of the commission, I soon resigned both posts for lack of a means to implement a fresh way of conceiving a universal history. Nevertheless, since I continued to follow the unfolding of the enterprise, and to participate, I was able to add, and as dynamically as I could, to what is taught by our present French school of history something of what has been produced by researches in the rest of the world.

Though I was interested in the totality of history, and especially in that of scientific thought, I was already too much involved in the study of the nineteenth century not to be more aware of that era than of the others. Now, it seemed to me that the basic problem of the period which separated the first industrial revolution from the second might be stated in the following terms: The contribution of capitalism was that it brought its system of production to the forefront without giving much thought to the importance of what was taking place at the same period in mathematics and physics, though there theories seemed to be evolving in a no less independent manner. Nevertheless, and notably in the past eighty years, productive society has shown itself peculiarly adept at picking up whatever is best and worst in the technologies spawned by the sciences. Thus, as much on the part of the laboratories as of businesses, the two have worked, though unwittingly, with this conjunction in sight. Society has been the author of an adjustment which it never formally proposed. Beginning with hidden movements within its internal structure, there issued the partial manifestations which were appropriate to science on the one hand, and on the other to the economic structure. This example so powerfully supported my reasoning that I did not doubt that I should find many others; and such, indeed, has proved to be the case.

I was beginning to think that I had brought all the preparatory labors for my book to a successful issue, and decided to undertake the firstdraft composition; but when it came to the test, I was soon forced to admit that such was not at all the case. There came moments when every page forced a general retreat. These difficulties arose from the fact that when I had treated each of my materials within the perspective which most clearly set it forth, that is to say, on the scale of importance which it seemed properly to deserve, it turned out to be impossible to accomodate a sustained, coherent, and stylistically acceptable exposition to such a combination of abridgements, stemming from such varying angles of vision.

At the same time, it seemed necessary to make the book shorter to the degree that it hoped to be more general, and again to write it in the language of the general public. Indeed, there was no question of instructing specialists, whatever their specialities (the least of whom in his own field knew more than I), but of offering them the opportunity of coming together on a neutral ground accessible to any man of education. Now, to renounce all specialization was to renounce my own. I was barred from introducing here those exercises in logic which had served me so well, but which were not accessible to the general public without a strenuous apprenticeship. Again, it was advisable to eschew the facilities of historical narrative, which are quite available to the reader, and the more so because when one refers to what has already happened, it eludes reason. Finally, from beginning to end, it was necessary to maintain a position at the halfway point between the demonstrative and the descriptive, and to control with a certain rigorousness the rather general and allusive propositions, so that perspectives might be opened on the major details and the highest principles.

I should doubtless have renounced an effort which was consuming far too much of my time, if the difficulty I was experiencing in observing these rules of composition had not proved precisely the need for them. I know now from experience why each science of man follows the specific path on which its language leads it. Today, freed of my task, and able to rediscover the use of specialized vocabularies, I am so much the better enabled to evaluate the advantages because I know the dangers. But the task for this kind of book was to break one's chains.

I rewrote my manuscript, therefore, as often as necessary so as to experiment with several plans, and to the point where it seemed to me that the text, as here published, and as compared with earlier versions, had become the most convincingly coherent. This impression required verification, and one method might be submit it to the test of a resumé. Certainly the meaning of a statement shifts with the dimensions one gives to it, but the best is that which resists every modification.

This condensation is offered herein as a table of contents.

The whole, as may sufficiently be seen in this abridgement, is neither as complete nor as systematic as I should have wished, nor as some other may be able to succeed in making it. For this reason, I hesitated to entitle it a 'Treatise of anthropology', indicating thereby, with the proviso that it be expanded to the study of all cultures, that such was the central discipline for all the sciences of man.

It will be noted that the body of this book falls into two groups of studies: Parts II and III throwing differing lights on the same problems: The one bringing into relief what belongs to the imaginative faculty, the other what arises from things. Now, to make the system complete, it was necessary to introduce here a specific analysis of the relationships between the power to imagine and things. I believe that psychophysiology, which is today making such great advances, will permit this type of research (sketched at the outset of Chapter 7), though to complete the task would require more competence than I possess. As for the rest, psychology and psychoanalysis may clarify the origin of conflicts and also of logics, but not the experience of the blast-furnace and the cannon shell. The path toward a treatise on a general anthropology lies through a historic anthropology.

Having opted for this latter, the present book devotes its first two chapters to the function of historicity. It concludes with two others incorporating the concise outline for a genetic history. On these topics it may perhaps be useful to anticipate a difference in quality and authority between the various developments within these chapters of introduction and conclusion.

At the start of this Preface, the notion of historicity was linked to a group of logical propositions, or rather to the way by which their correlations were transformed. Historicity is introduced quite otherwise in the pages which follow. Indeed, it seemed to me more convenient, more convincing, and more useful to present it as suggested by experience. Yet one legitimacy does not preclude another, and, without saying all that might be said on this same historicity, I believe that nothing is more certain than its importance, whether in the exercise of research into the sciences of man or into the theories pertinent to them. The term historicity will not often be used in the body of this book. But it will be sufficiently clear that it is always this term that is in question, and that it is this same term which permits us, finally, to reduce history to its basic sub-branches.

However, introduction and conclusion obey another purpose as well; that is, to find the causes of our present dangerous contradictions, and to discern why we may hope to surmount them, and at what cost. Therefore, the opening of the first chapter and the very end of the last are not entirely in the same tone as the rest, for there the optative mingles with the indicative. I have not thought it necessary to renounce these developments. Since the moral intent which inspired them was the stimulus to bring me to my research, they may perhaps have some value for those willing to read the results. It hardly needs saying that my wish here has been to have nothing in contradiction to what it is possible to establish. Such hopes are indicated only by the silences that linger after the sound information and the applied reasoning.

The central content of this book from the middle of the first chapter to toward the end of the last might more strictly have been published under the title of 'The Imagination and Things'. The plan that I first followed distinguished: imagination, words, things. However, I was unable to resolve the treatment of language otherwise than in the context of the imaginative faculty, even though language is the borderline element, the region of passing over the threshold at the point where the imagination leads to a better penetration of the real. Not every structure is to be identified with that of languages. There are as many illustrations to show that the collective labor of men may give rise to cerebral reasoning, where the interrelations have been most speedily established by means of words.

Such considerations of plans or chapters are in no sense secondary. On the contrary, it is important to push them to their most extreme consequences. That is why the section to which the present statement leads assigns a major significance not to the opposition of the imaginative faculty and the real, but instead to the possible versus the certain. This latter opposition is made still more explicit under the form here retained, the exploration of possibles and encounters with the certain. Exploration is here reserved for what is the less easily defined, encounters for what manifests itself in incontrovertible evidences, even when they are contradictory. This means, for example, that facts such as traditional history retains them are held to be irrefutable, even though, under the influence of different accidents, they might have been different from what they were. On the other hand, all the varieties of numbers utilized by mathematics, like all that internal experience teaches of existence, impress us with the feeling that a certain logic of truth is not an illusion, even when we cannot grasp it except in connection with scattered and poorly linked necessities.

In the most trivial as in the most basic circumstances, we are confronted by the indeterminism of our determinism. We know, when we throw the die, that it will fall, but not upon which of its faces. We know ourselves to be mortal, but not upon what day. All that presents itself to us as real raises this ambiguity. This is not because certainty and chance have each a distinct domain to itself, but that both are encountered in every domain. Seen from the angle of the possible, the world is full of actions launched to unknown ends, even though they make use of means which do not deceive. Seen from the angle of the certain, this same world seems governed by laws, which nevertheless, by their interactions, produce unforseeable results. And all is so intermingled that a great number of accidents of all sorts whatsoever do not preclude translation into uniform averages, while rational certainties are full of contradictions, such as the discovery of imaginary numbers to resolve an equation of the third degree, or the substitution of relativity for Newtonian mathematics.

We shall never insist overmuch on this enormous difficulty implanted at the center of historicity, where it defines the tragic condition of man at the point where the logic of his moral intentions encounters the incomprehensible as it presents itself in the course of a progression of which he is the agent but not the author.

Very long ago an experiment, itself still more ancient, suspended the fruits of good and evil on the tree of knowledge. To know is to know how to judge; that is, to know how to introduce order into choices as offered. Now, the order to which the individual subscribes may not be that which his group or his entire city is in the habit of preferring. Who knows when the order of a city changes? And who can decide that the change is enduring? Coriolanus, Caesar, Octavius violate the Roman law. The first will be destroyed, the second elevated then struck down, while the third will consolidate an empire, though it will not last forever. Only the passage of time will decide what value lies in an initiative taken amid circumstances which encourage the ambition of some new proposal, only sooner or later to give it the lie.

There is no moment of experience which is not rich in lessons of this sort. However, it is not at any chance moment in the world of great deeds that perfect illustrations of the tragic condition of man arise. Millenia were needed, for example, before chance ceased to be viewed as a gift of the gods and began to succumb to operative formulations. The successes of Aeschylus or Racine mark important transformations in the system of civil laws, but no less in the general development of logic from the era when it had failed in Greece to resolve, by means of demonstration, what were the axiomatics of chance, to that period in Europe when logic endowed mathematics with its inventive power and enabled it to surmount this most difficult obstacle.

Orestes is a criminal, but also an instrument of justice. The murder he commits breaks the sacred bonds, but it is done in obedience to Apollo. Pursued by the Erinyes, he is delivered from them when the time arrives for the spirits of vengeance to be deprived of the ancient power. But the laws of the city have not changed without also changing the fixed way of arriving at convictions; that is to say, after the art of syllogism has been discovered. This social shift is scientific as well as moral. At each event, the situation created is that of a certain statute or regulation which brings men into harmony among themselves, as if a kind of logic placed them in nature. Nevertheless, in ancient Greece this logic, however powerful over civic laws, cannot yet solve the mystery of human misery in the grip of things.

Thus, when the century of Pascal returns to Platonism for its institutions, it is no longer ignorant of what suffering means. Obscure movements modify the foundations of a society which will, nevertheless, maintain itself for more than a hundred years still; so well, indeed, that Phaedra believes prematurely than it is permissable for her to avow her passion and Hippolytus his. Theseus, believed dead, returns and in his punishment confuses the violation done his rights as husband and his rights as ruler. The hour had not yet sounded which would change the foundations of laws, though the scientific materials were already assembled which would transfer the oracular decrees of destiny from heaven to earth. Pascal could not escape giving utterance to his theory of the wager for the benefit of gamblers and skeptics whose habits he wishes to recall to the service of a Jansenist God, who would not reveal himself to his faithful except in situations without an exit.

The complete solemnity which characterizes certain expressions of the tragic condition marks a change of order at the heart of a collectivity whose systems of reasoning are also shifting. It marks a turning-point in the history of man in the grip of human and non-human reality. Greek tragedy on the morrow of the conquest of the art of demonstrative proof, classic tragedy on the eve of scientific progress, these signalize thus for us two great moments in the development of the intellect. They are the basic landmarks around which all is articulated.

In Greek tragedy, the roles of father and chief are on many occasions more or less confused. Nevertheless, the duties of the second prevail over those of the first, as witness Agamemnon as well as Oedipus and Creon. Actually, on the morrow of the conquest of the art of demonstration, the search for a rational city deprives the patriarchal family of its former legitimacy. The same ambiguity of the two functions dwells within classic tragedy on the eve of scientific progress. However, here it happens that the chief must take the place of the father: Theseus becomes such for Aricia,[8] Mordichai exercises a paternal magistracy with regard to Esther, and perhaps one might say as much of Augustus when he pardons Cinna. The preeminence of the father over the chief will come to pass through an atomization of society into families as the center, when bourgeois drama will give support to the new and original point of view. In these two major examples, the importance of the modification of customs and laws assumes an extreme character, pertinent to the history of the spirit of research; and in the course of this change, language most explicitly expresses the tragic condition, first when it finally adapts thy syllogism to itself, and then when it welcomes the nomenclature of the exact sciences.

Now we must ask why two great moments are marked by a striking simplification of representation at the moment when the tragic character of all destiny becomes precisely that of language. Could there be two ways of arriving at the level of an achieved intelligence, during which each mental process, as it becomes reversible,[9] proves also to be operative? Or, to put it more generally, might there be periods when it becomes less easy to achieve this result, periods when men would be less intelligent than in others?

---

8. Aricia was the daughter-in-law of Theseus, wife of Hippolytus, son of Theseus, subject of Racine's *Phèdre.* Translator's note.

9. *Reversible* is used here as it appears in Piaget. For example, if one adds *A* to *B*, it is clear that one will find *A* again by taking *B* from the sum. This reversibility, however, can raise apparently insoluble problems.

Every whole number multiplied by another whole number gives a third whole number, but this statement does not work for division, so that we cannot say that the 'rule' is reversible in all cases, and must have recourse to fractional numbers. The substitutes discovered toward the seventeenth century had to bring into question, beyond further doubt, the logical universalism of space in three dimensions, and hence the unities of time and space. Comment suggested by letter from Ch. Morazé, Jan. 13, 1971.

The hypothesis here maintained is that each mental process which is already achieved may be reproduced without demanding the same amount of effort which its invention demanded; but also that we do not have recourse to this effort except to the degree that circumstances permit, and that in the interim the impulse to invention may have atrophied. The presence of such favorable circumstances is linked with the active play of what I shall here call collective regulations. The fact that two epochs utilize them to the profit of two such different systematizations, one appropriate to demonstration, the other to the formulation of chance, may be attributed to two processes which are constant but not identical. The first, the more ancient one, is that of determinations,[10] an effect of cerebral psychology. The second, the post-Renaissance, is an effect of the more general order of things.

This analysis could not have been advanced in a brief and systematic way except by deciding on a sort of rationalized project of experimentation instead of the recitations of history, and by utilizing only as materials what we know of the past.

This work is not interested in action as such except in terms of gaining the necessary perspective for its reconsideration. The practical objectives of the book are perhaps not those of this century, but its intellectual preoccupations are for that reason but the more lively. The first of its goals will have been achieved if the reader accepts the idea that universal history is not merely the abridged sum of particular histories. History is the understanding and grasp of an expressive logic of development.[11] And it is under such a claim that history becomes essentially an articulation of a general theory of the sciences of man, touching also on psychology, of which it is an amplification, and on sociology, from which it awaits the investigation into those conditions which endow the illusory with such charm, and which add to certain systematizations a feeling of certitudes.

10. The French word *determinations*, Ch. Morazé points out in a letter, carries the connotation of *decisions,* or 'the totality of motivations that induce an actor in history to "make up his mind to act" '. It is thus opposed to *determinisme,* which is 'relative to physical nature and implies neither conscious knowledge nor will'. Letter from Ch. Morazé, Jan. 23, 1971.

11. Logic is at once *expression* (*logos,* language) and reason. As the first, it is shown in experiences lived through, that is, in history. As the second, it reveals that if each innovation that is to appear belongs to the mysterious, each past event is inscribed in history as comprehensible, and so authorizes a great number of possible explications. Note from Ch. Morazé, Jan. 23, 1971.

My students have been ever in my thoughts, and also the researchers in my seminars from whom I have learned so much, and the lecture-room audiences where André Siegfried made me welcome, first on the rue Saint-Guillaume, then on the rue Descartes. I have been the more aware of the high quality of all these folk as, in addition to the attention they gave to facts, they exhibited a special interest in the order of their presentation.

I must pay my respects to all those who have been able to find a coherence therein, especially by their ability to reconcile two such different experiences as those of the living present and those of the reference documentation. If the plan of this work belongs to the author, there is no sentence in it which has not borrowed from others or been inspired by them. I thought I had to proceed with haste, though depriving myself of an immense annotated bibliography, because I wanted to participate in today's intellectual conflicts. To those to whom I am indebted I shall endeavor to acknowledge my debt. They will further deserve my thanks by pointing out errors of interpretation, and especially the numerous occasions when I have failed to achieve a more effective simplicity. Precious friends, authors of books, some of them known to me, books that were the best companions of my hope, they impart to the spirit of the times the impulse and the onward movement without which man would be unable to envision himself except in terms of servitude.

NOTE

At the moment of entrusting this work to publication, it seems that I must return to two precautions indicated in the Preface. The first relates to the logical exercises which support the argument: They do not legitimize a total rationalization or formulation of history; they serve only to bring into consideration, by their logic, what is rational and what is not. The second relates to the examples used in illustration only to inject some relief into the reasoning. The allusive manner of their treatment involves an imprecise examination which runs the risk of the distortions of obviously excessive condensations. I shall only indicate those whose analysis I have pushed to the farthest point, and at such length that they should have no place here, but belong rather in the general theory. This book condenses thousands of written pages; if time permits me, and if it appears useful, I shall explicate the method suggested and shall apply it to specific historic expositions.

PART I

The function of historicity

1. Humanity as the problem

I. Man knows enough of the infinite spaces that surround him to know that they do not as yet put any living universe within reach; and also that if he has in some measure succeeded in breaking away from his planet to make the global tour in a few hours, this is because he has labored long on the efficiency of engines that can also destroy him. At the same time, humanity is trapped in the process of self-multiplication, overpopulating the earth in precisely those areas which, despite being well-endowed by nature, have suffered more than profited by the general enrichment of the globe. When a new, all-powerful political machine in that most ancient empire of wisdom and moderation, China, undertook to limit its excessive birthrate, it very soon had to call a retreat, because the measures taken were forthwith penalized by a dangerous lessening of production. Proliferation and poverty, like science and destruction, are correlative.

Some famous physicists have been disturbed by the role thrust upon them; some biologists, by the small attention paid to life. The warnings of neither have slowed up a process which always finds as many scholars and engineers to serve it as it needs, as if science, having failed to make happiness prevail, could not refuse its services to violence.

Nevertheless, there is something about knowledge and science which, in the long run, ends by prevailing over all else. Karl Friedrich Gauss may have appeared to be a weak reed in the Brunswick overrun by Napoleon's armies. Even so, mathematics and electricity are consequences more universal and more durable than Auerstadt and Jena. The scholar may not decide the destinies of the world, but science does, raising up its interpreters as they are needed, even when it appears to mock its prophets. Its contacts with politics are those of a creative continuity with circumstances which are aroused, destroyed, modified or transformed in the least foreseeable fashion.

Nothing is apparently so far from systematic as the political world. Events and heroes in it are not interchangeable; indeed, it is their irreducible singularity that fixes them in our memories. Nevertheless, there are not so many ways of asserting authority over crowds, of exploiting interests, of organizing states, of commanding war and negotiating peace. The actors in history, though clothed in different costumes, speaking different languages, exploring other means, plot to take over by but a limited number of ways of entering on the stage and playing their roles there. It would not be too difficult to draw up an abridged inventory covering the elementary operations of every prince, good or bad, devout or diabolic. The endless agitation which has disturbed the world from the distant Assyrian cruelties down to our century, on which Hitler put his stamp, is composed of a thousand repetitious methods, of interferences reducible to a limited number of types, all aimed at certain success, though a success often doubtful, and always ephemeral, however brilliant.

Granted that the scholar's world is no nearer a linear simplicity; but it is more progressive and less irresponsible. Its events are less sensational, but they have an infinitely longer range. Take as an illustration the enormous discontinuity which makes Fermat a successor of Diophantes,[1] though fifteen centuries separate them. Nothing is clearer than this link — Fermat writes on the margins of the works of his Hellenic teacher. Or consider that interim which sets Leonardo of Pisa more in the Arabian school than in the Greek. This kind of relay restored movement to science, and plunged it into its present accelerations.

Before Diophantes, Ionian mathematics, thanks to demonstration, reaches an end to the first long cycle of conceptual progressions. The origin of such progress lies in proto-history; and it took its form from choices among the expressions inspired in paleolithic communities by family, social, economic, and mental experiences. Now these people, insofar as we can infer from the rare, scattered evidences available to us, were less concerned to track one another down than to share in harmony the food-gathering and hunting resources of their territories, which must not be thoughtlessly depleted. The first successes in

---

1. Diophantes was a Greek algebrist of the third century, A.D., revived in Renaissance mathematics. Translator's note.

agriculture and the founding of villages broke the order of past millenia. From the moment when technical skills reach a certain degree of efficiency, such as permits a notable increase in the populations that use them, there begins that history whose story is one uninterrupted sequence of violences. Possibly these had begun before the signs are observed. But as far back as memory goes, this is the involvement in the advance of progress.

After Descartes, in the course of the past two centuries — a minute fraction of time in terms of humanity — scientific knowledge injects technology into our revolutionary progress. At the same time, in artificial fashion, it recovers that universalism which primitive societies would seem to have tested in their organizations back when these were directly inspired by the conditions of nature.

Between Diophantes and Descartes, history, amid its contradictions, is ready once more to launch that march of discoveries interrupted in the West when Rome imposed a civic order founded on military domination.

The most favorable interpretation of these facts was wont to attribute the still prevailing state of war less to some permanent condition of man than to the effects of inertia within a history structured on a reliance on the operative knowledge of the past — that is, on those communal, pacific, and primitive institutions which had endured so much longer. The intervening period which lay between the first mathematics and the sudden rise of our experimental sciences was a period, if not under the protection of and with the support of, at least inspired by, a transcendental monotheism, intolerant in its practices though ecumenical in its intent. Yet it did permit a certain return to the apprenticeship to *things,* a return which Antiquity, more juridical and warlike than experimental and technological, had interrupted. Under Christianity, even before the Crusaders and the merchants had speeded up the process, monks, theologians and popes had introduced into Europe experiments from Asia, where China in particular had invented numerous and admirable contrivances in all areas. Thus, even before the sea-faring expeditions had encircled and verified the unity of the globe, the world was preparing to reveal their solidarity to men of intelligent faith, however different their callings. Already the organic oneness of human technological skills was on the way to being suggested.

The era of bloody conflicts would thus turn out to be only a long but temporary transition, during which the most developed religions would mark the median and the high moment by offering men the highest compensation for the murderous chaos which hurled them against one another; that is, the promise of union with God, or, at least, a mysterious escape here or hereafter from earthly trials. The political activity then was intended to have constituted the necessary means for more profound developments, developments of far greater dimensions, designed to encourage not particular States, but a human unity under reason. We must also note that very few communal references had been offered for the dialogue between the man of State and the scholar. The first of these, the State, treats of circum-stantial conflicts, while the scholar represents the most profound and the most durable calling of man.

II. But it was impossible that two histories should exist, one political, the other scientific, as independent of one another. An immense reality unites all the details of the past, whose story continues to seduce us, but whose importance our present industrial power forces us to reconsider. This reality must be seen as composed of the totality of articulations with a place for man among them, under the pressures of his desires and tested by the natural milieu which sustains and nourishes him. This milieu further furnishes him with materials and opportunities for concrete successes, and dictates the methods of procedure. Humanity, therefore, in its most authentic dimensions, must be defined by the collective structures, the personal physiological functions which these imply, and the customs which are representative. All the rest is recorded as a consequence. Some structures are concrete and lasting; and especially when they are thoroughly mingled with things as they are, penetrate things and are penetrated by them. Other structures, occasional and fortuitous, after having impressed men in their time with terrific impact, survive afterward only as memories, to inflame the imagination, to inspire others to try again, and to encourage future growth from projects to projects.

Unfortunately, this great totality of interrelations, which stems from events so that science may appear within it to transform the whole, and within which lie things, men and their goals, has not yet been able to issue from a universal and objective knowledge. Every man and every people knows only partially what properly concerns him or it. Confrontations and interchanges of talk, memories retained from former lessons and the uninterrupted effort of criticism, permit a communal pooling of inspirations and experi-ences. But this they do at the price of creating worlds restricted by traditions and deeds in which the true mingles with the false, the rational with the passionate, the general with the particular. The imaginative, thanks to which man depicts himself, debates with himself, and projects himself into the future, is likewise the function of his wandering and his confusions.

Humanity discovers itself by dividing, in circumstances that force man to surpass himself. The idea, overrated from Plato to Descartes, is nevertheless only the reflection of a game of substitutions. Berkeley is the witness to scientific progress when he invites Kant to restore mathematics to experiment with conditions. And it is clear that Marx was trapped in idealisms when he forgot caution and claimed to transcend experimentation as well as living experience, and yielded so to the delights of introversion. A general utility is a more sure criterion. It guided savage men toward the living truth. It enabled us to escape from the overestimations of introversion, from the illusions of the good conscience which, believing itself endowed with some exceptional privilege, ventures beyond the reliable to be led inevitably to violences by which some other is made the victim.

Nevertheless, the idea is not purely illusion. It is not such, for example, when a creative cerebral physiology can find expression in myths to which communities cling at the price of their blood.

Unhappily, history does not have at its disposal that systematic experimentation by which science distinguishes the real from the illusory. Futhermore, the physicist himself, if he discovers eternal laws, does not know how to predict his own discoveries. He must resign himself to the inevitable; for we do not with sufficient certainty seize upon anything but reasonably stable functions, and are no better able to discuss their causes than their changing effects. The consequence is that the historian is not much worse off than the biologist when he is reconstructing evolution. No doubt Marx had this in mind when he proposed to dedicate his work to Darwin. Voltaire had already proved by example that accounts of the past find no way to escape the arbitrary demands which make the present credible. Like Montesquieu, he also guessed that cultures constitute systems comparable to living organisms, in which no element can be changed without correlative changes in the rest.

Evolution, so opposed in its first years, has been the more appreciated since it has been viewed as an antidote to Marxism. And yet Marx was already linking progress with the successive rejuvenations to be introduced by the renewals of class conflict. Thus he set up the ramifications of a design familiar to naturalists: a modern bourgeoisie called upon to supplant an absolute monarchy emerging from the same kind of transformation as permitted monarchy to prevail over feudalism. And if communism, not quite as he predicted, was able to establish itself only outside of the anticipated territory of the great capitalisms, from which it had to emigrate, it was conceived at the moment when capitalisms were taking form and before they had arrived at their real flowering.

Evolution does not select a single, simple path; it does not divide into fragments spliced one to another. When an evolutionary process runs its course, the defects which apparently interrupt it are the counterpart of the advantages which began it by particularizing it. The eye of birds and the instinct of insects are superior to those of man, but they represent limited and irreversible selections, and constitute successive options, having disregarded possibles already found manifesting themselves elsewhere in order to set up differing mutations. And this process, composed of cycles and stages, is sometimes without migration, and sometimes admits of it. The generative lines of innovation are capable of giving rise to several such, contradictory or complementary. The first to take form are not necessarily chosen for the greatest futures, though a delay in appearance is no better guarantee of greater success.

Finally — a lesson which implies the others — not all mutations are equally creative in all their stages. Sometimes evolution multiplies, sometimes it sets in order, sometimes it invents, and sometimes it brings about only slight modifications adapted to groups which advance no farther, and often regress. The first of these behaviors indicates that functions do not evolve in a unilinear manner. Certain ones among them, at certain stages, offer two or three solutions to the problem of their progress, and multiply the changes, such as those which created birds and mammiferes alongside the reptiles from which they issued, and from which they achieved their parallel development. These specializing mutations underline the importance of fairly simple branchings. The most striking of these in the animal world is that which contrasts the two lines of insects and vertebrates. On the other hand, and this is the effect of the second behavior, the evolutionary flowering of a species introduces into it nothing further of a basic nature, but adds an infinite differentiation of detail, effects of adaptations more deforming than creative, and the causes of the infinite variety in living nature, especially in its plant-life manifestations.

The first of these two patterns applies equally well to cultural evolution; like cultural evolution it is discontinuous, mutant, cyclic, not necessarily indigenous. The second pattern is less creative than adaptive, is infinitely recommencing, sometimes surprising, but ephemeral and relative in its manifestations. It applies to what history, like everyday usage, calls facts, noteworthy facts and divers facts, or, more precisely, innumerable circumstances, recommencing and fugitive, such as give birth to these facts.

It is more appropriate, however, to stress the close relationships between history and biology. Cultures do not have the autonomous and rigid structure of animal species, for each culture is composed of changing elements and interelations. No one is independent of the others; all of them interact to advance the general organism of humanity. In short, rather than speaking of distinct organisms of a paleontologic genesis, it is more appropriate to speak of the organs of embryogenesis.

The biologist benefits by the privilege of knowing the terms of a living evolution, which apparently no longer creates since the appearance of man. But he does not have the advantage of being placed at the center of phenomena. His superiority is less open to question in all that touches on ontogenesis, the life history of the individual organism: he can cause something to be reproduced under his eyes. But the historian is enclosed within his era and within his district, at the center of a grandiose and unique phenomenon which extends beyond his reach in all dimensions, and whose end he cannot know. History is thus dependent on biology. In certain of its aspects, it is the enormous, transposed enlargement of what the microscope reveals.

No doubt the appeal to present discoveries to explain past facts risks the charge of anachronism. And indeed, it could not be a question of denying the lessons of scholarship in the name of a systematization exclusively inspired by the present, but only of ordering the importance of historical realities less in terms of the aspirations of an epoch, a circumstance, an author, than as a pattern susceptible to verification, made precise by virtue of an experimentation which may always be checked. This attitude is as legitimate as the postulate implicit in all history: namely, the present does not revive the past, but it does permit that some part of it that it is important to know is remembered and understood.

As for the rest, we shall not insist overmuch on the constant changes in the pace and aspect of evolution. Even if we had to note only the mutation introduced by scientific industrialization, we should have to prohibit the affirmation that human action operates identically in all parts of its course. No less important were the identification of spoken and written signs, the discovery of demonstrations, the inspiration of monotheisms, or the invention of scientific nomenclatures. The discontinuities thus acknowledged would seem to accord badly with two necessary ideas: that which creates from the permanence of physical laws a postulate of their elaboration and utilization, and that which renders the human species as naturally invariable since its biological appearance. History belongs exclusively neither to the deterministic nor to pure chance. Collective and diachronic, it arises biologically from the one and from the other.

This primacy of the biological is of such a nature as to be reassuring, for it gives reason to believe that human inventiveness will not prevail over the more general destiny of life.

III. Nevertheless, it is hardly conceivable that humanity can purge its existence of all conflict. All that is needed to convince one of this is to refer to the past, and to the perennial and yet never exhausted lessons of those moralists who treat of the passions. The list of these has been fixed for some time, and, though brief, seems to take human motivations into account. However, the passions hardly explain why, if all men are subject to them, only a small number of them remain objects of memory. Even less do they explain scientific and technical progress. Passions are more subject to differentiations than are the creative advances of order, as is confessed by the problem dictionaries have in defining love or avarice, pride or envy. Even as they harrow us, passions cause us to feel the living unity of the self. Even so, they are not subject to circumscription within specific and exhaustive examples, but yield as many varied combinations as there are attitudes to be given representation. The millions of turmoils and agitations in the present drama of the earth lead us to suspect a still greater number in the dizzying depths of the past or the infinite perspectives of the future. We are no doubt fortunate that abstraction has reduced such an immensity to a few basic motivations, but it is scarcely rational to suppose that this has exhausted their significance. Since it is unlikely that among so many different ways of behaving any large number should turn out to be identical, all that we are taught thereby is that existence is explained less by reference to the unique than by what alters that existence under the effect of discontinuous and discriminatory pressures.

The contradictions that inhere in man's becoming collective insure that each finds therein the condition for his consciousness that he exists. By linking together the points at which his self-will clashes with the resistences he meets and provokes, he discovers his own contours. He defines the self less by the vague continuity of his internal emotions than by the attitudes, the gestures, the words, the faces of a reality of which some other is the witness, the confidant, or the scornful observer. He is made up of tentative attempts as detected, recognized, or denounced by others. Beyond the fact that all that he has been escapes from his will, he can only — and that within the restricted possibilities that are determined by his previous accomplishments — adjust his future growth to what surrounds him and what affects him according to unknown necessities.

This adjustment, even while it multiplies the possibilities of being, produces also an immense dispersion of events of all orders and magnitudes, incessantly and infinitely reformed; and this not so much because men change in nature, as that nature, modified by men, changes the conditions provided for them. The intervention of things in human existence differs according to the depth to which science has penetrated them. What are exact laws at a certain stage cease to be such at another greater stage, where the reality involves less the simple postulates than the changes within their system. Thus history has a character of starting over in those surface manifestations that are political facts, and that are always the more upsetting because of all that is introduced into them by the unseen agitations of creation itself.

This creative penetration places human evolution after the biological evolution, even though the former is continued in a quite different style. The living force which modifies species acts in and on them, but independently of their knowledge and will; the cerebral force is appropriate to the human species, but, even so, without becoming strictly rational. Every individual chooses at every moment among many possibilities, of which most will never advance beyond vaguely disturbing or regretted potentials. The totality of men multiplies infinitely the available potentialities for each, but those which the community realizes are not the same as those which necessity withholds from its members. Every man is the intersection of two worlds of possibilities mutually irreducible. The one, which is voluntary, is adaptive, chance, ephemeral, and always recommencing; the other, intellectual, extends the biological task, is creative, ordered and durable in its effects, insofar as it is governed by a necessity.

This ambivalence is fairly well evoked in the dual meaning expressed in the French language by a single word: humanity. Other languages have recourse to two vocables to name on the one hand the totality of living folk, about to live or having lived (humankind), organizers of a world subject to organization; and, on the other, a certain common and indefinable quality, postulated in each of us, and showing itself admirably among certain ones (humanitarianism).[2] In the first sense, humanity implies a progress; in the second, an immanence. This ambiguity is obvious in European vocabulary, rediscovering amid Renaissance confusions what Cicero said of the knowledge of *belles lettres* as suited to refine manners. In English pragmatism, humanity is opposed to the human race, and identifies in a restrictive way a certain quality of heart, invoked in favor of the abolition of slavery, or the legal protection of animals and children. In France, philosophic optimism had preferred to blend into one vocable a quality of spirit with the progress of enlightenment, and the conquests of equality with those of mechanical power; and this vocable became the standard of successive revolutions before disillusionments and skepticisms abandoned it to the abuses of rhetoricians. Nevertheless, in every case and in all countries, the hope survives that the superior qualities of men will enable them to surmount the divisions made so dangerous by reason of their instruments. In this sense, the word humanity has not lost the esteem of honest men who respect themselves in others, and who, however concerned they may be over their own deaths, can accept the idea more easily because of the assurance that just and upright men will survive them.

But not all has been said when we declare that man owes it to himself to be human toward his neighbor, for only within society does he know himself. The totality of men, far from constituting a single unit, is linked with others through a very large number of collective fields, within which enterprises and representations differ in space and time. Humanity conjures up not so much moments of grace in which essential truths are revealed to intuition, as a diversity of experience, an immense juxtaposition and an indefinite sequence of realities, neither absolutely in opposition nor exactly consistent, which, though they never entirely obliterate the individual, do place him in particular contexts. The inability of the normal man to

2. The English *humanity*, however, may also connote either. Translator's note.

identify himself with humanity, though he seeks nevertheless to do so for his full fruition, has justified his belonging to one or several restricted groups. The proximity and the overlapping of these add up to an extremely high number of borderline zones — natural areas of conflict, where the worst violences are at one and the same time both forbidden and justified.

Geographic space offers the most obvious example of these areas of conflict. In any one spot, at every moment, there occur clashes of interests and passions whose structures may be recognized by their opposition to other structures, differing in the organization of their elementary and analogous components. This process of differentiation gives to the human landscape its infinite faces. As a corollary to the historic movements so initiated, this process is, on the collective ladder, the magnified expression of the contradictions introduced by milieu which differ with each individuation; it also translates the restraints imposed by climates and geologies. But if it is above all adaptive, it is also educative, and therefore expresses itself in the preemption of organizational centers. Among nomadic peoples, the disposition of tents, huts, or houses in a village prefigures the effort within urban centers to preempt the high spots which best serve to polarize attention, and so to confer order and authority upon the official image. This process, consistent with its origin, does not halt with the concentration of efforts at the heart of, or in the environs of, a single city. It regroups several such efforts under the preeminence of the one among them which is privileged by a very variable combination of customs consecrating its priority, or of traditions and decorums which support the innovation.

There is no nation, even of recent origin, which has not entirely or in part traversed the path leading from the agrarian to the municipal regime, and to the choice of a capital city which eventually became the capital of an empire. The modern republics of America have in a few decades passed through the stages that were known in elementary succession to Mesopotamian proto-history. Geographic fragmentation is thus reduced insofar as a sure and constant need for unification, obedient to communal laws, invites that reduction. This need, appearing long after the geological transformations which moulded the face of the earth, is subordinated to the particular facts which that geology has inscribed thereon; but human experience renders that need primordial. Inheritor of the social instincts of animality, that need expresses these imperatives, adding thereto demands of a far more differentiated hierarchization.

But even this hierarchization cannot be attributed to the influence of the accidents of place alone. The distance which separates kings from their subjects, gods from the faithful, or the learned elite from the proletariat of the earth, involves a structural density far greater than the depth of passion, and not to be sufficiently accounted for by geographic interventions alone. If most of our planet's territories are found to be humanized, this is no doubt due to the resources and opportunities that they have offered men. And this is true even of territories purely useless, such as the conquest of a desert or a mountain, though not without a long series of efforts at conquests dictated by needs quite different from those of settlements alone.

Proofs may be found in the central role of commerce, which reorders all ecology. The profitable transportation of merchandise and valuables fulfills a dominant urge of mankind for exchange. Here one may observe the reduced image of a much larger reality manifested in the constitution of families, languages, and institutions; that is, all that which transforms dependence into interrelations, and transcends the organic by organization. It has frequently happened, notably in Roman antiquity or in certain Christian periods, that the man without profession or land who abandoned his penates or his parish to turn to maritime or caravan adventure was regarded with a certain suspicion, because he seemed to take himself out of his group. Nevertheless, he stimulates it, brings it unknown goods, arouses envy, creates needs, and, by making the feeling of differences more acute, transmutes it into aggressiveness. Thus enviable traffickings in goods may mark out the pathways of war; at the same time, by distributing goods and balancing the equation, they open the routes for moral and scientific understanding. Up to our own time, the first effect has prevailed over the second. Europe, swept along by the impetus of its merchants bent on the conquest of the earth, believed itself called to some universal legitimacy, under the pretext of a superiority which seemed to promise that by imposing its will it also bestowed progress on others. In fact, it exported its poverty and its divisions, and the contradictions that disturbed Europe itself before tearing it apart almost to the point of its destruction. To search into the cause of this disillusionment is to ask not only how merchandising had so laid hold on the men who began by distributing it, but also by what internal processes the particular characteristics of cultures became so irritated by what seemingly should have neutralized their differences.

Works of art surely constitute a common heritage of mankind; yet the greater part of these works register such special historical perspectives as to have known but fragmented existences on the earth's surface. Now languages and literatures, the more highly developed meanings offered to eye and ear, and the bonds of unity, are also bearers of aggressiveness. Esthetics at its most profound undoubtedly allows one to divine some common mental structure which crosses the frontiers of culture and epochs. Yet, just as we reach the inimitable when we seek the universal, so these arts, as they have become more embellished, have the more dangerously enclosed representation in localized worlds.

Finally, now that long experience with many sorts of interrelation has enabled man to discover science, demonstrable certainty, and rigorous experimentation, people still fiercely confront one another. Though scientific attainments spread to new continents for the benefit of all, the obstacles that science encountered in former times are no less present today. Yet already the great States in which almost the totality of man's industrial power is concentrated and developed have mutually neutralized one another. The rest of the world, which they once believed themselves destined to dominate, is left with the opportunity to work out its historic experiment amid the wars to which its people are driven by an aggravated poverty.

We must look outside of geopolitics, commerce, the arts, even science, therefore, for what it is that justifies the vague conviction of mankind that they are all one, carried along on the vast floodtide of progress which particularizes even while it oppresses. Men feel strongly, each within himself, that this solidarity, this oneness, is somehow linked to the existence of a specific function common to all. This function we shall call *historicity.*

The varying meanings of this word evoke the necessary or voluntary conditions which affect the interrelations among men, defining them as men, beyond their insularity, which is itself so dependent and ephemeral. Historicity, so understood, is indeed a function, or, if one prefer, a group of functions, which forces man to change, and which delimits the physical, physiological, and collective conditions of these changes and their consequences, and so circumscribes the domain of liberty, consciousness, and will. Historicity is that which assembles motivations into a synchronic perspective, goes beyond the reality which is properly human to extend itself to all that imposes, within the natural determinisms, a sequence and an order. From it arise rational and moral imperatives, even if it does not illuminate the secret of the conscience and the will. Its action directs history, without determining its every detail. As an internal function, it leaves men a certain freedom of choice. As influenced by things and the collective structures which translate its imperatives, it remains subject to events. But on each occasion, it is as much involved in the inevitability of excesses as in the necessity of the equilibriums which must be preserved within them.[3]

Some elementary lessons may be drawn from this permanency of the function of historicity. As regards its necessity, its historical validity and its political justification, it forces us first of all to pay our respects to the illusion that men should be happier today than in earlier times. From what wretched state would they have had to emerge if all the progress accomplished in thousands of years had been strictly parallel to the state of their happiness? We are forced to admit that in ancient times they might have found amid their lesser need and their lesser effort, and within societies assured of an order quite close to the elementary manifestations of life, what we seek amid the harassments of productivity and a dependence on goods whose multiplicity has become indispensable. Rousseau was partly right in his reservations: man, if he is the instrument of progress, is also its plaything.

There are two corrolaries to this moderation. The first is that it is vain to regret a change about which one can do nothing, but which permits a certain hope to exist, even if an illusory one, against the flagrant injustices of history. The second is that no people can arrogate to themselves the privilege of teaching others how to be happy. Such naive arrogance does injury to the disinherited who recall a one-time good fortune and find in that memory the impulse and the courage to plunge into the greatest risks, in the effort to extricate themselves from a thankless present. Generosity, where it is assumed — as it is every time one prides himself on his greatness of soul for granting what is either an obvious right or a common necessity — is a form of cruelty and invites its consequences. The art of giving gifts, which primitive societies enter upon with caution, involves a difficulty which has been described by eminent anthropol-

3. For example, one may see a war not as created by a collectivity but as a way of responding to a situation which has to be met in some way. Historicity, that is, has brought about a situation which can not be ignored, and must be met in *some* way. The 'choice' then may be called 'a certain freedom', though it might be to try to ignore any choice, hence to court destruction from outside. Thus Chapter 2, 'The event as datum'. Translator's note.

ogists. According to the ritual, he who gives the least suffers from that fact, and in consequence loses his prestige and his authority.

Finally, quite apart from these corollaries of political morality, the concept of historicity opens new paths for research. At this stage of beginning, we know little of historicity beyond its way of acting through differentiations. Starting, therefore, with what opposes itself to man, we must try to seize upon some basis for his hope of finding a common reason for being. This way of beginning may not illuminate the goal to be sought, but it does point up the most immediate object of our study: namely, the event, or, more precisely, what all events possess in common or as differences, into which are translated all that opposes us, reveals us, and changes us.

2. The event as datum

I. If historicity is a function, its organ is not circumscribed. To designate the organ under the name of humanity is to appeal to a vague, ambiguous and too restrictive notion, since in the history of the development of a man or of men, forces of a material order and logical constants intervene, such as belong not to humanity alone but to the totality of the real. Philosophers assign this force to God, to Spirit, to Matter. The ancients wavered between limiting destiny to the scales of Jupiter or the scissors of the Parcae. Theologians have debated without end on efficacious or efficient grace; the mystics on the correspondences between Quality and Being. Nevertheless, they have this in common: they attribute all existence to one and the same universal stuff. Neither phenomenologists nor marxists have denied the intuition which assigns all historicity to a totality as evident as it is indefinable.

Since historicity cannot be apprehended through its organ, it must be grasped though what manifests it: and that is, events. But we are confounded by their multiplicity. Assuredly, to that imagined gesture which scattered the fistful of matter out of which the universe is made, and with that same act created space, gravitation, particles, stars and the earth, we may as well ascribe also the virtue of holding likewise in its power the essential forces of life and of history. There would be no event, then, large or small, which would not be a moment consequent on that original and primordial deed. Before the popularizers had proposed that image, seers and poets had done so. Nevertheless, this image does not merit even the name of hypothesis, for if it can sum up everything, nothing can be deduced from it. Events cannot be reduced to a single one. There is no one which is not the secret of all. Closely watched by the man of State hearkening to his rivals or to the masses of people, by the financier scrutinizing the markets, by the scholar analyzing and reordering the data of his apparatus, events lead their existence from suspense to suspense, revealing nothing which is not also an interrogation; and their chronology, strict in its past necessity, remains problematical in conjecture.

This last feature we should attribute to men's freedom to give themselves over to acts of their own choice except that, long before they existed on earth, nature gave proof of a spontaneity that already defied all prediction. Beginning with the anthropoids, we may trace back over the trail of species as far as the simplest; but no reasoning permits us to deduce absolutely, by beginning with what the reptiles or fish had been, what the mammals eventually became. And even before life, matter had no less been constituted by events, and continued to be so to its minutest and humblest depths.

The human event, a specialized type of the phenomena proper to nature as a whole, appears in the very last eras of an immense evolutionary duration that disregards millions of years more freely than we do decades. Our existence is so brief in the scale of time that an accomplishment that appears long to us is scarcely perceptible in the unfolding of the great plants, and as for that of minerals, there appeared for a long time to be no connection. The duration of the totality of the human phenomenon compared to that which preceded it, supported, or nourished it, has the thickness of a finger on a mountain top. But the importance it assumes in our eyes is inscribed as a consequence of a major mutation, namely, that which introduced thought with the brain. Since then, we may classify events according to the role that cerebral activity has played therein.

Before man's appearance — the most important mutation since that which began life — this mysterious entity, life, produced thousands of organic forms, giving each a specific form. Successive creative waves gave rise to beings organized according to the appropriate acquatic, terrestial, aerial, pedologic and climatic conditions. And still the event excluded individuality; the behavior of a particular being was that of the species. And if the less enduring parts of the genealogical tree have been eroded, notably by bifurcations and what neighbors on them, no doubt the event, in its essential axis, was already ordered, though in no simple way. Some ramifications are involutive and produce nothing more than their own flowering; or, if progressive, they give birth to new ramifications. A whole universe of a depth still incalculable, whose dimensions escape our spaces, is intimated to us by constituted forces of increasing orders, in groups which are nourished and destroyed by one another, or project themselves into the future from equilibrium to equilibrium, by contradictory, complementary, or substitutive realizations.

The appearance of man by no means puts an end to a natural spontaneous and organizing process. The interdependence of species is not abolished, for man would not survive if animals and vegetables did not interpose between him and the mineral nature which is incapable of nourishing him. Thus the event retains in history the same mystery it had before history.

Life doubtless no longer brings forward new species on the shores of the known universe, and the organization which continues will no longer do so in the future except internally in the last of these. Within what surrounds this ultimate creature, all becomes adaptive if not regressive, and man is left alone in the world which gave him birth. Yet man remains still subject to a milieu which is still changing. The advance and retreat of immense glaciers, the descents and re-ascents between the poles and the equator, the zones which permit him to survive, forced him to adapt or be displaced. The pressure of these physical restraints exerted its influence during hundreds of thousands of years, that is to say, around a hundredfold more time than that of the whole proto-history combined. And still we must add that after the glacial retreat and the elevation of sea levels that resulted from their melting, the earth, freed from such great weight, rose. The relief, the modeling, the network of streams and rivers, the coating of sterile gravels or fertile mud, slowly became what they now are. During this period, by far the longest of its existence, humanity was forced by nature, led by her, toward the sites of man's unequal developments. One might think that this state of subordination to things hindered the progress of humanity, that the landscape needed to settle, so that humankind could conceive the first great progress of its neolithic age. Nevertheless, during the immense period that preceded, humanity had known several epochs of respite, hundreds of centuries in length. Now the traces left from these periods indicate a relative permanence of habits and archaic tools. This length of time, these pressures and intermissions of respite, are a part of nature's effort as it arrives at man and leads him by force to choose places through which, once he has become sapiens, he will soon be made historic.

Since then, human evolution operates in hundreds, then tens of years, in changes more important than those that had required thousands. Even so, the acceleration thus manifested does not exclude the pressures that originate in modifications of climate. These are not too easily observed because they take place on the scale of centuries or millenia, and because they are based on the whims of the seasons, for which it is difficult to establish meaningful ways of measurement. In perspectives of very long duration, the presence of insidious modifications of meteorological conditions can hardly be denied, and then the phytological which, in the long term, in other ways redistribute abundance or poverty. Such changes are also events, much spread out, and dragging with them slow migrations or modifications on the horizons of human labor. Traces of these last are found especially in legends which bridge the centuries, in myths like those of the deluge. History must have endured much that has never been deciphered. Infinite variations on the frontiers of tropical aridity have played with the destinies of great peoples. Perhaps central Asia, North Africa, Spain, in turn have profited and suffered from them. It is not impossible that the sudden invasions of Mongol horsemen and the Tartar empires, as well as their decline, the variations in wealth and poverty in the Iberian peninsula, the continuous progress of the rural yield in the temperate Occident since it surpassed Oriental fertility, were all partially, and in their first causes, effects of climatic variations, by which water was withheld or granted to pastures, fields, and gardens. Human labor, too, by its blunders, for example, by excessive deforestation, has sometimes aggravated the consequences of these natural imperatives; in any case, it has not yet abolished them.

The influence exercised by geologic and cosmic power on man's destiny is not one of variations only. The way plains and reliefs, the resource of soil and sub-soil, are localized affects all the dynamisms of human collective action in the conquest of its habitats. Geography intervenes in the human story by setting up obstacles and suggesting passages, by distributing or refusing plant, animal or mineral wealth. It predestines the places where they live as well as those where they confront one another.

Beyond these physical conditions, a living nature intervenes actively in the great collective accidents of health. Man, whose gaze has so customarily turned toward the skies to read there his destiny or the promise of his harvests, has no less consulted it for a further cause of anxiety, epidemics. Yet human behavior must bear its share of blame; it, too, has modified the delicate balances of the biological realm. Travels, the arrival in alien environments of physiologies not immunized to the local pathogenic germs and so causing them to become virulent, have carried trails of disaster across continents, to confound reason and to warn us of the tragic character imprinted on all that lives.

II. But if these difficulties, surprises and misfortunes have aroused fear, they have also provoked reflection and, in the very long run, remedies. Collective struggles undertaken against excessive dryness or humidity, as against diseases, have originated from these direful events, and given value to the inventions which have ameliorated their effects. On such a scale, history is made up of a very long succession of efforts. Thus, as a consequence of natural conditionings that could underwrite the survival of the human species and force it to develop a systematic experimentation, whose advantages are progressively perceived by human intelligence, the event is characterized by two extremes of behavior. On the one hand, by exposing an unexpected difficulty and challenging acquired habits, it shows confusion and arouses anxiety; on the other hand, it also gives rise to a process of reflection. And once reflection ceases to lay the blame on heaven, from which derives the concept of a cosmic infinitude, and applies itself to the purely earthly and pertinent details, it can pose the problems in precise terms, attach hope to solutions provided by earth, and open up new paths for expansion.

Still in the category of facts, then, are these insidious or brutal cataclysms that natural environment inflicts, these infinitely variable pressures which take so many victims before they provoke marvels of invention. Though such facts may not be simply and uniformly reproduced, they will reveal fairly constant laws for science to seize upon. Not being presented to science as rigorously identical among themselves, or in such a form that science may, so to speak, familiarize itself with them, these facts surprise and challenge, and constitute a menace never wholly to be banished. What they retain of the unforseeable, together with the spontaneous modifications of the environment, adds up to what may be called the natural raw facts.

Raw facts, it happens, comprise only a minor and poorly recognized part of what historians, politicians, and the public call events. Purely human interventions are much more often held to be the cause of events. Nevertheless, raw facts lie at the axis of natural events which they prolong. Envisage, for example, the succession of empires, or, what is still more meaningful, the proximity of cultures, sometimes productive, sometimes aggressive, in which nothing grows old or declines without having produced some means of arousing new summons in their turn to surmount some new level of progress. The image thus evoked is very close to what the naturalist observes in the selection of species and the genesis of their lines. Consider the end of the Persian dynasties of the Achemenides, then that of Rome, the establishment of orthodox Christianity and the renaissance of heresies, the rise of Europe, then that of new or revived worlds — no one any longer thinks of attributing these solely to the initiatives of military or religious leaders. In the hidden origins of these events, as in their spectacular achievements, a natural law exercises its power. Such a law implies not only a certain irreversible development of societies, but also a thousand discontinuities, innumerable wish-fancies of all sorts inspired by desire, yet limited by the needs of humanity in search of its own flowering.

The thousand events of history are inscribed within the general framework of natural raw facts. They are superadded to the facts, like those futile, erratic, excessive, or uncompleted tentatives within which biological evolution hides internal necessity under a surface appearance of a useless luxuriance. Men find in these, beyond what restrains them, their justification for being; there they test their ardor for living. They are the infinite range of vicissitudes out of which is created the immense representation in which all participate, the generators and regulators of our symbols. They issue from all the physiological functions, thanks to which and within which humanity, working with nature, seeks the paths of its own certitude.

For there are, finally, other facts besides the natural raw facts and those commonly described as historic. The discovery of a mathematical demonstration or a principle of physics, the rearrangement of medical symptomatologies or of biological classifications, the enrichment of systems of unities or of the nomenclatures of physics and chemistry, also constitute facts. And to those we must add the inventions of every successful expression that comes from the arts or the languages. Again belonging to the world of the event are the building of the Parthenon, and the procedure for resolving the equation of the third degree. For both of these mark an epoch, since neither Mesopotamian nor Egyptian architecture contained the sum of the first, nor Arabian mathematics that of the second. Such facts merit a special place by their being more specifically cerebral. Like the goddess of wisdom, they spring from the thinking forehead. They are symbols and signs, enriched and recreated, rather than substituted organisms or the disposition of groups in motion; and they resemble nothing at all outside of the human phenomenon, which they so preëminently characterize. They, too, take the form of a tree of knowledge strongly resembling that of the genealogy of species. And at least those belonging to the elevated order of mathematics offer the unique advantage of permitting a direct study, as detailed as may be wished, of the way they branch off among themselves.

Furthermore, if an author happens to date the birth of science, it is out of enthusiasm for some ingenious process for which he has uncovered the evidence. But whatever the importance of the successes thus brought to light, they always imply some antecedent. And this is so true that there is no moment in all of human evolution which can be recorded as marking a clear-cut first appearance of the scientific intelligence. At least there is none unless it be precisely that moment when man first appears as displaying those faculties which merit the name of man. Science extends over the whole course of history, since no other end except that of humanity itself can be prognosticated for it. By the same count, science covers the vastest ranges conceivable. The infinitely small and the infinitely large are implanted in the inductions of science, because it has been forced to express in rationalized proofs what the human world offers of the most intuitive and the most distant; that is, through arithmetic and astronomy, created by means of the syntax uncovered in the genesis of number and tested by the most impressive calculations on the positions of the stars.

When man was still predominantly religious in nature, his temples, pyramids, observatories, cosmogonies and mythologies, no less than his customs, clearly demonstrated that he still continued to hold as sacred the celestial and unknown causes that animated his existence. Nevertheless, from the endless reproduction of identical events, he had already disengaged certain popularized and secularized signs and tokens, which he used mechanically in his daily living. Such signs lent their practical efficiency to his working gestures as well as to his business dealings, and of course to his language. Even before what is called history began, a body of proven knowledge was already taking form, a testimony to obscure correlations that would generate logic as well as symbolic meanings. From then on, humanity continues to depend on and to scan events, nor will it cease enlarging this nucleus of self-creative and operative meanings. This mingling of events and meanings furnishes a basic stimulus to the feeling of mystery; also, thanks to conceptual thought, it makes action more efficient.

Much time must have elapsed before the return of the day, the year, the seasons, was accepted as assured. Breviaries of religion and civil holidays still linger among customs, remembered rites, as traces of solemn rituals, or as echoes of inherited fairy tales from the most remote times, to prove that each of these returns was taken as a reward for prayers or as gratitude for ceremonies. We must also surmise how much of fear and sacred awe were involved in the accomplishment of a calculation. The fidelity with which numbers responded in operations executed with their help and yet the difficulties they sometimes opposed, explain why gods were made of numbers. The immense fund of physical regularities, the condensation of water, the causes and effects of fire or weight, were not always left vague in a context so familiar or so fixed that they must have been taken as ordinary and reliable. Each had been the object of a conquest pursued through two stages: the first frees the observer from sacred reverences, the second permits him to perceive general laws. The rhythmical movement of an object suspended by a thread, the evidences of combustion, the origin of rain, must have ceased being treated as manifestations of the supernatural long before the principles of weight and mechanics, of chemistry and meteorology, were freed for the scientific spirit. And yet perhaps no less effort was required to stimulate the attention of scholars to these phenomena, long since a part of the unreflective knowledge of a daily routine. They had to be stripped of their emotive charge before the time could be quite ripe for secularizing them into the ordinary and customary. The stone which may serve to build or to destroy, the plant which nourishes or poisons, the beast which helps or kills, all have shared in a universal animism supposedly governed by malevolent or beneficent powers, or by demons and sorcerors. The innumerable evidences available to common experience must first have had to be withdrawn from the mythological universe and to have become familiar well before they could emerge into history as elements of systems proved to be constant.

This twofold process has indeed a significance at first all-inclusive, uncertain, and impassioned, as well as productive of poetic charms — at first awkward at reading causes, then more precise, rational, operative, able to uncover the shortest path leading from one effect to another. The laws of the physical universe do not belong to evolution because they do not change. But they do show what conditions it; and they are there for the progressive apprenticeship by which intelligence domesticates feeling and is thereafter enriched. In the circumscribed realm where natural orders most easily inspire symbols and then signs, the event, though conceived in emotion, becomes an invention, a discovery, and finds birth in expression.

There exist therefore at least two distinct categories of events. In the first, the event is rudely thrust upon man's attention by nature; or rather, it is at once both a signal and a constraint operating from outside, and pouncing upon man to command him. In the second, it is uncovered in exact expressions, in systematized orders made pertinent to effectual references. It appears as the conclusion of an unfolding and an effort at internal discipline, inviting man to produce further examples. Now these two categories of events join hands to educate man. The first, more suited to his emotions, elaborates them; the second implies a universe of reliable laws uncovered by reason.

In sum, to make a pertinent classification of all kinds of events, as one does of colors on a spectrum, leads to locating them at the extremes. At the one end is the raw natural fact, at the other, science; and all else is distributed in between. And since this rearrangement of the three groups pertains to the one reality, the way in which the knowledge of nature manages to abandon the older restraints must tell us something about the progressive function of innumerable facts customarily designated as historic.

III. Now the first condition in order that a scientific notion may be pertinently extricated from the flood of concrete data is that exact sequences of causes be found therein. Here a special difficulty intervenes, and perhaps the greatest of all those with which humanity must come to terms: namely, the most reliable causal series are not always those which best please human emotivity. For Aristotle, a moving body ceased to move when the force causing it to move ceased to act. As long as it was believed that he had enunciated a commonplace bit of evidence, no rational mechanics could be conceived; for the first condition was a conviction that a body in continuous and linear motion would sustain the movement so long as no force acted to oppose it. Involved here was a feature which offended reason even more than the heart. The effort would have to be even greater for one to admit that a beloved one could be the victim of chance. Between the loss suffered, the grief felt, and the trivial nature of the cause, reduced as it is by the theory of probability, all is so disproportionate that it is not difficult to understand why all human beings during so many millenia past, and most of them even today, should turn to a universe of beliefs situated beyond operative, efficacious, but inhuman reflection. Among peoples called savage, the individual killed by a wild animal or attacked by a disease passes less as the accidental victim of a chance meeting than as the target for an act of magic will.

Thus innumerable lessons of a long history thick with events were demanded before a working use of causality could be defined and delimited. The notion of chance came close to flowering in ancient Ionia; and it underlies the Greek feeling for the tragic. But we have to wait for the later days of the Renaissance before a rational working design of a causal series could be applied precisely to physics, and, correlatively, before all the indeterminate could be assembled under the field of chance or the contingent. When actuaries set up their mortality tables, indifferent to the reasons of the heart, the human spirit began to comprehend what causes are, in their relation to natural laws and great numbers. The measure of how much our present century retains of the Pascalian is how very difficult it is to exclude the providential from our knowledge, and to let the operative prevail over the emotive.

In other terms, it is by the test of historic experience, on innumerable and contradictory events, traversing the inspirations of art and religious belief, that human intelligence learns an impersonal logic and the postulates pertinent to its application. It was at such cost that physicists could make an inventory of their laws and their objects.

Such success is that of an analysis of every event. Time presents itself now as a cycle, that of instants, days, or seasons, now as a line which never turns back on itself. It invites us to distinguish all that repeats itself absolutely: the stone that falls, the harvests renewing themselves, pairs which beget their descendents, generations which pass in turn; and also that which changes without return, the aging of beings, of peoples, of systems of State or of representation. It suggests a redistribution of all according to the range of observation. Men, taken in isolation, appear free; in mass, their destinies are linked. The experience of civil laws, inquiries into guilt, the administration of justice and the development of law, all have played a necessary role in the progress that has led man to distinguish the fortuitous from the lawful, the superior force from responsibility, and, in consequence, the law of things and of chance. But law itself issued from a reflection still more elementary.

The date or dates of any event whatsoever constitute at first sight merely an external guide mark which does not penetrate to its substance. As opposed to its situation in time, men will speak of the content of an event; it has dealt us a blow, they say of it, or it struck us. Nevertheless, it does not consist of a block which cannot be decomposed. Once the moment of surprise has passed, the event lends itself to a closer look, a comparison, the establishing of a chain of causes to explain how what had been unforeseeable became unavoidable. The event, as its etymology indicates, is also an arrival or an outcome, the termination of secret movements whose course one is compelled to retrace, once he has felt the importance of their effects. It may then be penetrated in all sorts of directions; and to such a degree that after having been experienced as a block, the event then offers itself for analysis as a point of junction in a complex of vectors. It teaches that the weight of things conceals an articulated space.[1] It forces us to treat the emotive as the immediately concrete manifestation of a logically graspable reality. Modern psychology, it happens, has verified experimentally that these two lessons, the first impact seen as a block, then the analysis of the event as an element in a chain of causes, are essential to the genesis of intelligence.[2]

Furthermore, when an event takes place in the realm of the symbol, so that, even for an instant, all the poetry of the world is summed up in a brain to create a sign that transforms some aspect of the universe, the way for this cerebral conquest has been prepared by living through a vast number of ordeals. But this latest sign also makes use of symbols and expressions previously discovered. Thus, through these restraints and reconformations man creates his knowledge of things. The stages of this conquest are made up of so many elementary apprenticeships, articulated among themselves to touch the very heart of the infinite diversity of facts and deeds.

The lessons thus learned cannot fail to exert an influence on the interpretation of subsequent events, which from that moment on will be differently interpreted. A review of these earliest lessons leads one

1. The word 'articulated' is preferable here to 'structured', as being less static in implication, and as evoking a mechanism, the possibility of movement. Note from Ch. Morazé, Jan. 23, 1971.

2. Piaget has shown that the child is capable of reasoning accurately with regard to mass before being able to do so with space, and, a fortiori, with movements. The child undergoing his apprenticeship in the external world is in the same situation as an adult facing an event as a blow or a weight before it is analyzed as a part of a totality of trajectories which converge. Note from Ch. Morazé, Jan. 23, 1971.

to revaluate subsequent experiences, and to explicate them more successfully by cataloguing afresh the threads which bind them together. This is what one does after an accident, the collision of two trajectories up to then independent; or again, after an illness, the eruption of an infectious colony within a living organism; or, let us say, after a bit of good fortune, an arrangement of pleasures, or a pleasing combination of circumstances more or less anticipated. And yet illnesses or accidents, duly categorized, give rise to statistical methods, offered for overall predictions. What for the victim is a tragic surprise is for the actuary but part of a system sufficiently stable to permit insurance companies to negotiate the risks with confidence. The same holds for lucky coincidences; they, too, after the event, are explained and catalogued without offending logic, within the totality of what has occured.

Every event teaches men to rise above sensory appearances in order to achieve a more profound intellectual grasp, to reflect on the effects of mass in order to comprehend the structures of space; and finally, by altering the nature of chance, to deprive the gods of what now depends on objectively determined causes or on accident circumscribed by the calculations of chances. These lessons can, of course, be heeded only to the degree that human nature accepts them. Therefore, in the physiology of historicity, we shall find functions to correspond to their assimilation. We shall also find degrees of efficiency, corresponding to an increasing order of complications. The implication here is that collective experiences, more or less prolonged, had taken place before the proper conditions could arise — sometimes cumulative, sometimes mutually altered so as to be ready for some new conquest — or could be envisioned by the brains of those individuals most capable of turning them to good account.

History itself teaches us that millenia were necessary before the syllogism and demonstration were conceived; and twenty centuries more were needed to arrive at the conviction that laws of mass and space apply identically to the most ordinary mechanical effects and to the cosmos itself. However, this identification must never lead us to deduce with finality that the infinitely small obeys the stated regularities of the ordinary scale. Here too, we may perceive the primordial importance of the collective: to expel astrology from the heavens so that astronomy might entirely take over is to submit ourselves once again to reflection on chance. Thus the European collectivity, having finally grasped as a living experience the roundness of the earth, and approaching the moment when that fact is inspiring Newton to his principles, aids him in verifying them. It then becomes sufficiently involved to draw from all this the methods and definitions that will serve nineteenth century physicists, and already conceives the axiomatics of chance, destined to be so indispensable to the physicists of the twentieth century.

It has not been easy to find a place for the science of chance. It is too thoroughly mingled in with everything else, to which it is linked through the combining factor of the imaginative faculty; nor is it to be identified with either determinism or freedom. These two phases of all existence are strangely mixed. Conjointly, they have given rise to two vocabularies, and, as it were, two styles for treating of them. People, when they are outside of science, speak of God, of providence, or of fatality, within the daily setting of life. From these points of view, they will label as certain what is absolutely compulsory, and as chance what is assigned to the frontier zone beyond which lie the uncertain and the unknown. · The heart will find the first mode more to its liking, for within it something like poetry draws all toward the coherence of a supreme and unique Will, now fixing laws, now granting the grace of a certain latitude of responsibility. To accept the second way, one must refuse to look at the unfathomable, however glowing with fortunes and misfortunes.

As for the historian, he can only conduct himself as a scholar, even when he is considering what is not science. He must place himself as closely as possible to what separates chance or the providential from the certain or the determined. Whichever face he contemplates, it is the other that he must think of. For him, the certitude which he feels to exist, such as that each man dies to survive only in his children, that the stone falls when there is nothing to support it, must, like all things similar, be reentered into the unforeseeable sequence of events. On the other hand, every political action, all that which changes in beliefs, dogmas, as well as scientific hypotheses, and even to the least of ephemeral fashions, must be treated in the perspectives of the certainties to which each leads.

These considerations dictate the plan of what follows herein, a plan hewing in between what depends on the possible to lead to the certain, and what depends on the certain from which the possibles are born.

We shall begin by treating the first of these aspects: first, because during so long a time historiography has made its chief preoccupation the apparently gratuitous event. Certainly, knowledge is being reexamined today. Gone is the time when the historian stirred his listeners by presenting the lives of Genghis Khan, Lenin, or Ben Bella as a series of fortuitous circumstances. The cultural collapse of Arabian Asia, the senescence of Tsarist society, the obsolescence of the colonial system, are phenomena too immense to weigh as no more than the initiatives of the greatest men. The wonder still persists as to why these men were so indistinctly perceived by the majority of those destined to suffer because of them, even when they knew that there were prophets whom they did not believe.

The greatest modifications are hidden under the swarmings of their accidental embodiments. These latter, nearer to the dimensions of our interests and our abilities to comprehend, are the only ones we grasp immediately as events. And it is these which we shall now undertake to analyze.

PART II

The exploration of the possible

3. Memorable deeds

It is in the nature of historic facts to generate one another at the heart of the consciousness which apprehends them. There is no action without some kind of referential link to what has happened before; whether it be a humiliation to be revenged, a state or condition to be defended, or a conquest to pursue. If the hero is unware of such, friends or enemies who surround him will inform him of it. But, in any case, his information remains ambiguous in character. In the world of mineral matter, nothing of what was escapes from what is; and living matter records all that is appropriate to what it creates. With mankind it is different. Whatever his desire may be, he does not learn before the undertaking what he needed to know to be guided to success. And yet it is often his very ignorance that leads him into the undertaking. The historic deed brings into action mnemonic instincts and fragmentary and incompletely learned lessons.

This inconsistency of memory lies at the origin of one of today's paradoxes. The upper levels of life, the conquest of the cosmos, the inventions and tools to which the preceding are indebted, inspire in peoples with a great history their strongest communal pride; but when it comes to narratives of the past, they still grow excited over wars, though they fear and condemn them. This state of affairs mocks them on two counts, by leading them blindly on the path of their most unpredictable progress, and by lending a fascination to the abysses.

The risks and the speed of action never cease captivating the most reasonable of men and the most dedicated of planners. The reader does not seek in the narrative of memorable deeds the forward thread of progress, but instead, and first of all, the suspense between fear and audacity, enterprise and failure, something of that hesitation between contrary impulses which takes possession of the participants in a spell. Thus, moving from one extreme to the other according to the episode, they share at one moment in the frenzy of great dominion over others, and at another in the desperate resolutions by which they resist the same. Aeschines and Demosthenes by turn, they experience the tragic in historicity with the ambivalence of their humanity. As one may read the storms on the high seas by the waves on the shore, so the soul's agitation at listening to the story of great deeds from the past is in distant harmony with the actors of history who played out in the greatest circumstances the all or nothing of their existence.

The interest we take in the recital of deeds whose return we do not desire permits us to measure the degree of exaltation which possessed those who had to prepare themselves for such action as a necessity and as a duty. The memorable event lies at the crossroads of these two perspectives: that of its unfolding, opening out upon the future; and that of the memory retained of the past. As we observe each of these in succession, we shall keep in mind that memory and initiative are always intermingled.

I. The emotion aroused by the memory of an undertaking already brought to its conclusion is not exclusively of an ethical character. In the same way, the act is not concerned with the office of good or evil, nor with that of its usefulness or harmfulness. It is first of all a certain thrust of pure excess, which makes it fascinating even after the shock, and even if it had been criminal. Now, to brave the risk and defy destruction to satisfy a violent desire is not limited solely to great deeds which are celebrated. There are multitudes of little deeds of the same nature, performed by individuals who remain obscure. And if these are not remembered, it is because they are swallowed up in a profusion of similar and compensating initiatives, or drowned in an infinity of scarcely distinguishable interventions. They have thus the common and, so to speak, normal character that sums up the grand total of the ordinary. The event does not become memorable unless by a certain way of being exceptional. It must arouse a durable reality beyond its ephemeral occurence, and be inscribed on maps and monuments, introduced into laws and customs, and given form by commentaries and critical annotations. Having begun with the spontaneity of a gesture, it adds something to the expressive and self-protective customs of average behavior. It tends further to constitute a specimen experience, and finally to become an object of computations and calculations. In short, among all the explorations of the possible, and differing from those innumerable ones which remain useless, the great deed is a success. It opens a way perhaps brief, eventually frightening, but new, and yet one in which many have been in some way similarly involved.

The deed in general is more cultural than historic. Free though it be at its outset, it soon falls under the dominion of a community of pre-existing laws which regulate and balance all, and are appraised by contemporaries and historians as being in the ordinary routine. On the other hand, the deed is made memorable by disclosing the existence of a hitherto unknown collectivity, an original one, just coming into being, and obeying principles new in their nature, their degree, and their ordering. This rising phenomenon is recognized in young Rome in the tale of Gaius Mucius Scaevola,[1] or in Christianity by the rites instituted in honor of the martyrs and saints. If it is imperative that one durable portion remain faithful to that which was exceptional in the beginning, or to that which gave it its high significance and its power to attract, that is because the human milieu in which it occurred was shattered by it. Many of the slaves of ancient Rome must have had the impatience, the courage, and the talent of Spartacus; but they are not remembered as he is, the one who shook all by giving new life to a class. Caesar or Bonaparte, unique perhaps in their gifts, would not even so have become exceptional were it not by grace of circumstances which delivered to them a sufficient number of partisans in the midst of a divided State.

The only deeds that become memorable are those which a new collectivity makes such, because it recognizes in them the element that differentiates the deed from some more ancient one, from which it issued and is now divorcing itself. A living reputation is an effect of consonance within a dissonance. It implies a creative doubling of the numbers of admirers and despisers around a hero. There certainly exist famous reigns without internal discord, where the power is in harmony with the aspirations or the submissiveness of a whole people. Then wars alone, those perpetual interrupters, introduce salient deeds, and the rest appears to dissolve, in some great and unique event that presages an advent. The prince and his times

1. Scaevola, a young Roman of the 6th century B.C., having killed the wrong person in his effort to assassinate an enemy King, burned his hand in self-punishment. Translator's note.

mutually blend by an optical effect, and we are led to speak of the century of Augustus or of Louis XIV, or of the Victorian era. But what still captures attention above all are the deeds done, what is called a civilization. The event stands out in relief as such when the masses are divided and confront one another, when they give value and an immense brilliance to the moment. Robespierre in a few weeks is made more famous than many ancient kings. The Passion from which issued the Christian centuries lasted but a single day. Alexander or Lenin in a few years laid the foundations of a world.

Memorable deeds, collective dramas, in which humanity splits in two as did biological lines before them, are confrontations within organic wholes, of which at least one is on the path of mutation. One must remember that morality and merit, though they may have been of great importance among the obscure and the forgotten, do not play the determining role when celebrities step into the limelight. The Chinese custom of care and respect for moderation, as in its control of grants of special privilege by means of examinations and competitions, did not contribute to making the event stand out. The crimes of Genghis Khan, the deliriums of Hitler, the narrow spirit of Spartan or Roman enslavement, did not rob them of their high historical significance — that of excess.

The role of the memorable deed in human evolution is that of allomorphism in natural evolution. By exaggerating one dimension it endangers a whole order; but also proposes for it a new one, destined sooner or later to perish entirely, or to embody a necessary stage of a general progress. Though excess is far from being always memorable, especially if it serves an error, it is very generally dedicated to some immediate abolition. Unless it be from coercion or from some powerful urging, individuals and societies tend to persist in what they are. Their need for durable certitudes adds new laws to the laws of nature, explicit in codes or implicit in customs. This arrangement, which is agreeable to human equilibrium and suggests ordinary actions, is aimed at prohibiting every violation. Therefore, the mere appearance of some behaviors out of the ordinary does not suffice to guarantee an invasion into the existing order. At the heart of societies, savage as well as civilized, every excess which is judged absurd or unwarranted is circumscribed by the conservatism of customs or dissipated in the indifference or the contempt felt by the group. If the excess resists the first of these treatments, certain rites may still regulate the situation, or it may be handed over to the courts. The more violations of order are resented, the greater the vigor that is thrown into correcting them.

This concern is ancient. Before men knew how to pursue inquiries into reasonably justified responsibilities, a scapegoat, however innocent, was charged with the crimes that vanished with it. This punishment was not so much imposed as an example, for the nature of it was less moral than tragic. Ancient experiences indicate that it reestablished a threatened equilibrium. More recent examples confirm that the frequency of crimes is more a result of collective conditions than of penalties. Acts of purification and justice serve only to measure the exceptions by which the established collectivity comes normally to its end. If these are too numerous, or a critical threshold is crossed, then a state of insecurity or a revolutionary situation arises, to the point that the stability and structure of institutions have been radically changed. The evildoers of yesterday become the martyrs and heroes of tomorrow. The founders of a new order defy the old before they triumph in the area of religions, nations, societies, after the ebb and flow of violences whose energies they have polarized.

The dimensions of a system of institutions are defined by what it can dissolve or exclude of the exceptions, by the ascendency of its customs or the severity of it laws. The authority which it exercises in its day, the prestige it retains afterward, are proportional to the weight which it can summon against every illegality or interior disorder, to expel them to the exterior. This system may, of course, be modified from within. If, because of the growth of an area newly opened to activity, the number of exceptions rises sufficiently to allow a new coefficient of order, then, by evolution or by revolution, other usages and other laws will be inaugurated. When Draco wished to prevent the Greeks from deciding justice for themselves, he legalized retaliations and integrated excess as a means of extending justice. Christian Europe, like the Mesopotamian societies before it, when it was overtaken by the development of commerce, legitimized certain luxuries in order to control them, though they had long condemned them. Institutional evolution consists of an enlargement of structures of order in terms of the pressures it experiences.

For all that, progressions of order do not follow in a straight line; more often they are at once divided and cyclic. They experiment with preferences while suggesting finalities; they shed obsolete regulations to release more durable ones which will work along with the innovations. These restructurings recognize vocations and special callings, focus them, and guide them toward remarkable accomplishments. They also point up disparities, obstruct or prohibit relapses, and run the risk of being exclusive. Thus moments of choice take on values which may have a long future, or may sooner or later end in a blind alley. This aging process imposes its discontinuous character on history, which glitters from epoch to epoch and place to place, for shifting reasons. The mutual relationships between trials and successes are thus rendered obscure, incomprehensible, and abrupt.

The diverse thrusts of vocations or special callings would be entirely internal to groups if groups did not have a tendency to stiffen and become fixed so long as no shock jolts them. Progress, however, is made of competitions, rivalries, and attacks. Humanity, like nature, is designed for increases in order; but, also like nature, it resists this tendency and divides. Just as species tend to self-conservation, and do not overreach themselves without a struggle or without feeding on one another, so the despoilings, enslavements, tortures, and murders by which cohesive societies try to defend themselves from within become deeds of merit when societies collide. Frontiers of class, of States, are the points where differences confront one another, where the basic data of morality and the sacred in the community are reversed, and the excesses of aggression take place; they are also the areas where the growing cohesiveness of rising organisms is decided.

The most ancient inhabitants of the Euphrates and the Nile did not long defend themselves by numbers alone: they experimented with the need for a military frame and yielded to it in the structuring of the State. The lesson is not thereafter challenged. There are no more effective revolutions of a purely spontaneous nature. They only seem so because of the sudden disclosure of a virtual order evolved in the invisible background of the visible one that is being opposed. Memorable deeds cannot be separated from collective hierarchies, obvious or latent, which are made up of oppositions and revealed by the event.

The extent and duration of the Roman Empire is not to be explained by obvious technological progresses, but first of all by a certain quality of institutions, joined to the art of war. By its conquests and its law, ancient Rome will long endure as an object of reference and of nostalgia. The same might be said, perhaps, of the Assyrian Empire, as, finally, of the France of the Sun King. The capitals of triumph celebrate the superiority of one State over another rather than the power of man over things. Indeed, sometimes true creation appears even elsewhere, in neighboring regions destined to be conquered. The growth of the political organism is a specific phenomenon, engendered by conflict and sustained by it, and menaced by the delights and relaxations of peace. If then, in sum and over the very long term, scientific invention and technology prevail, it is not by a direct effect of selection, but in the course of a complex and ambiguous process; and, in these respects, the process does not differ in human collectivities from what it has been in living species.

In the area of human conflicts, groups, cities, States, in their effort to consolidate their own order, expel disorder beyond their frontiers; and there they keep it, if they can, the better to protect themselves from it. Celtic villages surrounded themselves with a defensive desert, the warriors facing outside; and by this important function, they justified their claim to the control and command of the interior. The use of force externally applied conditions the interior, orders it and creates hierarchies. The interrelations between constituted bodies, sometimes peaceful, always challenged, at times violent, test, augment or abolish the cohesiveness within them. Every geographic expansion, by this process, sanctions the spread of symbiosis, bringing together more men under more complex laws. But conquests and assimilations cannot enlarge indefinitely the field of legitimatizations; defeats or withdrawals are finally the lot of the greatest of empires. Seen from one point of view, the general action is summarized in actions directed from the internal toward the external. Seen as a whole, all is the play of interactions confronted by chance; a success here, a set-back there, slowly defining the geographic dispositions and the hierarchies of communities in conflict.

Human cultures, like living species, live off one another. Victory supplies the city with slaves, subordinates the peasant to the city, elaborates the hierarchies, always the more differentiated where the merchant discovers his interests, the artisan his vocation, and the thinker the leisure to devote himself to his meditations. The simply predatory victory is sterile; but without the structurations which it builds, progress would not have taken place.

Evolution changes the panorama of action from era to era, but does not reverse the essential data. The manufacture of arms, objects, and tools, the accumulation of wealth, modify the respective relations of violence and creation, and make necessary a certain equilibrium among them. Even so, up until a recent period, war and peace pursued the same goals by different means. Every path of changes is strategic.

An abundance of goods does not necessarily guarantee strength. It does generalize comfort, stabilizes the group and the general level, but eventually weakens it. In times of abundance, the liberty of each endangers the resistance of the whole. So it was in early Asia, in Iran, India, China, where successive waves of rugged tribes structured for war imposed themselves in the form of monarchical and princely dynasties. The same occurred in early Europe, where aristocracy for a long time rested on the barbaric sword. Close to half the human race today is still commanded by military powers, and the rest remain largely conditioned by the same. However, if external violence, or even only the threat of it, builds up or consolidates the internal hierarchies, then there will appear areas of demarcations open to conflict between the social strata thus superimposed. The plebs on the Roman Aventine negotiate with the aristocracy, the slave revolts, the peasant roams the fields in arms, the bourgeois reject the court, the people rise.

The organization of production and distribution has likewise its imperatives. But since it is a constant that an unseasonable revolution delivers a city over to its neighbors, or that a successful one makes it the conqueror, and since also, inversely, a victory reassures the internal order which a defeat compromises, wars and revolutions are allied in destiny. They are the two greatest ways of assuring a testing; in identical fashion they bring into question the resources of groups or States that are in continual competition. There is tested what the strength of peoples and the systems of organization, the reserves and the production of goods, are capable of. There, too, men are recalled from the explorations of the possible to the happy or unhappy verifications of the reliable by the objective reality which governs the issue of conflicts. An imminent order then superimposes itself upon what had been blindly initiated by chance engagements.

Following upon the immense duration of non-historic ages of stone artifacts, humanity of the first millenia of history turns into an intense fermenting, creative, and aggressive activity. It concentrates and organizes itself in the geographic sites where all prospers; but there it also becomes fragile, a prey tempting outsiders who are subject to harsher conditions. These latter bring that order into question, and eventually rebuild it to a higher form. Violence does not build; but, for better or for worse, it clears the ground, and permits a society involved in its own way of being and doing to substitute another, a different and eventually more capable one, originating out of a previous stage of evolution and destined to travel further on an unencumbered course. War is a test of vigor. A successful overthrow substitutes for a too self-satisfied elite a new class in the service of a regenerated productivity.

Violence, whether it destroy or liberate, lies at the two ends of an evolutionary cycle reproducing itself in a hundred ways according to times and places. Sometimes the cycle occurs on the spot, where it superimposes epochs; sometimes it shifts to new lands and brings vocations side by side. Of the two phases of this cycle, that of production without aggression dooms people to longterm subjection; but that of pure aggression does not make them masters forever. Consumption lies waiting in the wings. Finally, the process sometimes contracts or accelerates, and its phases overlap, as happens naturally where population increases and techniques are rapidly perfected.

All these cycles, however, come finally to creating progressive realities. Unfortunately, these realities cannot always be recognized at the moment when the action launches its process, whether to the advantage of evolution or of involution. The outlines of great cultures are no more immediately defined than those of the species would be if we did not know their outcome. From a distance, we watch Mesopotamia and Egypt, where the world's might was summed up, become victims; see Rome, the dominator, whose sword conquered so many slaves, become the frail city of the servant of the servants of God; observe the kingdoms of Europe, leaning upon the bourgeois before being defeated by them. Events appear to be offshoots of disorder; they are, in truth, conflicts of order. They are incessant selections among constant pressures or opposing pressures of organizations, where each density is accomplished by a reversal of what had sustained it. Often, even well after the blow, no one has knowledge of what end the drama might have been capable of serving.

It needs much perspective to be able to evaluate the event. Thus each epoch chooses, classifies, and interprets differently what it retains of the memories handed down by those who preceded it. Indeed, it is not enough to speak of epochs. Just as each profession once had its patron, each nation and each social class has its heroes whom its sets up against those of others. Now if one tries to distinguish between these various commemorations by referring them to types, one is led at once to the general problem of the event, and invited to go beyond it. One finds himself further carried beyond the point of view of the accomplished deed to what memory has retained of it.

II. Though men are equal before nature, they are not so in history. In each place and moment, history advances a very small number of men, to whom the others are attached by complex bonds, difficult to define, but acknowledged by the evidence. After the event, memory retains only a feeble portion of what actually happened; and it often occurs that structures which were unimportant in the eyes of their contemporaries turn out to be of prime importance in the light of their subsequent action. This double choice, and its apparent whims, express a double imperative of evolution.

If humanity wished to cling to the totality of what is, it would be so absorbed in self-contemplation that it would no longer advance, and would sterilize its memory. A certain denial of inequality and distortion goes parallel with the relative fixity of so-called savage societies distant from the epicenters of history. The societies which get into history are those which change by opposition, which repudiate themselves by developing hierarchies, and finally renew themselves. They are also those which change what they celebrate.

The most common holiday or feast days remain still what they were: the seasonal ones marked on a lunar and solar calendar. The peasant status of the vast majority of its faithful helps us to understand why the Christian church made a feast day of the winter solstice, of which Saint Augustine made no mention. To the celebrations of the Passion and the Resurrection, which a doctor of the faith would find central and sufficient, the people add Christmas. Thus is restored the rounded cycle of the natural condition out of the experience of millenia. It is said that Tarente had more holidays than days; Christianity has its daily saints embroidering the whole year, around the great moments of the existence of Christ, themselves adjusted to a very ancient system of ritual. When every moment of the year thus arouses a memory, the need to commemorate is as imperative as the particularity of the thing commemorated.

One must either enter into the particular of each family and each individual, or rise within the hierarchy of intellectual or political activities, to escape the determinism of the seasons or, independent of them, to refer an anniversary to the event which sets its date. The weight of history has its effects. Israel, with so much to justify it, celebrated the Maccabees, Esther, and the memory of the ruin of Jerusalem. The brilliant conquests of Islam determined the success of the Hegira. But tradition does not easily relinquish its systems carved into the communal convenience. The French Revolution could not very long impose its Year I, even upon the French. Napoleon, like the Bourbons, was congratulated on the day of his patron saint, and not on the day of his accession to the throne; and it took almost a century for July 14th to become a national holiday. Since then, however, certain historical dates have been inserted into the official calenders; and their number increases in the modern world.

This success is nevertheless insignificant as compared to the place taken by chronologies in what is called general culture. Now, if the domain of historical knowledge increases to such a degree in scarcely more than a century, even though remaining divided from country to country and from one social order to another, and especially if it is self-sustaining and can detach itself from stars and seasons, this is because an important innovation has been introduced. Legends and tales, formerly all mingled in with history to inspire communal behaviors, tend today to be no more than the treasures of childhood or of scholarship. Because of this shift, religious information, even when it has not changed the references of its faith, has had to modify those of its missionaries. The facts and deeds most useful to remember now find their legitimacy not in the always recurring periodicity of natural existence, but in documentary accuracy and a rational credibility. Their significance has thus been changed.

The deed originally commemorated was inspired by the living experience of those who celebrated it. The historic fact is established, sometimes with great difficulty, by starting with what one can know of those who participated in it. This reversal of perspective accompanies a multiplication of informations on the past and makes each of them irreducible. One comes to know that humanity is not limited to the inherent rebeginning of itself, such as satisfied the philosopher of Antiquity; or, after the high period of Christianity, the skeptic fatalist, so proud of his strong mind. A new interpretation of the nature of time, which views it as creative within the acceleration of history, now joins this creative character to the absolute and irrational value of what it creates and what it challenges us to comprehend.[2]

2. Ch. Morazé adds the following note to this passage (letter to translator, May 26, 1970): 'Time, that is, is no longer seen as circular. It issues from a past never reproduced, but indefinitely prolonged toward an unforeseeable future. Each moment in time is the creator of something new. Moments are never exactly reduplicated, but go on indefinitely adding new weight to an accumulating experience. The scientist, therefore, is called upon to inquire what experimentations may be able to suggest of a common element, even while experience is rushing on like an acceleration without a brake.'

This transformation of historic feeling allows us to escape from the conservative effects of illusion, and to a more reliable concept of what the past was. When Titus Livy recites the origins of Rome he believes he is narrating what was, and writes down only what has been imagined about it. His heroes are but symbolic creatures, anthropomorphisms which permit him the more easily to summarize the evolution of functions and the relationships of classes. The naivete of his good faith teaches us that there are times in which to invent heroes, and other times, no longer inventive, in which people grant belief to the invented and inherited figures. Finally, there are others in which the pressure for rationality is stronger than these emotive attachments, and which destroy these optical illusions. But if they succeed one another in this order, these three moments do so in accord with an infinity of ways of remaining relative and partial. It is two millenia since Euhemerus[3] found a positive explanation for mythologies which the masses of his time re-imagined differently but consistently.

We no longer invent gods; we scarcely promise any success to founders of religions, and our critical spirit exercises a certain caution toward even those who claim to be founders of States. But we still make heroes out of those on whom success smiles; and, from acquired habit as much as the need of the dream, we claim our full share of transfigurations not so long ago completed.[4] Historic objectification does not follow a linear or continuous progress. We recognize therein interruptions and retrogressions, according to cycles whose movements disperse rather than disappear. All in all, however, the distance tends to decrease between the hero and the idea built around him. The average man in his turn is also carried along by history; and if he still creates idols, it is only insofar as he knows them to be, despite their embellishments, like himself.

III. Several corollaries follow on these considerations.

If events are the shattered manifestations of the swings of the pendulum, varied in nature and importance, numerous, juxtaposed, compounded, each within its own terms apparently long in its

3. A 4th century Greek, B.C., who taught that mythological personages were human beings deified by the fear or the admiration of peoples. Translator's note.

4. That is, needing heroes, we make them out of those whom destiny has clearly favored. They reassure us, even though they often are but fleeting impressions from causes not easily understood. Note from Ch. Morazé, May 26, 1970.

launching and sharp in its recoil, achievements may be compared with the arrest of linear motion in pure mechanics. A force interrupts an effect of inertia. Yet the mechanical figure is not strictly pertinent. At the outset of a series consisting of events of the kind that become institutionalized with time, an accident might or should have intervened: Alba might have been able to conquer Rome or Antony Octavius, Louis XVI might have had the genius of Bonaparte, or the latter have been captured on his flight from Egypt. But if a single episode is changed, the others must also be; so much so, indeed, that step by step, all reality evaporates. Under its apparent movements, history plays tricks in which collectivities participate without knowing the reason why, movements which they ponder and comment on from the need they have for representations. With other librettos and other actors, the theatre would remain the same, with its scenery and its machines, the expectation of its public, and the inspiration which links it with the unfolding action. If Cleopatra's nose had been shorter, an episode would have been changed, but neither the face of the world nor its course, nor scarcely at all the destiny of the Roman empire.

The event is a movement of a wave in the storms of the ocean's enduring reality. When a great destiny takes form, it may well be the effect of pure freedom of choice or pure chance; but once it has taken form, necessities take over, ensnare it in their web, subdue it to systems and causes so thoroughly that, when the outcome is reached, all within it appears to have been determined. It is useless to attribute the Roman decline at the time of Romulus Augustus to chance, nor does Victor Hugo convince us by treating Waterloo as an accident. In these two such different illustrations all is acted out quite apart from the gestures of emperors.

If, as has been said above, great deeds can be placed between natural facts and the facts of knowledge, that is because though both are free and contingent in their origins, and determined in their conclusions, they amount to so many explorations of the possible. In their initial launchings they challenge the actual; in the result which is their conclusion they meet a new limit. They inaugurate the double apprenticeship of chance and causality; they instruct the intelligence striving to detach itself from the fascinations of chance, so that it may discover itself by conforming to the immanent lessons of causality.

Historical experience teaches men still more. If something of the will may be seen in every moment and every place, there are few occasions where it gives birth to a memorable reality; for the will's intervention must be in collective reality ready for division and destined to conflict, in a system or order challenged toward being differentiated, abolished, or passed by. No matter where or when, the possibility of great deeds is promised only as illusion. When choice does take place at the center of discriminations of too little importance, these latter are usually very numerous and very banal. Their quantity and insignificance soon erase the consequences of the free gesture which the choice permitted even while drowning it in a mass of analogous attitudes. It is only when the confronting forces — and then not so exactly equal as to forbid any voluntary act — are sufficiently powerful on the one side and the other that an initiative can develop into a great result and a persisting memory. This stipulation amounts to an axiomatic of the probable.

The magnitude of what has been accomplished when a great event is completed provides the measure of the weight of the forces in confrontation at the moment the event came into being. The decline of the Roman empire, for centuries a puzzle to the Occident, seemed like an exception to the principle which makes turning points brief as compared to the very long periods which prepared for them; it is like a slow dilution of tiny, scattered episodes, with no startling or grandiose deed to mark it. But that is because the passage of what is called the Middle Ages, if we stretch it out over some centuries, announces not only the end of five or six hundred years of Roman conquest, but also the end of several millenia of an experiment begun with the division of the ancient world into cities, stranded on the nostalgia of a collectivity that failed. The immense presence of Asia supplies the dimension for this failure, which will not be resolved until the encirclement of the globe can be realized. Thus, in connection with the Byzantine or Bas Empire, to speak only of the decline of manners and morals is to misconstrue the scale of the relevant phenomena. Actually, manners at the time of the emperor Julian were no worse than those of Cassius, Lucullus, or Verus. The long ferocity of the circus games developed naturally out of the brutal heroism of the first Romans, and their unfortunate contempt for the amazing fecundity of spirit in the Mesopotamian millenium. The same is true of the Arabian decline in Asia at the time of the Mongolian invasions, which was not the effect of the moment, but the end of an era inaugurated by the Arsacidae.[5] Much the same

5. The Arsacidae ruled in the near East, opposing Rome, from the third century B.C. to the third A.D. Translator's note.

might be said of Christian Europe, the Napoleonic ferment or bourgeois colonization.

Every deed should be recorded on its own scale. In very great
events, several evolutions emerge, of unequal duration and unequal
magnitude, disclosed, though not without pain, by a view opening on
immense horizons.

Now, even when they are not distinctly seen or clearly expressed,
the intricacies of evolutionary wholes unconsciously instruct men in
the part they must grant to chance, will, and necessity. The feeling
which progressively results from this understanding is not to be
caught in operative formulae to reduce politics to a mechanism, since
science itself is more than that; but the result is a narrowing of the
margin left for improvisation. The door is less open to the heroic
imagination. The focusing of attention concentrates to the point of
accepting scientific experimentation. The function which sharpens
this precision is naturally the reflection which precedes decision.

Two statements must be made in the subject of this function. The
first is that the effects are not the same in the development of the
sciences and the modifications of action. In the one, the function
gives place to a cumulative process in the course of which memories
of the past are sorted out rationally in order to increase the pertinency of what serves the future. In the other, all the mistakes are
repeated, and brute instinct plays a large part within the whole.
Nevertheless, in the one application as much as in the other, at least
since more than a century, the number of events increases and, by a
reciprocal influence, all history is thereby speeded up. To grasp how
this bifurcation operates will be the object of the studies which
follow. A consideration of this common element of effects will
doubtless provide the means of finding the order of our research and
its primary object.

Furthermore — and this is the second statement — every decision
is taken in the imagination. There the memories of past experience
are summarized and the adjustment of plans is elaborated. There
reflection on the watch for the event, scientific as well as political,
learns to distinguish the occasional accident from the true effect. The
imaginative faculty, nourished by representations at first uncertain
and vague which give form to the sense of beauty and the inspiration
of faith, gives rise also to explicit conceptual systems, appropriate to
natural conditions. This refining process increases the number of
inquiries which one may, within a same lapse of time, submit to
destiny. It speeds up the return of more understandable answers to

questions better put. Thereby history advances more rapidly.

Better organized memories permit us to pass the sooner through the stages of evolution. By discovering itself the more promptly, humanity also contemplates from a higher and a more distant perspective the paths on which it has been swept along. Since history is the proper instrument for its own shaping, it takes stock of its internal possibilities when it projects itself in memorable deeds. Furthermore, this is clearly the reason why history, when it had not yet arrived at knowing its own past, invented it on the model of its present. Since that time monuments built and inscribed to celebrate high deeds are narratives of experience behind which evolution finally permits itself to be discovered. And in the political order, it is enough that events become more numerous and that we remember better those that have occurred. For thus, assuming that they remain of the same nature, scientific reflection on them may be rendered more prompt and more fruitful. The most eccentric event is a flowering of the obscure genetics of life which man prolongs into history. In these terms, it acts usefully upon the unconscious, even when conscious knowledge finds nothing rational in the deformed image that it presents of what happened.

Valéry has said that man enters on the future backwards. It is true that he is not disposed to adapt to that future, nor to build it out of anything but acquired experiences. However, he prepares for it only by taking it as an objective. Functioning in terms of himself, he chooses among the elements offered for its accomplishment; and before he realizes the future, he pictures it in imagination. He has no other means of preparing for what will come, except this admittedly arbitrary function; but it would be of no service to him if it limited itself to visualizing the past exclusively, no matter how accurately. Nor can this element of the indefinite be reduced entirely; for without this hazy illumination, man would not undertake to transfigure living experience, and to reconstruct it from new events.

As an active ferment of memory, the imaginative faculty kneads the past as dough to force the future to rise from it. Surely, if it is unfaithful to the past, the imagination is a poor guarantee of the future, which it can never decide by itself alone. But, since imagination is its inspiration, there is no human deed which is not, at least as far as concerns that part generally assigned to the will, hatched out of its action. Strange and disturbing chemistry, whose most active products are likewise the least pure, those in which present desires most effect the truth of what has been lived in the past, to create from that a way to live in the present. The epoch arouses more enthusiasm than could the incident which was its pretext, and the recital of a great deed cleanses it of its mud and blood.

Faith gives to the accidental the dimension of the eternal. When the Orient, proud of having anticipated Greece by so many centuries and proud also of having victoriously resisted Rome, was conquered by Islam, it rewrote its history in an epic style in the manner dictated by the new faith. When Spain returned to being Christian, it had to have its paragons of fidelity — namely, the Cid. A long and stormy past career was made to appear loyal and young, though not without disavowals, on the frontier of two opposing worlds of interests and beliefs. A deviation and a decomposition, like that of a prism submitted to a ray of light, makes us see in the direct past the chosen origin of what a present discomfort creates by reading it on the bias. The alchemy which Europe owes chiefly to China it attributes to a Hermes from a more familiar antiquity. In the same way, the dissatisfaction provoked by a bourgeois reign gives rise to the Napoleonic legend. These illusions are necessary; they compensate for troubles of the soul and relieve the paralyzed. They nourish the future on an innacurate memory, one fragmentary and transposed out of deeds accomplished.

Nations of our day do not escape this optical deformation. Citizens of the United States still believe that their technological successes are the rewards of their struggles alone, and that, as in Asia or in Africa, their ancestors, before their independence, were the victims and not the beneficiaries of Europe. And more recently, the Soviet Union attributes to Russia and its revolution what came to it from the capitalist Occident. Each unit of humanity takes satisfaction in particularizing what it owes to the general evolution.

Memorable deeds have the unknown as their condition, and the imagination as their first means. Only at the cost of mistakes and illusions can man in his weakness confront the supreme power. But illusion also comes finally to recognizing the reality within itself; reflection penetrates progressively into the order of things. Nature, by endowing man with the privilege of imagining, has given him the promises of reason and the reasons for his hope. The data for his actions and the logic of his progress are made manifest and are united within the imaginative faculty. It is now the appropriate time to draw up the inventory of this power to imagine, by noting the stages of its transformations.

4. Conquests of the imaginative faculty

To recognize the essential place of the power of imagination in history, and to add the legends to the annals and the works of art to the archives, is to throw light on ancient and obscure millenia, and to lend depth to the judgments based on chronologies. It is also, quite aside from statistics, to survey the fields where man's nature intervenes in his own concerns, even though it diverges from his most apparent reasons.

Not long after Macedonia had been made a vassal by the Persians, Alexander in a few months reached the Indus river. However, after Alexander, Roman proconsuls and emperors, though having resources easily superior to his at their disposal, failed for centuries to reach or to cross the Euphrates. Finally, that Orient, which for so long had resisted the greatest military empire of those times, yielded apparently at one stroke and completely to a handful of Arabs. Any further piling up of details and facts only obscures a problem which becomes simple when linked with fairly elementary emotive structures. The experience of a deified monarchy had in the course of time so weakened the will of peoples that they were overcome by the youthful ardor of a little nation united within the continental borders of Greece. Yet in their hearts there lingered a nostalgia for the time of their own autonomy and power, now betrayed by the imported Hellenism. This feeling the Arsacidae and the Sassanidae partially satisfied; but it was the poetry of the Prophet that most responded, elevating Allah above the world and inviting the humiliated to the heroism of combats promising victory and paradise. During the centuries which follow, the Koran will be evoked and invoked, as much for the glory of great empires as in the devotions of those toiling cities which will follow in succession on the original site chosen for the first great cultural confrontations.

Defeats and victories are imprinted in the hearts of combattants in terms of evolutive systems of representation and their equilibriums. Before battles are completed each one senses whose turn it is to obey, to cease, or to rule; and this it is that decides the issue. Under the same conditions, it is not force of arms alone which allows a few conquistadores to seize the pre-Columbian empires of America, for they might well have been crushed under numbers — but from the start the effect which simply the sight of them produced. When the two worlds of representations confront one another, the one is galvanized, the other neutralized. It has happened that the very presence itself of a foreign peoples affects savage peoples with mortal illnesses, organic states of despair, the preludes to annihilation. Biologic resistance is a certain criterion of hierarchies of culture, because it depends on the relevancy at the moment of a system of beliefs.

The power of the imaginative faculty resides below the images which illustrate it, in the passions which sustain them and cling to them. The passions draw their strength from the agitated depths of being, in a physiology of functions involved in an environment which is as much human as material. Thus the passions are supported or deceived, and charged with an emotivity communicable from one member to another of the same group. They also furnish the matter for speeches and attitudes, and teach the efficacy of the symbolic content and burden. The living substratum which feeds the passions has its own internal logic, created from the material conditions of a place or a group, by influence, tolerance, or opposition, along with what is developed in a similar way elsewhere or in other groups. As fits the event, symbols reunite, assume an order, and attract collectivities, for which they sum up an identity of desires and possibilities appropriate to what is happening. If they are misunderstood, they disconcert and undo all. Two groups thus brought face to face may have many elements in common, so that wars are made long and uncertain, and never resolved; it is what they find incompatible that determines the strategy of the conflict and the significance of the outcome.[1] Images are the expressions of power; their history is that

---

1. That is, as in civil wars, a certain equality of power and identity of ambitions makes conflicts all but insoluble. An example is the internal wars of Europe, an expression of what has been called 'the European equilibrium'. Note from Ch. Morazé, Jan. 23, 1971.

of hates and attachments, victories and surrenders.

The structures of order, and their resemblances and differences, are reflected in the structures of images. Determinations, decisions, are founded on the first and embodied in the second.[2] The evolutive laws of the first act as corollaries of the second. Representations are the translations of what is. Institutions support them, the arts embellish them, beliefs sanctify them, every undertaking tests them, confirms or modifies them, by prefiguring through them and registering through them the embodiments of authority.

The world of the imaginative faculty is sensitive to the promises and prohibitions enclosed within the reality that confronts men, and gives form to something of that reality. The miracle of birth, the mystery of death, the imperatives of family and of society are stamped upon that world, whether vaguely or in large characters, and so confer upon myths the energy of life itself.

I. Myths are all that is left to us of the story of more than nine hundred thousand years of prehistoric activity. Since they express the elementary forces that drive our being, it is but natural that psychoanalysis has from its outset accorded myths a considerable importance, confirmed by the cures that have relied on their lessons. Nevertheless, it would be dangerous to identify the beginnings of a man's life, his first months or years, with the immense previous duration of humanity; for he would then become its quintessential summing up. A life history of an organism (ontogenesis) is not a reduction of the history of a species (paleontogenesis); it is rather a greatly differentiated composite of the elements of earlier ontogeneses. Certainly, among the unhappy effects upon sufferers who are unable to surmount what are called complexes, such as function at the origin of every deed and act, we may discover driving forces peculiar to the very nature of man, and hence at all times operative. But these compulsions exist as such only by the resistances which the cultural imperatives impose on them; and these have now greatly changed.

For example, man has not always concealed references to sexuality. Instead, they have tried to give weight to what has progressively been discovered to be of importance. Drawings and statuettes of ancient paleolithic times show that sexual organs and attitudes, far

2. For a note on the French word *determinations* see Preface, p. 49 fn. Translator's note.

from being stamped as forbidden, were strongly emphasized. Exotic religious representations still retain traces of this freedom. Disguises, transpositions, sublimations were not invented until after an infinite number of experiences, strengthened by hard-won esthetic successes progressively brought under order. If the deeds of that pre-history, which has left such profound traces on the symbolic world, now escape us, it is also true that they could never have been brought to us except by the records of history. Across a long sequence of generations, they have been born of chance tentatives and regrouped into institutions, and have encouraged to the greatest possible degree a vast host of explorations of the possible, each one interrupted when the resources of the way chosen were exhausted. This last way is then replaced by another, itself the result of another choice, often just as ancient, but different, or in opposition. Before sexuality was stamped with prohibitions, its connection with fecundity had to be established as a certain datum. And if it took a great many millenia to accomplish these necessary gropings toward a satisfactory adjustment within the human milieu, that is explained by the immensity of the unknown which confronted ancient man. The great number of objects successively or concurrently held to be divine, elements of landscape, territories, hills, plants or animals, stones, waters or fires, likewise indicates the extent of the domain of that hesitation which underlies still many of today's credulities.

In certain paleolithic cultures not so ancient — savage societies still preserve traces of this — the pregnancy of the female appears not the result of intercourse with man, but with the earth itself, to which all fecundity is attributed. Perhaps at the time when humanity remained small in number, and scattered and weak, a necessary respect attached to the origin of every kind of generation. The dead were buried so that they · ight be reborn; and if it was necessary to kill an animal, it was done according to a rite appropriate to preventing the extinguishment of all life. The fear of a general destruction, the obsession with death which was tamed by propitiatory sacrifices, served to deify the springtime, the earth, or the sea. A forward stride was taken when the biological renewability of the family was recognized, not as a discovery consequent on others, but as a general acceptance of a sparsely held belief, as ancient as its rivals and mingled in with them before its hour to prevail arrived. The universalism of mother earth is not abolished at one stroke; it lingers in certain places, reappears in others. But it is opposed by the manifestations of social entities, on the family pattern, which put a restraint on customs, usages, and images, and then develop into more complex wholes, built on competition and opposition.

When the masculine principle triumphs, the father becomes also the head. As men become more numerous, they are less sensible of their frailty as a species than of their mutual rivalries. Cities, once they are built, oppose each other with manly vigor, whether god or goddess rule in their greatest temple over other divinities, now assimilated or subdued. The preference for the pleasure of riding horseback, or of combat and pillage, over the agricultural work left to women, may not have led to the invention of war; but it did make it prevail as a necessity and as an expectation of the supreme rewards from it. Elsewhere agriculture, commerce and artisanship prevail. The system of representations translates these ancient and confused experiences into simple terms, so that an equilibrium is sometimes achieved at the same between the order of force and that of production. The world of the divine is divided into hierarchies on the order of kings, warriors and producers. In countries blessed with fecundity it happens that a feminine element, at least, endures in this established triad. In Rome, the three Capitoline figures are male: Jupiter, Mars, and Quirinus.

The difficulties encountered by this triple symbolizing of the social order may be measured by the number of ancient religions which appear to have sought it without finding it. Others, having arrived at it, have nevertheless retained or rediscovered a number of other divinities to throng on Olympus, or to hide within the secrets of their mysteries. For all this, the importance attached to simple as well as to what we may call magic numbers, grows no less. And when this importance is not obvious at the center of the religious world, it reappears in the details of the construction of temples, or in the ways by which the gods are represented.

The dialectic of the imaginative faculty is naturally historic and collective. Each people, according to its manner of living, invents its own world of the divine. Under clear skies this is solar. In countries of irrigated and fertile soils, it is earth-bound, chthonian. In variable climates, it is meteoric. And in the seductive yet fearsome desert, it is sometimes also nocturnal and astral. The cosmological suggestions show the greatest variety: the same moon which for the caravaneers of the night symbolizes a supreme god may, in the eyes of the warriors of the steppes, be but a minor goddess of femininity. For some, the waxings and wanings of the moon are manifestations of will; for others, its swellings are those of fecundity. The bull whose horns evoke the crescent is sometimes a force that subdues, sometimes a promise of abundance. But since all lends itself thus to ambiguous interpretations before a sufficient knowledge has introduced precision into life and things, the symbolic world is subject to a thousand inventions. Each has taken long to ripen, and the faithful followers of each are bound by bonds of flesh and blood. A city conquered and forced to change its god becomes in the eyes of its sons a mother betrayed or compromised. All epochs have had their Orestes or their Hamlet, as well as their Oedipus, and have been culpable or beneficiaries of an apostasy on whose consequences they dare not look. And yet the changes of gods are inevitable, for their embodiments are those of history and of societies, according to the unceasing internal conflict which forces the transformation of the illusory.

The organization of divine hierarchies, with their parades of secondary powers, is not only the magnified reflection of established societies, stabilized and for a time legitimized by their fairy tales, but it is also the expression of an internal self-knowledge and an external knowledge of things. The prolific gods, warriors, arbiters, are among themselves parallels of pleasure, action, or meditation. The gods of the earth, of tempests, and of the sky with its great regular movements, mark the initial appearances of the three spheres of law from which arise the civil order of growing wealth, the abuses of political conflicts, and the physical constants.[3]

The world of the imaginative faculty is like a map on which are shown the paths of competence and knowledge. During the millenia, a god was assigned to each number, and the numbers called primary were marked by a special reverence, for they gave birth to the others by multiplications. The three smallest play the greatest role in the complex of mental operations identified with the ruling Trinity, from which the feminine is banished when the fecundity of the intellect succeeds in supplanting that of the body and of nature to which all had so long been referred.

The passionate structures of representation continue to operate between self and the rest, between men and things, the most commonplace custom and the most divine mystery. Every passage from one system to another presupposes a bringing into doubt what was once believed true, the logical search for a more pertinent certitude.

---

3. The classical *ius civile, ius gentium* and *ius naturae.* Translator's note.

This is an effort of abstraction and reconstruction. The artist does not produce from mere whim or even from his will; his whole being guides his expression. There is no form sketched, built, sung, said or written which is not strictly commanded by the obscure internal structures, fashioned by the dominant and accepted representations into which these structures insinuate themselves, there to add what is demanded by a newly born need arising out of anxieties and unaccustomed desires. Whether it be figures of animals or men, imitated or idealized, monstrous or given geometric form, or finally abolished in favor of abstract mathematical concepts, none of this is an arbitrary effect of fashions only. Across the millenia, these divers phases so often repeated in one sense or another, point to the profound labor of complex elements which knit and unknit and recompose in the brain of the artist. There, with more or less success, he designs the images needed by the group to give form to its wishes, and a future to its past.

There is no esthetic embodiment which is not that of societies and of logic. Almost up to the moment when history begins, Egypt and Mesopotamia, the plateaus of the East and the Mediterranean shores of western Asia, had furnished much of mankind what for centuries would be the essentials of their religions, morals, arts and sciences. And then an important divergence, a branching off, becomes visible in the evolution of representations.

In the East, the sovereign monopolizes God and masters great empires, but cuts himself off from his people. The dynasties follow one another from age to age, superimposed from outside on societies long boiling with activity, but unable to impose order unaided upon themselves, still inventing but no longer discovering. Enamored of monotheisms, dissatisfied with the pretensions of monarchism, they share in the spread of Hellenism, though they oppose the arbitrary and artificial polytheism of Roman enslavement. These peoples will gladly rediscover themselves in Islamism, the promiser of equality and victories under the guidance of an abstract and unique God. In the West, each citizen has the gods he prefers, framed to his own measure in the cities or in the empires. Thus the gods are permitted to proliferate to the point of draining each of them of his divine attributes.

Several paths lead to or restore the unity of God. There is a certain stage of culture in which a divine imperialism disorients, and in which a democratic polytheism satisfies no better. When the Roman elite ceased to believe in their augurs, though they had not yet questioned their own civic legitimacy, then from the despised Orient came the beliefs which troubled Rome. As if stunned before the might of the Sassanidae, Rome abandons its emperor Valerian to that Orient and brings back its myths. It becomes Mithraic at first, and then adopts the cross as a symbol, that instrument of torture which had been reserved for its slaves.

Between East and West monotheism persists among the small peoples of Israel. These peoples had been at the mercy of Canaanite beliefs which, however, they rejected, and had been enriched by the experience of powerful neighbors whose captives they had been from time to time. Later, by a surge of syncretism, they gave rise to Christianity, which developed at their expense. This new religion, within its three great dogmas, encloses the mysteries of three contradictions over which all its previous experiences had stumbled: namely, the logical ambiguity of the one and the multiple, the conflicting emotive appeals, and the sincere inability to comprehend the transcendent and the immanent, as well as suffering and death. Under its law, scarcely understood nor much observed, but still venerated as the supreme product of a mysterious Antiquity, new peoples develop the virgin lands of Europe. There, during the Christian centuries, the representations of East and West mingle until they rediscover a certain general spirit and ardor, that of a heroic and mystical, yet at the same time dogmatic catholicity, one that provokes competition and debate, amid which each party has recourse to arms, sometimes the worst that passions can propose, to support its cause. By such means Europe strives to reunite the ancient and the new. It rediscovers a secret lost by Rome and the Barbarians, and resumes the tremendous drive of inventions and discoveries whose basic impulse had derived from that Babylon which had given birth to so many marvels, to be envied, plundered, imitated, misinterpreted, lamented and cursed.

This foreshortening of evolution permits us to interpret the profound transformation introduced since the Renaissance into European representations, and the conditions which made this possible. Among these latter we must obviously count all sorts of material conquests, the forests cleared off, the lands cultivated, the cities built. But neither in agriculture nor in artisan skills were there introduced advances as decisive as those of the neolithic ages, or the ages of bronze and iron. They labored, they harvested, wove, forged, with tools not fundamentally different from those of proto-history. More important, no doubt, were the commercial developments. The bronze civilizations probably radiated out from Mesopotamia to Scotland, the Baltic and China, but central Asia from that time on became the scene of a much heavier traffic; for political and religious wars define the territories of common interests and retrace the paths of wealth that flowed from Asia. Still more significant is the increase of new populations stimulated by Europe's merchants. However, the successes of modern Europe are not explained by that fact alone.

For surely, in the surge of modern Europe we must recognize also the lure of luxury and profit which had seized upon men who had exhausted their mines of precious metals and sold so many slaves to produce the elixirs of a long life and the ravishing objects and rare products offered by the markets of Asia. The Crusades were not merely plundering, it is true; nor were the daring of Columbus and Magellan purely commercial enterprises. These men were inspired by a faith, a faith cruel toward heresy yet sensitive to novelty, open by its original syncretism to new syncretisms, and assimilating to itself the best that infidels and pagans had preserved and produced. It did this, however, at the price of remorse, punishments, rededications to virtue, and excesses. Now, in ancient Ionia, in contact with the great continents and the sea, the Greeks, having turned to good account what the Orient had to offer them, uncovered the latent secret of demonstration, along with the joy of being naked and the pride of being freely valorous. In the same way, the humanity of the Renaissance, becoming conscious of the immense resources included within its Occidental heritage, and in the acquisitions from the Orient, unclothed the beauty of man, submitted dogma to reason, and dared the forbidden oceans.

The anxieties and fears which had surrendered the arts to stylization and brought moral reflection to the parable and logic to theology lost their dominion. Here again, as in all evolutive phenomena, the new current did not spring up abruptly. Its course can be traced centuries by centuries, through the intellects of monks, popes, crusaders and merchants; but it unfolds, when the hour is ripe, to give prominence to a new complex of representations, which do not destroy the rest at one stroke, sometimes even revive it by challenging it, yet which do attack it, become enriched by it, and take strength from it. Monsters are still painted, but less to frighten than to demystify them. Paradises are no longer skies of gold but landscapes of flowers. Poverty in the Flemish paintings wears real rags, though the comfortable interiors are like tableaux. Faces are exhibited in their daily living, and the Sixtine chapel is hung with tapestries of beautiful tormented bodies. This self-confidence, however, at a time when all Europe is stained in blood, is no pure tranquility of soul. The scenes of the life of Christ are imagined in palaces or marvelous landscapes, as if to reconcile piety and luxury, or by the riches of the century to embellish what debate is already beginning to bring into doubt. Inversely, the artists respect majesty when they work for kings and princes, but subject it to their realism. By such transposition Heaven withdraws from earth, God becomes abstract, and the real presence is challenged. Criticism achieves its full authority and, in the age of Machiavelli, its legitimacy loses its moral character to become that of fact.

The movement does not come to a halt in this striking if indefinable moment, historic, though it cannot be dated precisely. But, if it continues, it is in a sense quite different from that of the period inaugurated by the Greek miracle. The Greeks stabilized a discovery of humanism following on centuries of intellectual inventiveness; the Renaissance rediscovers it to launch the swift rise of science.

History is a slow act of balancing from one trend to another. The moment of meeting between Virgil and Dante is that of the memory of an ending and the hope of a new beginning. After twenty centuries of a pagan inspiration carried to such heights that Christianity had to reverse its whole course, new centuries begin at the point where the exclusivism of the State's predominence returns increasingly to impose on representations what the State had been before the invention of monotheisms as a universal trend.

But history does not fluctuate on a single plan. After the millenia in which a multiplicity of myths become concentrated in a single great one which summed them all, the imaginative faculty relaxes. spreads and diversifies, and is made so local and so personal that one assumes its reign to be accomplished. This necessary transformation is the work of an internal process which dominates all or a part of the evolution of mythology, and amounts to an apprenticeship of historic times. Since nature has not endowed man with the reflexes appropriate to immediate adaption, he adapts by gropings. Memory allows him to retain its lessons, but because it is not instinctive in him, as with insects, only over time, little by little, does it lend itself to chronological inventory. It must have been difficult for the original ages to become aware of the three dimensions of space; and traces of that hesitation are still with us. But still more difficult was it to distinguish linear time, infinite past and future, now no longer cyclic and circular such as the ordinary bodily sensations (coenesthesia) would teach, and peace of soul would like to believe.

By illustrating the reasons for human vicissitudes, the ancient myths enlarge and transfigure an indeterminate past, rich in universal causes and almost foreign to the earth. Between these imagined marvels and the actuality, there is interposed a mishap and a fall from grace: Titan is defeated, Saturn is exiled, Paradise is lost. But since myths also renew hope by inspiring piety, they easily give rise to those eternal returns accepted by Plato and systematized by millenialisms. They teach that long periods separated by sudden revivals succeed one another and repeat themselves. The appearance of each is believed supernatural, the terrible end but the promise of resurrection. Tribes of Oceania have voluntarily destroyed themselves to be reborn like the Phoenix. Saint Paul founds his faith on the resurrection of Christ, the pledge of everything else. Christianity has lived already for a long time in the feared yet hoped for expectation of an apocalypse. Nevertheless, Saint Augustine had already shown how much the mystery of the incarnation especially opens new perspectives on history by inscribing in it a fixed point. This point becomes a guiding mark for past and future, and suggests a universal calendar to be offered by European customs to the centuries for adoption, and to the nations for imitation. The optical illusions responsible for imagining an ancient reign of giants or of great ancestors, or a lamented golden age, are softened and blurred. The predecessors of the founder, far from being envied, are now pitied. Mosaicism, Buddhism, Islam, also enrolled within the living data, have never so fully as Christianity reversed the axis of attraction. It was above all at the heart of Christianity that the ambivalence of time was established, with the about-face which locates the better in the hereafter and the beyond. Perhaps this is because its point of origin is more easily dated than is that of some others, more enveloped in mystery than are the others; or because the conjunction of Redemption with Incarnation not only reconciles linear time with the two sequences of numbers, negative and positive,[4] but also imparts value to suffering, rescues labor from servitude, and divinely consecrates the duration of time in all its moments.

4. Ch. Morazé appears to mean here that redemption for the darker past and the introduction of divinity into humanity and its future linked past and future in a linear concept rather than in the old cyclic or circular concept; and thus negative or minus dating going back from that moment is reconciled with positive dating looking to the future. Translator's note.

II. When this result is all but accomplished, when the belfries of commonplace villages as well as the cathedral steeples sound the hour, when each profession celebrates its own saint, then the way is cleared for the chronological perspectives needed for a renewal of the critical spirit that accompanies historical analysis. The Greeks and Romans had had a try at it. But the reborn rationalism is better assured than it was in Antiquity; for it was accomplished by disowning the last servants of the Hellenistic heritage. Under these conditions, the myth appeared to be banished only to rise greater and more universal. On the contrary, Europe, having reassembled in one dynamic flood tide the acquisitions of West and East, joined the spirit of experimentation to that of history. Since then, intellectual evolution seems to converse with itself, and scientific and technological progress imply, as if automatically, the revision of systems of representation.

It is in the name of such assurances of his time, proved by science and industry, that Voltaire challenges dogma and jests with the golden legend. He teaches a historical positivism which does not contradict itself, attacks credulities as scholars did magic charms when they explained alchemy, while, at the same time, Fermat and his successors were offering a powerful sequel to the lessons of Diophantes. The development associated with science and historical knowledge promises the abolition of myths. Nevertheless, if science succeeds in bringing about an intellectual revolution by substituting its new scientific systems for ancient certitudes founded on Revelation, it in no way abolishes the claims of imagination, to which it has unceasing recourse to embody and to enrich its own certitudes. Kant, in his *Critique of Pure Reason,* does justice to the illusion which confused logical truth and reality. Indeed, the great mathematical, astronomical, and physical hypotheses are operative only to the degree that they are held to be products of the imaginative faculty. As for history, by claiming to subordinate all to scholarship, it does not escape running into a thousand obscurities and illogicalities across which the power of imagination, though supposedly suppressed, spreads to invade the field of political representation.

The new development of the mythological function amid the inadequacies of history is insidious. At first it assumes a form too naif to be feared. When Bossuet tries to legitimize absolute monarchy by the appropriate words from holy scripture, the myth presents no new danger. His fashion of resorting to tradition is no better grounded than that of Titus Livy; the sacred text is not the means for any better critique by the defender of the faith than is the legend by the champion of Rome. But the text is taken less as a chronological index of events than in its role as a summary of inspired experiences. Objectivity asserts itself in the next century. Then scholarly research experiences a truly admirable advance. For now, devoting itself particularly to the annals of kings, princes and great families, it puts scholars and monasteries at its service to establish the genealogy of its examples. The Revolution permitted Michelet to open the archives to the public, and to draw therefrom the data for a general and popular history. From this social as well as intellectual mutation there appears to be born this time the strictness of assured interpretations, developed later to the rhythm of that industrialization whose changes it had to endure.

Nevertheless, critical history remains in Europe a corollary of the rise of the bourgeois. Michelet, a son of the people, writing for the people, exalts his native land, proclaims it an example to the world with a candor that distresses foreign opposition, and which will be the despair of German militarism. This is because, like Michelet, though not according to his views, Germans, as well as Italians, Magyars, and Czechs are rediscovering their past, rehabilitating ancient languages and reviving memories of glorified ancestors, heroes of a less universal character than those of legends and tales.

Everywhere, the effects of scholarship and of historical concentration are quite different from what their promoters were anticipating. Augustin Thierry escaped into the study of Merovingian times or the time of the Norman conquest of England, as if he were fleeing the distractions of the present. He obeys them just the same without being aware of it; for his work places the emphasis on the idea of race and justifies the claims of noble families returning as conquerors on the debris of the Republic as, according to the count of Boulainvilliers, their Frankish ancestors had done on the ruins of Roman Gaul. He also introduces a racial myth whose virulence will in some degree corrupt France and much of Europe. In Germany, Hegel and his contemporaries and disciples will claim to transcend history by a philosophy which shares the exacting analysis of Immanuel Kant. All of these, nevertheless, express the intellectual aspirations of an ambitious and active social class, caught in the capitalist surge coming from England, incited and inflamed by the French example, and hostile to those petty courts so detested by Schiller. They defend badly their ambition to accept as a teacher an industrious and ambitious state like England, on the model sketched by Fichte. The young German universities call themselves liberal and demonstrate against the Teutonic spirit. Nevertheless, their punctilious erudition, which will be recommended by Renan for imitation by his compatriots after they are conquered by Bismarck, gives circulation to the inaccurate idea of a culture originally Aryan, and prepares the way for the worst pan-Germanisms to come.

Before the great monotheisms, every city, every clan, had its God. Modern Europe does the same; the nations draw apart in the name of their Paradises of heroes, strip them of the challenged Christian God, and transfer the energy of the Crusaders to their patriots. The difference is that heaven is no longer considered a guaranteed reward. Locke and Berkeley promise liberty and pragmatism to the English, Voltaire and Rousseau abundance and fraternity to the French, and the German philosophers power to their compatriots and others. The peoples need representations, the new dominant social class offers them those that seem suitable and that by this bias legitimize the liberal and national State from which it draws so large a share. History confirms the new imagined worlds, by instilling in its beneficiaries an image of what it was: in England a profitable conquest of commerce, an ethnic symbiosis in the sumptuous glitter of a dynasty in France, a crusade against the Slavs in Germany. The images of nationalisms in Europe are produced in much the same way as those of the most ancient mythologies had been. Marx undertook to fight against this power of illusion and jeered at the vanity of the philosophers. But, carried away himself on this torrent of the imagined which he had hoped to dam, he promised the internationale to the proletariat of the industrial countries of his day, even at the moment they were swearing to destroy each other in the name of right and liberty. The inexorable law which he had suspected, but which failed him, will not bring success to the communist system of representation except in countries with a communitarian tradition and, before it can unify the world, will but accentuate its divisions.

The operations of the imaginative faculty go as far on the path of differentiation as they had been on that of syncretism. The great religious myths in the epoch when they served as a general reference, even if they were expressing and linking with the fundamental aspirations of the soul, were not immobilizing action or pointing the way to its decisions. To legitimize the daily routine, the collective imagination invented tales, legends, narratives, whose moral tags eventually borrowed from ancient beliefs what the dominant faith

was failing to explicate with pertinence, but which bore a resem-
blance in that each appealed to the supernatural. Supreme power,
occult powers, guide and sustain the hero, and so assure his triumph,
or at least his preservation, as a reward for his indefinable but
obvious virtue.

The obstacles opposed to the hero arise from the empire of evil
and its wicked spells. In the simple world of the tale, as of the era,
the characters are determined. One has to introduce into them the
uncertainty of noble demands so that a magnified danger commanding the whole scene restores the ambiguity of a tragic destiny;
even so, there too the human hero depends on the divine order.
Comedy, born of low jokes and banter, following a reverse path, does
not drag heaven into human affairs. And if it leaps over a period in
which it is summed up in characters, the *Miser* or the *Liar*, the
Misanthrope or the *Turcaret* of Lesage, it secularizes life, puts epic
poetry out of fashion, and introduces the romantic novel. This last
genre is in its origins contemporary with positive history; it wishes to
portray on the level of the daily scale what history tries to establish
on the scale of great moments. The romantic wholes are images of
societies, reflections of manners in which the familiar and the everyday carry on their existence in the midst of memorable events, and as
a consequence of, and alongside, them.

The methods of history and the novel are not identical; that is, to
establish chronologies and to delimit true personalities submits to a
documentary discipline far stricter than inventing them. But this
strictness of reference excludes the flexibility of the imagined experiences that are needed to explain the internal motivations of actual
living. The power of imagination makes its way through the gaps and
errors in history, and is followed by history, which submits these
fictional experiences to its own way of testing the concrete. The
activity of the romancer in a certain way extends that of the
historian. It shares in his task of demystification; but the novelist's
work, imagined like the scientific hypothesis, and tested by the
critical inspection of the reader, is nevertheless also a creator of
myths, sometimes on the scale of the folk, but especially on that of
the individuals whose dreams and behavior it inspires. And if the
legal action against Flaubert is not sustained in law, the explanation
given is that such action was demanded by moralists who were
disturbed by seeing what arose as 'Bovarism' because of a too callous
narrative of the manners of *Madame Bovary*.

When imagination is attacked by knowledge it loses its freedom, but not the need for it nor its strength. When dragged away from its transcendent preoccupations, it is only the more active in the service of reality. It gives value to the existing, the moment, the ephemeral; and it speeds up the future. Imagination multiplies its own power by fragmenting it, and opens the paths of a scientific world as vast and unknown as concrete nature was to the gropings of the first men. It involves the minds of today in efficient and rigorous causalities, leads them from success to success therein, without further defining the central point of the human community of efforts. It substitutes scientific hypothesis and its experimental demands for religious myth and its consolations and its experience with exaltation. But it also cuts science off from life, and involves life in an infinitude of adventures liberated by the intellectual initiative, and united by the solidarity of great classes and nations into great dramas.

Nevertheless, the divorce between imagination and knowledge is not total. The hypothesis of the astronomer is less illusory but just as symbolic as the astrologer's recipe. The importance of the result achieved by the last great conquest of the imaginative faculty, that which gives birth to modern science, can only be attributed to a new way of interpreting reality. This manner is more appropriate to technological activity because, instead of granting first place to the expression of emotions and passions, it more accurately establishes the bounds, perhaps not of the real itself, but of the conditions for whatever wishes to deal successfully with the real.

Here, then, the high point of the imaginative activity resides, whose evolution may be summed up as follows:

The imaginative activity, the inspiration for events and inspired by them, began first by establishing abstractions of events, or rather, types of models in the legends whose often contradictory episodes testify to the difficulties which confront the rational understanding of the living experience. Then, not having found the logical center of all, the imagination draws the Olympian world closer to the daily experience. The empire of the divine is then emptied of its composite monsters, expelled by the immortals with the faces, the characters and weaknesses, as well as the organization, of men. But the need for a perfect unity is not yet satisfied. The search is once more launched beyond the images borrowed from earth, though not denying them all, insofar as astral and solar nomadism had been made aware of the simplicity of its passions, by introducing into them the mysteries of birth, of suffering and death, as well as those of numbers and calculation.

This transcendental imagination, without cutting itself off from the earthly, locates still farther from it the all-powerful which justifies the irrational, compensates for injustice, and atones for transgressions. This immense distancing of the divine center orients all in its direction. Thus, in an effective manner, it contributes to encouraging confidence in the operations of reason whose very sophisticated use of the syllogism has enabled it to measure its own inadequacies, while linking them with the aspirations of the heart. Thus, beginning with this very great multiple, research is made possible step by step into the smaller elements, not so much logically deduced as found pertinently useful. While handing over higher truth to God, man permits the rationally irreducible factors to play their part. He familiarizes himself with these latter, whose acceptance encourages the progressive admission of the chronologies of history as well as the abstract definitions of scientific nomenclatures.

When this reversal has taken place, the imaginative faculty aims at being not so much a logical totality as a very orderly catalogue of experiences. After having striven to contain all humanity, the imaginative faculty feeds on its own disparities now that science has learned how better to extract its certain correlations and their points of contact with things.

Now during the same time, if action changes its rhythms and accelerates, it does not modify its nature. It is not now in action that one must seek the directly valuable results of the power to imagine, which action contributes so much to feed. For alongside action, which is incapable of changing its gestures, expression, so greatly able to refine its elementary components, draws also on the power to imagine, fixes it and nourishes it. And since expression unites men less by its character as mass than by its subtle, ephemeral network, its innumerable elements and its power to convince by its articulations, expression is to be viewed as especially suited to advancing the organization of what man learns and reflects on, when what attracts him is no longer so much supernatural as at the very heart of his communities.

Finally, before undertaking the third and last study of what relates to the exploration of the possible, it is useful to note that the evolution of the power to imagine, by making experimentation with the particular prevail over the common dream, concentrates the attention which man projects onto things, and teaches him how best to direct that attention. This concentration of the effort of discovery, and this acquired pertinency, mark the two great stages of the history of successful expressions, to which we shall now turn our attention.

5. Successful expressions

The greatest deeds of the past and their imagined worlds would have been forgotten had it not been for works of art able to survive through time. Without these, every age would have had to undertake all over, each for itself, the exploration of possibilities forever returned to their first steps. Humanity might perhaps have aged less, but it would also have had fewer conquests. Without durable expression, the repeated search for reality might perhaps have carried its elementary gropings to an extreme degree of perfection. It would not have gone through so many successive miscarriages of the illusory, nor have experienced those of industrial science.[1] But expression does not shield historic evolution from raw facts, nor the power to imagine from its first charms, except by extracting beauty from the imagined. The churning sea of possibilities throws up not only institutions capable of controlling deeds, but also works capable of seducing men. Poseidon, son of Chronos, is made sovereign of the fluid immensity out of which Astarte, his bride, is born.

Nevertheless, differing thus from the institutions fashioned by deeds accomplished, the perfected work came into existence before it became an event to be exhibited. In the world of men's productions, the work is indeed a logical effect of their actions, but it enjoys a certain chronological precocity. It shows an already latent aspect of the power to imagine at work to give itself form. The

1. The image is not precise. These miscarriages, it should be said, bring to mind the periods which needed to be traversed, some because of discovered symbolic representations to satisfy the needs of the heart, others under the pressure of logical representations in the creation of science. Ch. Morazé, note to translator, May 26, 1970.

ambiguous nature of its invasion into casual time is a glimpse into the depths where the determinative forces of expression find their application.

The field of knowledge is free and open only through the expressed; that is to say, toward the center of a vague zone where the perceived and the felt take form, and where what one believes mingles with what is. Internal experience teaches us the existence of an obscure mass preceding and as if below what is done and said, nebulous with faltering observations, a mass which now eludes and now presents itself by throwing off toward consciousness thrusts of certitude that call for formulation. Before what is well conceived can be clearly expressed, a long labor has to be undergone, made of badly composed sentences in a language in search of its words. Purity of style is not immediate and spontaneous except in privileged moments when the development of the work, within the author, meets that of the understanding, in the setting for which he intends it. Then only do the resources of form, elaborated by the collectivity and mobilized by the author, clarify for him what he has found to be transmissible to others.

What is not expressed, what burdens the I with its unconscious weight, totals up all the impressions which physiology has received from the environments that condition it. It contains the destiny of each, related to that of others and that of things. But it is perceived only as a play of shadows, hidden beneath the shifting surface of our pleasures. It is shown in an elementary way in brief outbursts, it affects attitudes and words, inhibits gestures which one had thought controlled, causes the unexpected to start up, and reveals by means of incidents which psychoanalysis calls *actes manqués,* abortive acts, a reality as powerful as surprising.

On occasion, the unexpressed brings about an act of grace between two beings, when a certain brilliance of glance, a tiny movement, gives to each a happy certainty of an identity sharply revealed for an instant, accepted in the evidence of what is communicated without speech. A nothing, then, becomes a plenitude such as sentences and commentaries added after the moment will not achieve. A certain very incomplete similarity, though at the time profound and filled with mystery, constitutes the value of these ineffable, ephemeral and sometimes delightful encounters. They have their opposite, too, in repulsion or hate. In these two cases, a limited unit of experience is for an infinitely brief moment made up of harmonies or oppositions and set apart from its environment. It is instigated by an internal sentiment of pleasure or pain, of penetration and a fleeting certainty, which is usually dissolved in a soon reawakened criticism or skepticism.

The thrusts of the imaginative faculty toward the concrete, when they do not go beyond these brief flowerings, would not merit mention if they were not already manifesting the power that every human milieu has of crystalizing at the points where the attraction of communication recombines the materials which the event has shattered. When they take on somewhat more stability, these thrusts impart even more importance to the distinction between gesture and image. This image unfolds better when every tentative move toward action is intercepted in the isolation of reveries or in the sleep of dreams. The same cause, though it often escapes attention, gives rise to an air sung, a lively step, some expression of contentment, or, inversely, of hostility. However tiny this material fragment, it is already the rough draft of a creative work. These odd bits may join and combine, may complete themselves by elements borrowed from the already known, or may compose a drawing, a text, a song — secret trial attempts, most often soon forgotten, of a nature no different from that of appreciated works of amateurs or even of certain effects of art. The German language gives the term *fantasieren* to this improvised realization of reveries, assigned by Beethoven to a genre.

But, aside from rare exceptions, we must again go beyond these tiny consolidations of the imagined to consider the successful expression destined to be long inscribed in the world of the real, there profoundly to move a great number of people. All proceeds in that world by stages, the effect of each being to adapt to the next. The work, then, even more takes into account lessons accumulated, even if unconsciously, from many precedents, remembering which, yet challenging which, man thereby adds new lessons.[2] Thus, when it comes into view, finally realized, given form and completed, an art object, a musical score, a literary text, it has already adapted a creative privacy to a collective reality. Such a powerful result is not due to chance. It is not by throwing together just any trial effort that an immortal work is created. The great work appears in the very midst of a thousand productions of minor value, in which are also found something of the colors, forms, sounds, or expressions

2. The latter part of this sentence is added to that in the text, following upon a letter from the author, May 26, 1970. Translator's note.

appropriate to a milieu and an era. The great work is neither the sum
nor the residue of these, but instead the perfect exemplar, which
brings several of the above together, and takes on value from the
original and overall unity of its creation.

One cannot too much insist on the difference between action and
creative work. The final result of creation confers on action the unity
which conditions the appearance of the work. The power to imagine
is nourished on what humanity remembers having destroyed in order
to change. The work springs forth from memory endlessly de-struc-
tured, the witness to fractures already understood because given
expression, mended because comprehended. It is a certitude being
born and an innovation achieved.

The work is the evidence of a modification seized at the moment
of its springing into existence. Not all changes find their interpreters,
but without them there is no interpretation. As for the author, if he
seems to translate all into visions, personalities, situations, that is,
indeed, a system of expression which takes place within himself. It is
an active reality underlying and preceding what he does with it, the
inspiration for a simpler and more communicable poetry as it is the
more communal in nature. At this degree of depth, the genius arrives
at self-forgetfulness, so that which calls for expression within him is
united to the means to express it.

In due time we shall examine what concerns the act of expression.
But what makes the work objectively possible depends on a certain
agreement between what moves the power to imagine and what
characterizes a moment in the evolution of a system of expression.
Under these conditions we find here a *constant:* namely, that it is
not given to every moment to produce any and every type of perfect
expression; and again, that there are periods when art is figurative,
and others when its value is to be non-figurative in order the better
to give new life to its symbolic components. Thus, having considered
how the power to imagine changes, we must now examine how the
modes of expression affect it. We may also fix a certain goal for this
clarification: namely, to seek how the expressive effort arrives at
logical formalizations whose syntactical disciplines have the value of
certitude.

I. The successful work has the strength of deep and orderly relations
which have found their precision by obeying the most subtle of
appeals. It is a transparent crystal nourished by the imaginative
faculty, a pure solution in which the expressive structures give the

work form in order to reveal its original nature. The author here can be called the creator only by reason of the respect due him. Actually, he is but the carrier-agent of an organic combination modeled on a new and still secret articulation of the milieu which shaped him, and from which he detaches himself in order to make his word understood in its shocking, fascinating, and unanticipated strangeness.

Spectators are well aware that they are not a part of the intimacy set up between Velásquez and the royal family of Spain; but, as they contemplate *Las Meninas* [*The Maids of Honor*] they recognize the quality of relations established between the painter and majesty; for the painter, though an inspired witness, was no more a part of majesty than the spectators, and is separated from it in order to give majesty its distinction. This is more evident still in the case of Goya, who is less the great nobleman and paints a more belated monarchy. Admiration is a relation to a relation. The first relation, that of the painter, for example, grounds itself at the start on the mystery of personality and poses problems of a physiological order; the second, as in the case of majesty, is much more social in nature. Certainly the one and the other are correlative, and the biological and the social are factors in either case. But since, aside from the duration, neither the difficulty nor the pertinency of the relationship would be perceptible, it is through history, that is, the social, that we must approach it.

The painter does not exist simply as a consequence of his particular model and his connection with it, for he belongs to all painting, to all those who have preceded him and accompany him in this art, among whom he is distinguished by being quite different even while remaining one of them still. Every artist is surely a moment in the general evolution of the imagined, and also in the evolution of procedures. He excels among his predecessors and his peers by borrowing lessons from them which he carries to a greater perfection. Every successful work is a witness to the importance of representations in the human whole. Also at the heart of a broader society which accepts or mistrusts the work of art, there is the specific dedication of a group which inspired the work.

To grasp the importance of this division which specifies and supports the quality of expression, we should return parenthetically here to the fundamental problem posed by the imaginative faculty as capable of throwing light on the question of form. An illustration will elucidate better than reasons — for example, that suggested by the Israelite communities reduced to ghettos within Christianity.

Caught in a movement deliberately hostile to them, or at least alienated, they often seem to be held back as compared to Christianity. Yet, placed in this critical position, they discover better and sooner than any other the weaknesses which will challenge Christianity. Thus, when the Western world finds itself rudely confronted by the contradictions within its social regime and its moral habits, certains sons of the Jewish tradition, Marx and Freud, find the most considered expressions and the most exact statements to propose for the difficulties which embarrass that world. Every great artist of whatever sort belongs to a particular social group, and is enabled by its exaltation or its suffering to perceive the active innovation. All differential situations may furnish stimuli to arouse the generations of artists and inventors; for they constitute so many specific wholes made sensitive to the least emerging differences. By lending themselves to the expression of these situations they are the better prepared to resolve them.

The cleavages within a collective whole predetermine the outcome. They also constitute the differentiated structure in which each element is, in its way, the analyst of the others. Certain of these elements, withdrawn from the action which they will reencounter only indirectly, become the suppliers of signs destined to fix certain characteristics within the mutual confrontation that was thus brought about. When society seeks to reabsorb the exceptional into the institution, it not infrequently happens that it either fails in the face of the growing event, or that it succeeds only partially. It excludes the deed that is feared, but not a certain prophetic manner it has of expressing the latent possibility. The world of signs is thus established beyond political institutions, and is created more out of usages and fashions than out of laws. It is also the more subtly imperious when it depends less on imposed commands than on the effective appeals of its pertinency. Academies, schools, are its most visible but not its most effective organs, since every system of expression is given value particularly by what alters it. Unusual methods of sketching, of painting, of working on material and of using language then take the form of exceptional structures.

The same is true of ordinary expressions as of petty deeds in which institutions respond to the dominant trend. The materials of arts and of language are effectively reassembled in bodies of meaning, in colors, forms, dictionaries, and grammars by the ant-like labors of many, but the great works, being of a more subtle nature than great deeds, have more spontaneously found the converging point for their pertinency.

The paths of meaning and those of imagination are not identical. However, though they most frequently diverge on the innumerable occasions when expression succeeds but badly in its purpose, they recombine in works destined to endure. The evolution of the expressive is less arbitrary, closer to the central flow of the imaginative faculty than it is to that of deeds. Like all evolution, it experiences periods of birth, or progress, of diffusion and of decrepitude. But since the matter which it appropriates to its use is more fluid, less burdened with restraints, more independent of the mass of concrete experience, it is also less protected from fantasy, even though, by compensation, it is more suited to rediscovering a lost order. By its increasing power and quality, it reveals the lost and rediscovered value of the problematics of invention.

We may see an example in the history of architecture. The ruins of Rome are in the Corinthian style of those great civic or religious wholes which complete the Doric and Ionic discoveries in the colossal and the decorative, and whose models are conserved in the grandiose remains of cities, temples, forums, and the Palatine. Then the first abrupt return to an elementary simplicity gives birth to the basilicas with flat, timbered ceilings. Roman art then becomes more confident, spreads to the provinces and expands, and is expressed in forms that have rediscovered boldness and ornament according to an ecology conforming to local conditions. As these multiplied experiments draw toward the end of their successes and their movement toward the new urban activity of northern Europe, there arises the art which will be named Gothic, only in its turn to be differentiated to the point of exhausting itself in stylistically flamboyant fantasies without a future. This is followed by a new return, this time to ancient origins; and the Renaissance, along with the freedom of the seas, rediscovers the art of cupolos and colonades. Then the rococo follows on the baroque, Versailles on the Escurial, and Sans Souci on Versailles. So, for a second time, all returns to an ancient archetype, the style of the antique and of the Scotch Adams, which once more spreads abroad in the fantasying freedom of romanticism and the composite luxuriance of Victorian taste. But beyond this third deviation the new research for the authentic is no longer satisfied to return to Rome. The era of 1900 imitates nature, its aquatic flora, conquers exoticism, seeks the form before the form, and brings all into question.

Several cycles are thus offered for our admiration, short or long, incomplete or radical, linked to modifications on the cultural frontiers from Euroasiatic Christianity to the West, from Europe to its conquering universalism. Each flowering corresponds to a condition born of the power to imagine: first and second Christianity, the reconquest of humanism, the revival of science. It is a time, in short, of surprises brought about as much by historical experience as by experiment in the laboratory. Each exaggeration marks the exhaustion of an embodiment which has lost its expressive power, and which, by its path to the bizarre, often makes necessary a return to an elementary symbolization that refuses all inherited figurations.

Here, in sum, we see reflected the vicissitudes of collectivities in which certain moments stand out dramatically as those when order is reasserted and drawn tighter after having lost itself on a spendthrift exuberance.

In this process, the major and minor arts are included with architecture no less than with literary poetics, with the appropriate nuances and displacements sufficiently known to all.

There is an intrinsic evolution of styles. Oriental societies have not evolved in the same way as those of the Occident, but their styles similarly present a cyclic succession, even though simpler, especially toward its end. This is shown, for example, in Moslem countries by the succession of semicircular arches, pointed arches, or even the horseshoe arches associated with the Caliphates, the Meljuk empires of the eleventh to thirteenth centuries, then with their principalities, and with the Persian restoration. Oriental taste, in its Ottoman composition, is stimulated by Byzantine survivals before it responds to the baroque feeling of Austro-Bavarian Christianity. Also the Safavides, those restorers of an autonomous tradition, though without submitting to the same direct influences nevertheless rediscover the models, the decorative themes, and the techniques inspired by the Pompeian models. The art of Ispahan corresponds to that of Bernini (1598—1680), even though not at all resembling it, for both express the same revivification. Only the circumstances of place, the more or less direct contacts with ancient reminders or influences of the Far-Orient, the incentives rendered so different by soils, climates and societies, cause them to choose differently what they will bring into order according to an identical rediscovered taste for the ceremonial. The Orient expresses itself in illustrations that complement those of the Occident, and is marked by cyclic phases of events correlative to our own. Inspired more by the way gardens may be arranged than by interior dispositions, the Orient supplies more fashions for luxury than models for study. No explanation is of value which does not include in the general principles of cyclic evolution that of manifestations opposed by some characteristic, or inspired by milieux which differ, and sharing, each in its own way, the hazards offered by an evolution adapted to new-born variations.

What is said of style in general naturally applies to graphology, the manner of forming letters, and to writing, the manner of forming and making use of words. Here, too, there are clear epochs, and, so to speak, elementary ones, in which sentences are simple and signs schematic, and others where all is surcharged. Thus it is, for example, in the Carolingian and the Gothic. They complicate form and foundation up to the return of classicism, which printing will stabilize. In the Orient, too, the manner of written works is transformed, sometimes by avoiding redundance and sometimes by returning to it. The angular script of the Kufic was suceeded by the fanciful, sloping script of the Nastaliq. For lack of adding something new, they embellish the already acquired.

Again, the study of languages reveals their nature through their history. The way in which monosyllables, whether agglutinating or inflected, are distributed over the map convinces that, within the immense field of spontaneous creations and the practically infinite possibilities offered by the resources of phonation, multiple systems are expanded by derivations, and made unique by their differences. Each language possesses in its own right a certain manner of being arbitrary, the result of a necessity for differentiations. At the center of a network of affiliations, ecology suggests a broad epicentrum situated at the crossroads of three ancient continents and at the meeting place of the movements of their peoples, in a zone from which languages separate by irreconcilable processes, each diversified by adaptation to its milieu. This epicentrum, remote from the zones where expression is still dominated by the pictogram and the ideogram, acts on idioms from the more recent invasions so as there to differentiate the Indo-European from the Semitic, the Finno-Ugric from the Uralo-Altaic.

This evolutive fission corresponds to an elementary linguistic phenomenon: namely, to qualify for being named, a concept must be abstracted by a shock from the total environment in which it is submerged, and the sounds which name it must be clearly distinct. Since this two-fold necessity of breaches of base and form is more acute between neighboring ideas or notions and closely similar sounds, it is there, also, that the meaning and the art of distinctions are sharpened by the clashes imposed by conquests and invasions.

Thus a progressive evolution is involved. But since the fear of not sufficiently asserting the self and the pleasure of play diversifies each system thus defined into excessive fantasy, the evolutive cycle ages as soon as it is generated. Even more than its erosion by wear and tear, its allomorphy by misuse forces a reconsideration of the expressive, beginning with the elementary imperatives of precision.

Linguistic evolution is more complex than that of other instruments of expression; it is also more instructive because it more clearly applies the principle of least effort or, what comes to the same thing, of an increasing economy. The effects are not at first evident, especially as concerns writing. The pictogram brings an immediate and general solution to its basic problem because it is, in principle, universally understandable. But, aside from the fact that the ornamental or esoteric refinements of scribes subtract from its quality of being direct, it proves to be inadequate for indicating the complex relationships which are better resolved by the infinite articulations introduced by time into the spoken language. From there on, the search for economy gives preference to the flexibility of sounds arbitrarily linked to a meaning. The figurative becomes understandable to more speakers, but less satisfactorily penetrates the correlative depths of notions and ideas. The alphabet, with some twenty to thirty signs which taken separately lack any meaning, succeeds in expressing the correlations where the idiogram fails. Between the two systems of oral and written form there is established a play of interactions demanded by the need to express the more complex and more profound interrelations. This leads to a renunciation of the advantages of the obvious but inflexible meaning in drawing.

In this two-fold labor of the abstraction of meaning by relation to the image and the mutual adaptation of spoken and written signs, we may safely affirm that of all the materials treated there is none lighter, more flexible, less costly, than the word made up of sounds. It involves, also, a thoughtful attention which makes it the most economical means of control of the pertinence of a relation or the validity of a concept.

Now, considered in its creation and in its everyday use, the word arises in the thread of discourse like the gesture on the thread of time. Pursuing this same comparison, the sentence is a deed and the narrative a coordinated sequence of events. Words are like men, and the men like kingdoms, which seek to captivate. Put otherwise, what historic action suggests of experience at great cost and heavy losses of lives and time, speech experiences at small cost, at small risk, and in the space of a moment. Language multiplies and lightens the trials and tests to which it submits the imaginative faculty. Indeed, being almost free, it does not become involved with reality as does the deed, and hence to a lesser degree enriches the stock of the imagined. But it does much more easily inventory reality, analyze and order it. Language is the first to produce works that are revelations or even premonitions capable of informing men on the nature and the scope of what demands their involvement. Thanks to successful expression of this kind, men are brought to know a particular aspect of what they are, even while they still remain prisoners of what they do. By such more restricted participation in historicity, speech anticipates history and informs us of the value of all art, that pertinent reflection of an element within the imaginative faculty, linked to the destiny of a collectivity.

In all its manifestations, and from epoch to epoch, if the work of art may be admired by those who no longer share the situation out of which it was created, that is because one is capable of recognizing in it the universal value of the expression whose quality reveals how a certain secret of a communal nature was found. The work of art blazes forth in luminous high lights the immense evolution by which the lived experience is summed up for all. It sets up for each of us the most flexible way of putting one's own historicity into form.

Art does not force imagination as imperatively as action, but it draws from action more prompt and more pertinent lessons of order. It is thus at the center of the realm of expression, rather than at the trough of action, that the effectual relationships of reality are the sooner discovered, to be the more easily translated into operative formulae. The world of expression is not only in an eminent manner that of beauty, but it shares also, by its unceasing search for economy, that of the pertinence which leads to exactitude.

II. Beauty has no age, but its objects have fashions. It is not possible to decide on better or worse between the Parthenon and Notre Dame, nor between Fragonard and Corot; but one knows that metopes, those ornamented spaces between friezes, are out of place in the second, and stained glass windows in the first. It is not that the subject treated is forever fixed in its demands, a nativity may be as beautiful under the thatch of a lean-to roof as between the colonnades of a dream palace; but certain objects do not please except in the appropriate setting. The child's swing would be incongruous on a base of gold, as would an arm-chair by Pluvinet in the Taj Mahal. That is why the best arranged museum puts admiration under a strain; its walls do not protect one from the noises, the colored and explicit suggestions, coming from the city outside. The works of art lose the power there that they had at the time of their creation. Even left on their original sites, drawings in grottos, columns of temples, Gothic arches of cathedrals, do not affect us as they did their first faithful. Tastes change with the reasons for adoration, and if our admiration has become more general and more liberal, it is because historical reflection has penetrated the web of our emotions. Thus a temporal dimension acts as a compensation for contractions of space where are confined the remains of works once harmonious in the unlimited worlds of the imagined of their own time.

As for the word, it is not only in syntactic agreement with the rest of the sentence, but is resonant within a whole system of representation. To paraphrase Horace or Boileau so as to extend their intent, one may say that each image has its place. To transfer the symbol of the bull Apis to a butcher's shop is to substitute amazement for contemplation, or rather to provoke to laughter. Such games of displacement are among the resources of the comic, whose jokes disconcert all veneration and free us from the hold of tragedy. Such is not only a gratuitous iconoclasm, but a reaction of secularization and rationalization.

The pertinence of a symbol is an effect of very complex relations, extended into all the dimensions of a culture. Even the savage village proves this when it appears in a sort of perfection of what it is in its totality. The dance then reconciles art with science, and reality with system. It is worship and commandment, hate and reconciliation. Men who are seeking not so much to produce some great work as to be able to exert themselves more economically on every ordinary occasion thus serve an apprenticeship to what will create out of their studied and graceful gestures something supple, light, appropriate, and of minimum cost. The dance was primitively a total art, comprising ethic, aesthetic, and logic. Only later did it become a matter of profession, in which all apprenticeship will have been made specific by a division of labor, and abundance will have deprived a total society of the feeling of communal participation, because it is divided and diverted to professional groups in the theatre. But even after this mutation, the stock of all successful expressions is no less composed from moment to moment of firmly united wholes. In the time of Descartes, for example, great painters entrusted geometers with the task of dividing their canvases by rule and compass, into spaces within which their inspiration is precisely inscribed. Architects, renouncing the Gothic raised between earth and heaven, rediscover the cupola in Florence. This they impose on the Escurial, in London and Paris, notably at the Pantheon, where Foucault's pendulum will mark on the ground the circular movement of the earth. But it is landscapes of stone that they find best fitted to suggest the nature of the globe recently encircled by hardy navigators, affirmed in its movements by Galilei, and soon to be situated by Newton in the universal pull of gravity. Similarly, when music fixes its scales and brings order into genres, refines its harmonies, becomes contrapuntal and completes its orchestration, the era is open to the mathematics of the continuous and the differential. When finally Euclidean and Cartesian spaces are challenged by science, the artists, too, begin to question the techniques of perspective, so admirably prevailing at the time of the Renaissance.

Now if, and in such way, beauty and precision join hands, it is for different results, according to epochs and periods. The fact is that the aspirations and movements of the collective soul find their most necessary interpreters in music, which Plato would have banished from the city. Beethoven, in Goethe's judgment, agitated feeling overmuch; the fact was that he bore witness to a change in the world. As for language and its poetry, fixed in its durability, but also translatable into signs and falling back on the image, it sums up in its ambiguity the flux of passions across the order of things.

The author of a narrative convinces his listener only by virtue of a certain quality of emotion which links one to the other. If he sufficiently touches feeling, he holds attention to his tale; he is not interrupted, for the impulse to ask him questions is less than the desire to learn what he still has to say, and the heart listens better than the reason hears. Carried away by emotion, the imagination forgets to be critical. The discontinuity of deeds like the difficulties of logic are founded on the intuitive and living continuance. It takes an extreme effort on the part of the critical to force the mysterious nature of these unions to yield to judgment. Even mathematics, like all things spoken, is in some manner enhanced by narrative. It has often happened that many centuries were needed to discover within the secret of a fully formed locution, or even of a single word, the sudden burst of meaning hidden under the quality of style, the precision of syntaxes, and even under the formal strictness of syllogisms. But it is no longer true that the mind trapped by phrases will forever forget its supreme questioning function. Never for long satisfied, nor yet indifferent, the mind responds to the message by an interchange of speech. It seeks certainty; and having found it, thanks to this dialectic, then brings it under question.

The varieties of relations between the charms of listening and the organized perspectives of looking, aside from their being correlative to the differences of emotive charges, depend on the collective situations. If the chanted dance is at the origin of other expressions of beauty, each particular art, before it is individualized into authors, depends on the ways in which the collectivity is structured, split up, made specific in interdependent groups, or stirred by the reactions appropriate to the way fashions and styles are also defined. The articulation of signs in closed systems, their classification into apparently separated categories, are correlatives of social specializations. These latter, being the more sensitive when they have not yet become habitual and, as it were, intermingled, remain quite fresh fractures and affecting traumatisms. It is when they are in this condition that the artist is moved by them, and fixes them in a creation which becomes an event, that is to say, the coming together of two developments, the one expressive, the other imagined — in short, a great work, when the change involved is great, and when the evidence of its manifestations is easily accessible. Even when we no longer participate in the storms which gave it birth, the work touches us, because of that same simplicity which integrates it painlessly into the totality of our feeling.

Every lasting innovation of expression is born of a certain communion which consecrates it. But once it has become object, it also provokes a critical examination of the feelings which gave it birth. From then on, it lends itself to the evolution which explicates myths, and donates its functional significance to the very ancient quarrel of universals. At the beginning, things sacred and sacred signs are identified. To recognize oneself in a totem is to represent it to oneself with that particular kind of reverence which distorts the reality to give strength to a symbol; it is also to fix a concept whose denotation will remain the accepted one even after one has rid himself of its magic. Thus, step by step, when the feeling of mystery is exhausted, the arbitrary but pertinent system of a general representation is completed. By dint of such experiments in the course of which the critical spirit strips the sign of the emotions with which it has been surcharged, concepts are defined by their mutual situation at the heart of a world particularized only by its axiomatics.

Now the overlappings of the worlds of representation are innumerable; and out of the least expression, whatever its nature, they fashion the visible part of an invisible, and arbitrarily fix a choice, capricious in its appearances, sentimental in its living reason, and always further linked by the order of the context. This ambiguity multiplies the uses of a word, and constitutes the frontiers and the superimpositions of meaning around the core of what it signifies, even to the point where the topological and the specific prevail over the representative. Thus the emotive is banished from the imagined, and the word finally arrives at expressing a completed abstraction.

The effort of the logical strips off the sacred to arrive at the rational. Languages lend themselves to this the better because of the rapid dialectic which they inject between what arises from the time the word has existed and the synchronous intervals of comprehension. That is, language keeps words alive that change through time, but permits specific meanings at specific times. Again, a cultural branch will have had to modify its system of expression, and to test its phonetic resources correlatively with the needs of interpretations. Words so eroded will be the better apprehended when they have become perfectly neutral, and find their place for a consistent result within the articulations of structures themselves irreducible. Rational expression is less the effect of faithfulness to a popular speech than to the lessons drawn from divers uses and modifications. Everything that changes the relations of words tests the validity of the relations of meanings. Thus it proceeds from ardent criticism that makes what must become a true correlation more flexible, and so discovers in language the durable material of pertinent entities. At the bottom of these transignifications and transliterations, the syntax of certainty is disengaged from the play of sentences, while symbols give birth to algorisms, namely, the art of calculating by notation. Historic experience, therefore, by a kind of fractional distillation, successively deposits the means of reason and the objects of knowledge, the logic of propositions and the basic elements of language, the semantemes on which history practices to corroborated results.

We may consider all that is fabricated by men of a same people to be similar to the signs of a language becoming the more quickly operative as the accepted transcription is the more arbitrary and the more detached from the emotive desires that gave rise to its use. In this experimental context, each contact between cultures and each transmutation from either of them takes on the value of a signification. A completely new culture whose inexperience strips its borrowings of the artificialities more appropriate to emotions not shared or no longer shared, does not necessarily select the elements most suited to the development of operative processes. And scholarship, for our information, rediscovers these errors or omissions in the misinterpreted documents; yet each time such study contributes something toward rationalizing the symbol.

Thus the Asians working in the mines of Sinai on the command of Ammenemes III dedicate their offerings to the goddess Hathor with votive inscriptions written in their own language, but are satisfied to make use of the phonetic part of the hieroglyphics, though the scribes, as was their privilege, guarded the useless and sacred figurative secrets. Thus the Asians invent an alphabet by virtue of the single fact of not belonging to a superior caste, the guardians and beneficiaries of the jealously guarded rites of their written language. In the same way, the Greeks, no doubt, did not recognize the best of all the arithmetic of Asia. Even less did they comprehend its mystical syncretism which, since it was so obscurely animated by the logic of correlations, would have prevented the Greeks from acquiring a fair grasp on the art of the demonstrative intellect.

The logic of propositions was the residue, as perceived by Ionia, of a thousand experiments in language imposed by numerous substitutions made by peoples and social classes ignorant of what they were producing.

Since the imaginative faculty as a whole incites man to express himself, languages, like all expression, no doubt unload certain myths only to burden themselves with others. The passage of one system of signification to another people, while progressively discovering the residual, resistant, and basic structures of the operative language, also gives rise to the new poetics of still unexplored areas of the unutterable. The already developed axis of the syntax of the certain thus makes it way through revivals of the beautiful. To strip the sacred from signs and their accepted combinations and to experiment with the arbitrary within such signs is to become aware of concepts and settled correlations; but above all, it is to enrich the fluid world within which images, forms and sounds endlessly recombine.

Only the dead languages are fixed in their lexicons and grammars. They linger as preserved relics of what they once served to say. But speech is only life and its risks. It parcels out its phonemes, reworks its order, and wanders among fruitful experiments and useful borrowings. Finally comes the moment when, renewed and transformed, it is durable and ready for a culture — one that has been itself remade and stabilized by the imaginative power whose economy it expresses. Thus a culture finds by itself its coherence in a society that is finally and usefully established, and on the road to a reasonably long duration.

A language is a confusing mixture of all the esthetics of a people, as an institution is the stable residue of the politics of a State. All that impels man to seek the pleasures of which the event has deprived him thus combines to conduct him on a widened track, through many schools of dialectic and the overcoming of many obstacles, and to guide his advances in precision of expression through the felicities of his efforts to express beauty.

In this journey through contradictions, the passage from shadow to clarity is not entirely a reversal of a success in dominating things. What it does is merely to testify that one is better aware of what one must attribute respectively to determined causes and what to the encounters of chance. In the immense incomprehensible turmoil of deeds, the pleasure in the beautiful identifies a healthy stage reached in the organization of the imaginative faculty and its portion of the contingent and the certain. The world of the sign is a place of marvelous adjustment between pain and the conditions of pleasure. It is the plan for reconciliation where the experience of the possible dominates sufferings, and enables one to live a moment of plenitude.

This world of the sign, infinitely more expanded in the human milieu than in the world of flora and fauna where the procedures are worked out, transfigures in the realm of the imagined the evolution of men's interrelationships. By its brilliance, that world announces the existence of a certain coherence. It describes that situation in which the borrowings from the past are affected by the experience lived in the present for the inspiration of the future. Now, if language is the work of the people, the use made of it and more precisely the manner, the style of the author, like all that inspires him, can be relative only to one of the groups which compose that society. At the heart of the general collectivity, many smaller and more specialised groups thus discover, thanks to this one of them, the expression of their certitudes, anxieties, and ambitions. There is thus neither genre nor work which is not expressive of social situations.

Furthermore, and finally, it is thus that scientific innovations are produced — that is, from the mutual encounters of all these respective dispositions such as characterize the process in its highest form, and are compounded of the agreements and conflicts introduced into a common destiny.

The correspondence between art and science is subtle. If science appears steadily ascending its slope while art is passing from one height to another, it must be added at once that this scientific progress passes through its moments of cleavage, its tunnels of the irrational.

When the Pythagorean school, inheritor of the successes of Babylonian numeration, encounters irrational numbers, how futile it was of it to demand the death penalty for those who dared reveal the depth of the difficulty which brought all its dogmatic authority into question. It was forced to prefer the continuous magnitudes of geometry to the numerical discontinuities which split its rational world in two. After the Roman and Christian periods have passed, Descartes will reconcile number and linear extent.[3] But always a new illogicality is inscribed as a preliminary to mathematics; this time that of complex numbers by which one is forced to confer meaning on the square root of negative numbers, even though this is so obviously incompatible with the accepted definition of powers of coefficient even numbers. In the modern progress of mathematics, mathematicians know hardly a decade without their stumbling over at least one difficulty of the sort that no axiomatic could overcome until their failure invited the demonstration that it could not be done. Rigorous deduction still remains the syntax of certitudes, but, for all that, it is not the assured expression of the reality whose resistances are not overcome except insofar as they are contained in the formal unity of a sign-symbol — itself treated as an assured object because, and insofar as, the experience of reason and arithmetic make it such.

Good sense is perhaps the thing best shared in the world. It will never, outside of mathematical experimentation, take into account that the infinite sequence of integers has the same infinite number of elements as the sequence of even integers, which are nevertheless but a part of the whole;[4] nor that the number of points on one side of a square is as large the number of points on the four sides.[5] For a

---

3. E.g., the square of the hypotenuse of a right-angled triangle is equal to the sum of the squares of the two sides, yet this always ends in an irrational number for the diagonal of a square. Descartes, viewing points as inifinite on both sides of zero, i.e., with negative as well as positive numbers, runs into the illogicality of the square root of negative numbers. Translator's note.

4. For example, as shown by the infinite series of $2 \leftrightarrow 1$, $4 \leftrightarrow 2$, $6 \leftrightarrow 3 \ldots$ to infinity. Translator's note.

5. For example, the number of lines drawn from a line AB, representing all

stronger reason, only long labor on things could have worked out the nature of, and the definition of such terms as oxygen, hydrogen, the volt, the ampere, and entropy.

If scientific development goes back to the very origins of man, and if it exhibits this hard and most constant nucleus, this is not as the product of pure deduction only. Logic, hidden in the heart of beauty, is revealed by the imperatives of expression, but what it puts into a work comes from elsewhere. Among the words most worn down from having been the most used in syntactic articulations, there are those which resist all further reduction. No progress has wholly arrived at the end of the usefulness of sexigesimal numerations, already in use among the Sumerians; and no one can or will ever be able to dispense with the numbers and operations which begot them. By thinking to have discovered numeration on a base of two, our modern age rediscovers a procedure long ago in use, one still retained in use in many savage villages. The fact is that such notions are relative not only to customs and languages; what gives them their support and validity is nature itself. Dialectic discovers them in the imaginative realm where action introduced them as a consequence of a law of things. History is the revealer of these objective necessities. It is not the exceptional processes of genius which confer this high importance on them, but actually the most communal collectivities.

The numeration of position is not a possession uniquely ours. Central America, though cut off from us, learned how to utilize it well before we had investigated it. The difference of pace between scientific progress on these two continents amounts solely to the fact that our historic embodiments have been much more numerous than those across the Atlantic. In the last era of the Sassanidae, India, inspired by Greece, was importing into Persia the numbers which remain ours still. Then, on the morrow of their conquests and in the first period of their glory, the Arabs, whom the desert had made unresponsive to the debilitating subtleties of the cultures now open to their domination, encouraged the simplification to the essentials of certain bodies of knowledge overloaded with the speculative, and so assured the practical success of these same numbers.

An analogous process will permit little Europe, emerging rather late from its barbarism, to discover the bonds and the web and woof

---

four sides of a square, through line CD, on side of the square, to a distant point X, since all must pass through the shorter line also, must represent an equal number of points. Translator's note.

of its own scholarly stuff in the lessons, glosses, and commentaries of the dazzling ancient world. In its eager youth, it was able to extract the essential from the Asiatic and Greek heritage, and to unite it successfully with its Cartesian triumphs. Not satisfied with this, it added thereto a thousand demonstrations and arithmetic procedures, opened and refined the glossaries of new words, and of biological, physical and chemical nomenclatures.

For, beyond the words which have undergone reshaping by the machinery of syntax, there is the greatly increasing quantity of words, especially in a little more than the last two hundred years, whose use is imposed by things. There is a history of the most exact vocabulary, as there is of the most reliable mathematics, plus a history of each language. But whereas mathematics is relative to all the mutabilities of the possible, language is of value especially for its bonds to the very nature of things, some of those bonds unshakable, others of the greatest solidity. We must now inquire why the method discovered late in the day, in one of the smallest districts of the world, so rapidly took on a significance so general in nature and so universal in human cultures.

The great deeds of history, by sharing in the possibilities which nature offers to human action, feed the imagination which explored and translated by expression. The certitude encountered at the conclusion of this process, a certitude demonstrated by the successes of our present techniques, could hardly fail to make its presence felt in so many adventures returned from the frontiers of the impossible to the very center of a concrete reality. Furthermore, the nature of cerebral labor must be such that when a certain degree of formulation has been achieved, efficiency sharply increases. It is these modalities of evolution which we must now examine.

Yet what we have just said about the exploration of the possible has left some problems unsolved. How does that regulation operate which so progressively concentrates attention on the essential? In the flow of efforts at rationalization, how may we recognize the point at which it accelerates sharply? How does the reality become the accomplice and the agent of this sequence of success, and especially of the most decisive of all? One must assume that the social nature of man, that the nature of his physiology and of the brain which commands its functioning, and, finally, the order of things, are all involved in these queries. These three factors dictate the plan of developments which are to follow.

PART III

Encounters with the certain

6. Collective regulations

Less than five centuries after Europe discovered America on the ocean voyage to Asia, and accomplished the first encirclement of the globe, men will reach the moon. The roundness of the earth has become as familiar as it appeared unbelievable to almost all of our ancestors of only a few generations ago. Our stock of certitudes is being always more rapidly enriched, and the present has only begun to take its measure. Nevertheless, humanity has not passed abruptly from a state of doubt to a different one of certitude. It has never ceased being sure of a certain number of given data. It is true that methodical doubt is necessary for the conception of new discoveries, but the greatest of these are but fragmentary within the totality retained as assured. There are verities which reach back to prehistory, run through all history, and remain absolutely what they were. It is not only numbers we have to think of here, or certain elementary notions relating to weight and space, but an experience still more primoridal. Though science has so greatly changed, there was never a need of science as such to be assured of certain obvious facts. The list is not so long as a too simple-minded good sense might lead us to believe. On the contrary, it comprises the most basic realities, the only ones we shall need to retain on the scale of this study: that one is born, that one will die, and that one must make an effort to keep himself alive.

Among all the other certainties none can ever endure which is incompatible with these, which are as constant as they are simple. Furthermore, what we know of evolution suggests that these first verities must in some sense be the source for the others, under conditions which we shall need to explain.

Two preliminary considerations regarding these demand attention.

The first is that if science issued from them, that was solely in its beginnings and even then in an indirect way and by difficult abstractions. Otherwise, it would not have been necessary to traverse so many events or to go through so many perfected efforts before science could be extracted from them. The progress of knowledge proceeds by many detours, or loses its way beyond some point arrived at, until it becomes aware of the errors and inaccuracies it has committed. Then it returns to its central course, and most often does so in accordance to what has happened in the evolutive process, and by going back to a point prior to the former, to start off again more successfully and to a more fruitful advancement. The cyclic movements of these returns are sometimes brief; but not so for others in the rest of human evolution which, for the most part, present a greater time-length of oscillation. They may occur also in the individual, and we shall see that they do so in actuality, but the true locations of their expansion can only be in societies or, more exactly, in humanity itself in its entirety, across all kinds of cultures to particular vocations.

The second consideration is as follows: in human society, these most commonplace certitudes are also those that naturally exercise the greatest power of attraction. Everything is periodically returned to them. It is true that science assumes an independent, autonomous, and specific body; but it still remains linked to all the rest of existence across the lived, imagined and expressed organic wholes which, as we have seen, guide its development. In the ultimate justification of its order, science is of value only in terms of what binds it to the growing efficiency with things. As a consequence, and despite errors in the course on which science too often leads thought, all that guides and sustains science, that is to say, the most general and the most positive collective, has as its main function in its service to the certain that of bringing all conceived systems back to the truth implicitly hidden in the elementary experience of human living. Its function is regulative.

Like all life, science is governed by homeostasis, that stabilizing force that no physiology, and, naturally, no cerebral activity, escapes.[1] As a result, the basic data, what is soonest recognized as such and the most closely attached to the living realities, are also,

---

1. Homeostasis: the tendency of an organism by its own mechanism to maintain conditions within itself at a relatively stable level; for example, its temperature or its bodily chemistry. Translator's note.

and primordially, the direct manifestations of these regulatory principles.

We must learn, of course, how the behavior patterns of this living substratum are related to the pain and labor it costs and to the productions which keep it in repair, as well as to their different successive, regressive or progressive forms. However, that will be the object of the second part only of this chapter; that is, after we shall have recognized under what conditions life itself, by its most elementary imperatives — birth, hope, generation, and death — confers on every historic phenomenon its cyclic character. The first object of the present study will be, therefore, the cell of all society, the living point where it is begotten, bestirs itself, and is swallowed up or succeeds — the family, in all its irreplaceable reality.

I. The bonds of affection between husband and wife, between parents and children, and the way in which they are accepted, dreamed and lived, determine the growth of the group. Whether the family is happily balanced, or is too improvident and too prolific, or again too avaricious of the future and barren, it is part of a destiny more general than itself. The family takes on the image of the customs, whether they be neglected or pauperized, timid and aging, or confident and progressive, as when the comportments of love are at once generous and spontaneous. All depends, then, on material conditions, on the degree of security which they seem to represent, but also on what they hope and dream.

It is now nearly thirty years ago that statisticians and sociologists noted a rising figure for children among peoples where death comes early, and fewer children among those where life is longer. True, we are as little informed on the fertility rate in very ancient times as on the biological causes even in modern eras; though we do know that prenatal and infant mortality remained very high up to our own day, especially at the center of the underprivileged classes. Buffon could still state, in the countryside of Montbard, that the hope of living lengthens, especially beyond adolescence. This situation is extremely ancient, especially for the immense majority of workers of the soil. In its origins, it has influenced all society. Births, in the beginning, could be the more desired as the chances of survival were less. Then, too, less importance was attached to the single child than to the number. The scandalous sacrifices of the newly-born were accepted as a means of rendering the gods favorable to the general security. Baal fed the flames of his bronze furnace with them. On the other hand, as the group became more secure, thanks to exceptional privileges or to a general amelioration of the level of life, or simply because it was inspired by a livelier faith, such barbarous rites were rejected. Each child became irreplaceable in the hearts of its own. This process of attachment to one's own children can even reach the point where the parents are careful to have fewer in order to raise them better.

Thus there could exist two demographic systems, the one handed over to nature, dedicated to its caprices and made uneasy by its demands, the other held to arithmetic and submitting to the wish to avoid its surpluses. The passage from one to the other is neither uniform in space nor continuous in time. Instead, it is constituted of cycles of differing lengths and of varying modalities. Sometimes a family passes on its customs from father to son; or even a whole group, a whole class, a whole society, does so. Sometimes, on the contrary, one or several generations take the path opposite to those which preceded them. Each time, an evolutive regulation may be recognized, which, perhaps, will give rise to the millenarian myth. Again, the evolution, after encouraging fertility to prevail, favors longevity and prudence with well-being, and causes a branch-line to run the risks implied by its aging process. Between these two extremes, customs in equilibrium may maintain themselves for a long time. The feudal customs of medieval Europe, up to a fairly recent period, obliged the serf, and eventually the freeman, to seek authorization from his lord to take a wife; thereby indicating, under such arbitrary usages, an effort to limit the proliferation of human beings to the scale of the food-producing abundance. Regulations of births also find as many ways as there are cultural systems, sometimes explicit, sometimes implicit. Their failure gives rise to two dangers, a reckless pauperization or a fatal excess of precaution.

Every social situation implies a certain modality suitable to the treatment of this basic problem. Bonds of affection and respect between spouses, between branches of the family and the generations, project ambiguous concerns into the aesthetic and ethic; for here are the confrontations of needs and wishes, the satisfying of necessity and the ambition for luxury, the recourse to flights from the group, or the self-assertion of the individualistic. Royal families, aristocracy, the bourgeois, the common people, the peasants, all adjust their behavior to the changes of the times. But this accomplished, they live subjected to the simple, basic mechanisms which, much more than events, dominate the growth and decline of groups and societies.

Influenced by the conditions of their power, uneasy dynasties seek the security of their futures in the disposition of their families. After the Seldjuks had lost their empire from having divided it too frequently among their numerous children, the Ottomans take care to reserve all to a single heir. The rest of their descendents whose number they mistrust after becoming fearful of their absence, they assassinate. This cruelty renders the existence of the last sultans one of fear. Less violent procedures, but more subtle, are concealed within the customs of the dominant classes, sometimes fortunate and sure of an unlimited future, sometimes anxious to strengthen an unsure legitimacy by narrowing the routes of its transfer. Groups recently come to power, upper classes barred from new resources, need a zealous confidence and a constant recourse to action to resist the debilitating anxieties over dropping behind. In Rome, Augustus, weighing the dangers run by the upper classes, wanted to provide for them by laws. It is difficult to estimate the result of this action, which may have been less than that of the imperial peace. Yet, in the long run, all of them lost strength by an accelerating process when the increase of private and public expenses weighed on an always more thinly scattered elite, neglectful of its conquering vocation and its gods.

Voluntary or fatalist, certitude sustains the vigorous branches which uneasiness leads to death. History is made of blossomings and senility, because it is the record of elevations and decreptitudes of lines sustained by faith before being undermined by anxiety. History travels, too, from stage to stage. What is more, when an elite is cut off from a body of people in order to embark on a brilliant destiny, the living mass, less actors than onlookers, play but a small part in its success, but also escape the degenerations which are, finally, the price success pays. Thus a reserve is maintained. For a very long time in the West, this reserve was the great peasant majority of the population. Today it is the Third World, the commonalty. It supplies the quota of rejuvenations, re-beginnings, and renewals.

Only exceptionally does a phenomenon of resonance carry the entire collectivity along with it in a single movement, as was the case with the Paraguayans in the terrible events of 1870.[2] Perhaps these

2. In a disastrous war with its three neighbors, this small country of some 1,200,000 was reduced to an estimated 28,000 males and 200,000 females. Translator's note.

people offered a modern illustration of what happened to certain cities of antiquity, too thoroughly dedicated to the exclusive concept they had of themselves. In such cases, the mass of the living group perished, carrying with it its system of representation. A cultural cycle with its biologic support is completed. There are even more dramatic examples of archaic peoples surprised by invading colonizers who violated their representations. An extreme stage in the regulative oscillations is then overreached, and arrives at a zone where all is broken off. The biological organism is no longer self-supporting, and an ethnic group disappears body and goods.

In sufficiently sizable territories, populated and fertile, it is rare that the destiny of privileged classes affects the whole mass which feeds on the outburst. In China, India, or Persia, dynasties which have come from beyond the borders have frequently changed. Imposed by force, they do not greatly penetrate the world that they control, but isolate themselves in their prestige and are encysted there and enfeebled, until some other disputes their place with them. On the shores of Lake Nemi, the priest of the old temple of Diana, in order to exercise his office, had to assassinate the previous incumbent. If this strange rite is not the remains of a very ancient experience, it is an adequate image of what survives at the head of very explicit wholes, where the popular mass, very little involved with its chiefs, watches them destroy each other, knowing that they themselves will survive the contest.

Change within the conditions lived through determines the variations in the symbolic world. No less does it assure the great social stages of history, beginning with what remains faithful to its most traditional habits of producing and its ways of love. Change incites the lively zeal of a conquering class, and possibly maintains its fertility for a sufficient time; then, in its turn, it withers what must disappear.

In a group on the rise, assured of authority and power, it is desirable to have many children. Then, when the time comes to worry about preserving its privileges, its customs sterilize it. Then, among its sons, a single one marries, very late; the last male of the family, as in Venice in the seventeenth century, or the eldest of the European aristocracy of the eighteenth century. Such behavior announces the rise of a replacing class. Later, monastic chastity being in dispute with religion and the celibate being unpopular, the European bourgeoisie reinvent contraception. Many families are identified with the ideal of rivalry, of climbing, of practicising a strict economy or being dominated by a drive toward saving, investing, or making a show. The number of children is reduced so that they may live better and give the children a better life, and a longer preparation for the highest offices. The consequences of such restriction were at first the less felt, because the amelioration of material conditions that followed as a result, and which it augmented, prolonged the duration of life and thus increased the population. But it also aged the population, made it more sensitive to the blows of fate and to the inroads created by crises and especially by wars. In a people of a low birthrate, a generation of diminished fertility encourages a less numerous generation. Every twenty years, the group of those at the age of new adults exhibits a feebleness designed to attract a return of the misfortunes that had weakened them. The Malthusian mentality of Europe was not without its consequences at the outbreak of wars which gave the Russian proletariat its opportunity, and awakened the fertile peoples of a colonial world to hope and to combat.

The forces of production combine with those of representations, which they also inspire, to define these fundamental characteristics. As families decay, generations follow on one another, sometimes with the promise of an indefinite future, sometimes with the agony of a destiny of threat. Sometimes they yield to the sentiments which prevail in the group, sometimes they resist it. The symbolic world acts like a differential between the real, material and economic support of their attitudes and the manner of enclothing them at the heart of the diversities of the collective behavior.

This modifying of the tonicity of families, of groups which families sometimes succeed in setting up, and of social classes which arise from this achievement of recombining interests and beliefs, is of concern not only in the realm of quantity. It is not always, nor exclusively, translated in terms of the growth or decrease in the number of children. It has also a certain qualitative manner of manifesting itself in the relations of husband and wife toward one another.

In all moments of history, confrontations and disputes arise from an excess or a lack of energy. Thus the relationships of power are founded, compounded, or overturned, as determined within collectivities or among individuals by an attitude of activity or passivity in the face of a given deed. Such oscillations of spirit are the cultural effects of a modification in the relationships between men and women. Girls are born slightly less numerous than boys, especially perhaps in a period of activity, but they are also exposed less and live longer. This prevailing fact seems to represent the respective roles of both sexes as history apparently suggests it: the event, by the workings of chance, is primarily masculine; culture, by its rooted character, is primarily feminine. Furthermore, according to genetics, the child is born male by the fact of his father, but takes from his mother somewhat more of acquired characteristics. The two sexes are embryologically very little in opposition, and not all by the dispositions of intellect and will. Each is finally more or less ambivalent. There have been matriarchal societies, and there are still tribes with manly wives, and men adorned like women. But, since protohistory, it has become normal for the accepted suitor to conduct himself as master, and to adorn his companion with what he owns by taking advantage of the abundance with which he surrounds her, as also to assume responsibility for her poverty. The way such customs have become commonplace underlines their character as more cultural than natural; but it also confers a special significance on events in which the feminine prevails.

When a people long subordinated to an invader recover awareness of their own strength, it is the women who have galvanized them. Illustrations have appeared in the Orient, in the Byzantine royal family, in the shadow of the Moslem harems, or the gardens built in the palaces of China. The West, too, had experienced the same when the Anglo-Saxon threw off the Norman yoke, or when the French refused an English king. Societies, like individuals, suffer from frustration, not so much when they undergo humiliation as when they are chained to a rigorous regimentation. And this is especially true when the tyrants begin to show exhaustion and, victims to their own privileges, open the paths to revolt by becoming enfeebled, and by allowing the dominated to become aware of their present misfortunes and the possibility of their own revival. And it is the woman who is the more sensitive to this latent hope, and to being on the brink of structural changes in power and domination.

Such revolutions may turn out to be only episodic; they are always difficult to interpret. Nevertheless, they are most commonly manifestations of regeneration by a return to the mass: thus from Cato to Catullus, Sulla to Heliogabalos,[3] Rome moves toward the

3. Sulla (138—78, B.C.), dictator, conqueror of Mithradates, reformed Roman law in favor of the Senate and the aristocratic party. Heliogabalos, three centuries later, born in Syria, a debauched and effeminate emperor, 218—222 A.D., introduced the worship of Baal into Rome. He was assassinated. Translator's note.

feminine before giving way to the Church. European feudalism at its height celebrates many vigorous love affairs before courtly love accompanies the rise of the urban classes. This is an excess not to be surpassed. When a collectivity is too feminized, whether it be after the triumphant return of the cults of the goddess in the ancient Occident, or in the twilight years of the French aristocracy at the time of Sade and Laclos, it abandons itself also to a fatalistic naturalism which turns it from action, and dooms it to successors who lie in wait.

Femininity now arouses, now weakens, the virile world. It plays a regulative role, whether, like Lysistrata, it refuse unrestrained aggression, or, like Chimenes, it reward reckless courage at the heart of a troubled world. At every opportunity and on every scale, history turns the light on this compensatory function within the play of forces which in demography as in mechanics, is designated by the same word: the couple.

As regards this word, one must deal with as many nuances as behaviors suggest, within the infinite variety of that living vigor which organizes groupings of beings in terms of their ways of feeling and acting, into alliances, oppositions, and compensations. The social complexity is a simplified and magnified image of all that physiological desires arouse in minds and spirit.

II. All these movements have as their substratum material needs and whatever it is that satisfies them. And since these concrete realities are most conveniently reduceable to figures, they are the more easily grasped. It becomes, therefore, relatively easier to consider the relations of a society with what it produces and its methods of production than to consider the relations of the spirit with the vegetative functions (growth, nutrition) by which it lives. It is true that the two project themselves in a common representation; but the material elements are the more easily grasped and are, in the beginning, the guides toward the analysis of the second.

Since one must not only be born and love in order to live and work, economic imperatives, the primary natural functions in family relationships, play their part in the incessant discords and adjustments within states of mind and spirit, as well as in the elements of the social landscape. These relationships, which constitute societies, like them evolve between two extreme and opposing models. The first places a whole communal lineage under a dependence on its oldest member, and inspires a cult of ancestors at the heart of a conservative order. The second reduces the family to its irreplaceable nucleus: father, mother, and young children, and places the emphasis on an active confrontation. Now these two models correspond also to two ways of possessing and exchanging. Rural folk retain traces of customs which must have been in their origins exclusive of all others. When natural selection prevailed at its brute level, and the progress of a people remained below the resources provided by the earth, many a region was uncultivated even when accessible, or even known. Men then were attached to their abodes more by custom than by necessity, and lived less within defined frontiers than in zones to which their ways of living had brought them. Personal ownership of land was not so devoid of meaning as when men were hunters; but the community was a better guarantee of a distribution of effort, a fusion of needs, and the sharing of resources. Exchanges of women between families, exchanges of work and gifts, were no longer subject to extensive rules as they had been before the agricultural era. But if distant alliances were no longer sought, as providing the largest possible number of families among them, the emphasis was the greater on the solidarity within each familial group.

As in every evolutive process, something of this innovation must have preexisted in what went before. Preferential marriage between cousins, formerly exceptional even though approved in certain cases, now becomes normal. Men guaranteed the defense and the movement of this community, now queen and mother, strong and reassuring, embodying lessons of experience infinitely ancient, and not too different from certain rigid insect societies. Even to our own day, and among the greatest of peoples, the security resulting therefrom has left yearnings for a golden age with its guaranteed happiness.

But the growth of populations and their concentrations in environments rich in agriculture brought about conflicts. At this stage, a further important division, scarcely prefigured earlier, came about in the way of looking at marriage. Polygamy, the general rule in so many places, obviously changes nothing in the structures of according ancestral lines to families — a child has but one mother. But it does affect the rules of possession. A prince or a rich man may gain extra prestige by guaranteeing the support of several wives. Mohammed set up this state of affairs around himself, and endeavored only to regulate it strictly. Inversely, the needy man, wishing to increase his possessions, enlarged his harem so as to have more women working under his orders. Such was the answer of the man in ancient Iran to the shah who, having enriched him, asked him what he would now do:

'I shall buy another young woman,' he said, 'and then I shall feel more comfortable.'

In societies the most assured of their progress and the best adjusted, however, the statistical fact finally prevails which shows girls and boys almost equal in number, and hence pledged to the primordial monogamy.

In all cases, after the warrior man has left the land to the woman, and also later, when classes consisted of the dominated and the peasants as opposed to the dominant and the military, every wife by the end of this era shares her husband's destiny. The exchange of goods is no longer made equally between families: a part of what one group produces is reserved for those superior to them, the amount determined by the stronger. The processing of the differentiation involved is to the profit of the one who holds the function of arbitrating differences, of directing the conservative ceremonies, and of reckoning the date of such with that of the seasons. In accepting rank, the society introduces transcendental qualities into its representations by endowing them with expressive forms around palaces and temples. Princes and priests become not only the beneficiaries of what they are offered, or claim, but from their wealth they draw an increase of prestige — that of being able to give.

The gift, so important in the consecration of primitive authority, was at first exercised only on the occasion of productions, and that not of the soil alone. Nor did the new masters at first arrogate to themselves the freedom to dispose of lands from which the communal toil extracted the resources which kept it alive, to the profit of village, city, or empire. But once the masters became sufficiently entrenched, they could prevail by eminent right over the free or conquered cantons which they offered to their chosen faithful for their use. All this has important consequences upon the agrarian modalities; for the original community finds itself limited in its movements, and is as fixed on its land as is the State on its frontiers. As for the beneficiaries of the privileges granted by the prince, they exploit their new domain by the use of manual labor separated from its traditional affiliations, fetched from the slave markets of war, or enslaved by law and the tax levy. Personal land ownership is not immediately separated from this seignorial power; but the process that leads to it is on the way.

The need to own is no stranger to the animal world. But if the higher vertebrates are distributed over areas of settlement which on occasion they defend bitterly, socialized insects, on the other hand, capable of some kinds of agriculture and cattle-breeding, hold their resources in common. It is therefore incorrect on the part of some to have wished to found private right in nature; for there it is ambiguous. According to circumstances, man takes on himself sometimes one, sometimes another of animal behaviors, or rather, experiments with them one after another and combines them. Before all land-owning right, every man might keep as his own at least a part of what he had produced or won by force, but the soil remained the possession of all. The men of the steppes, or those of ancient Italy, like those colonists of the La Plata prairies almost thirty centuries later, owned herds of animals before formally appropriating lands. The passage from one stage to the other appears in ancient times as in modern history as a corollary of the growth of population. When a certain level of population is reached, and with it a certain expansion of exchange, it becomes necessary to modify the custom and to install new laws. The symbolic world is thus transformed with the State. The level of living rises, at least for the privileged, and the birth rate is reduced by the desire for social advancement. What demographers call capillarity, a response to surface tensions, sets up a process of a swelling of the middle classes with the assurance of private ownership of land and the reduction of the family to the essential nucleus.

Sometimes, in a society structured in a way that might be called vertical and submitted to an effect of mass, the responsibility of a monarch is set apart. His house undertakes to govern families concerned with alliances of the same rank; and these, on the highest level and across all frontiers, constitute systems of alliances which in some of their characteristics recall those of the original predatory societies. The privileged princes, by the use of force, but also by virtue of symbolic representations which legitimize the weight of their commands, keep the workers on the land in their customary role. Again, we sometimes find a society structured horizontally, where authority is exercised preferably in a probabilist manner, that is, left open to variable decisions. Here responsibility, very flexibly articulated, permits a great number of proprietors to be their own masters, free to choose their wives and to make rules for their descendents, free also to sell, buy, produce, or do nothing, as citizens of republics organized at all levels for competition and with a view to such. This second phase of the cycle comes to an end under the pressure of invasions, conflicts, wars or revolutions, which force a return to the mass. These extreme violences have sometimes been forestalled. In

China, the sovereign, after having permitted the establishment of a controlled proprietorship, has on several occasions decided to put all the land under rural communalities.

Events take on a character as different as those of the evolutive processes themselves, which they date, and which are broadly determined by natural conditions. Such events express the vital destiny of privileged families which are not only tied to the problem of possession but are also linked to representations which guarantee or threaten the coherence of the political whole from which they benefit. In addition to the consequences of the risks of abundance and its distribution there are those of emotive symbolisms. The incentive which pushes a pretender to the conquest of power is dynamic and expansive, and is associated with some imagined and claimed superior right by which he hopes to convince his faithful followers. Once success is achieved, the myth is reversed. Now it is the success of a previous founder which is puffed up by his heirs, whose legitimacy loses its transcendence by calling upon the past. As it loses in fresh energy what it gains by referential authority, uneasiness arises, the rivals grow bolder, whether sons of oppressed families or even conquering outsiders. The same process, after being lost amid the intrigues of a too refined court, encourages bourgeois decay, as Thomas Mann has pictured it for us in *Buddenbrooks:* the last scion of great merchants, sprung from a stock which won its vigor in business, declines into estheticism.

But from the economy of rural civilizations to that which dominates in the bourgeois period, many other structural elements undergo change. The great number of peasants gives to the former its aspect of mass, and throws light on the vertical dimension of the political organization, with the King at the top. The way money circulates, the values, and the means by which the advantages of credit are distributed are also entirely specific. Taxation plays a primary role here. It weighs most heavily on the humble, and profits most those who attach themselves to the court treasury of the prince, whose natural function is to drain everyone. Under such conditions, business, by and large, finds it fresh resources either by the favor of power or by pre-levies on the fiscal circuits, winked at or submitted to by the authority. Then either a Colbert of a farmer-general and his partisans may make the decisions on business activity, on its forms and regulations as well as its innovations.

England, however, in the century of its revolutions, begins to offer a new model. Here many individuals, favorably situated on the shores and estuaries of the ocean, and too numerous to be kept under strict control at a time when Atlantic traffic is enormously swelling, masters also of endless resources of coal scattered almost at the surface of the soil over the whole land, seize upon the flood-tide of new wealth. In vain, then, does a monarch who believes himself still absolute, after the example of his continental neighbor, claim to enforce his rights in matters of tariffs, taxes, and monopolies. He is compelled to submit these matters to the approval of his wealthy subjects, soon called upon to be his bankers. All tends to become the fact of entrepreneurs successful in their undertakings. Finally, communism, even though it has dreamed of the dissolution of the State, will return it to its high financial power at the same time that it wants to make it the incarnation of the masses.

At each stage, the conditions of economic risk are found to be profoundly changed.

When population and production are primarily agricultural, the larger share of the risks of economic activity are chiefly the effects of climate, the round of seasons, and the kinds of weather. If the harvest is good and the peasant comfortable, the internal commerce is active and the master's need for artisans numerous, nor are workers unemployed. Abundance makes living cheap, and the city is peaceful and busy. The whole third estate is satisfied. On the other hand, if the year has been bad, there is ground for complaint all around. The peasant barely harvests what he needs to reseed and to survive for a year. There are no purchases, nor is there work in the shops. The entrepreneur is anxious, unemployment wanders abroad with scarcity. All is expensive. Faced with the solidarity of those who live by their labor in good or bad times, the interests of the privileged classes and of those who benefit by a landed income shift to their opposite. Since the nobility are paid in kind and by fixed amounts, their revenue is higher because, as wheat becomes scarcer, it is also more expensive. The landed proprietors with a greater power of purchase dispose at will of artisans in difficulties. Under such conditions, one can understand how a fairly long sequence of low agricultural production in France at the end of the 18th century reunited the people with the bourgeois against an aristocracy living its best and last hours.

Of course, things do not appear so simple in their details. Internal commerce is still mostly barter; the wealth from maritime traffic is not dependent on the severity of the climate. An infinity of nuances and even small mutations of condition find expression in the varieties of enterprises in the cities, capitals, manors, courts, or the open country. Nevertheless, the general aspect of material existence remains dictated by nature, and the parishes supplicate the Deity in the hour of Rogations.

The perspective is quite otherwise when production is primarily industrial, and when the earth's goods are feeble in proportion and comparison to those which pour from the factories. It is not that crises do not appear, but that the physiocrats are no longer acknowledging them. Rain and dry spells are no longer the dominant factors. What counts much more is the degree of adaptation between what is artificially produced and what can be consumed. The demand of the market, or its saturation, depend on the opportunity for undertaking manufacturing, which may be launched with full strength to satisfy a need, on occasion stimulated, or checked when the supply exceeds what can be absorbed. To put the machine into action again, then, either its destination must be changed or a new region opened to manufacturing, or a clientele recaptured by a lowering of prices. One must produce a new product or produce differently, change machinery so as to perfect it, or dismiss manual-laborers who will be reemployed in smaller numbers. In the beginning of an industrial system, the working people are the victims either of an always shocking rivalry, especially if it comes from another nation, or of the bourgeois entrepreneur. Depending on the specific cases, the system supplies the conditions for reactionary movements and for national wars, and even for class conflicts.

The haunting memories of competitive rivalries or of crises of progress caused by them exacerbated the passionate oppositions between classes and peoples. And it was this that justified the Marxist hope of ruining Europe in confrontations of nation against nation, a hope doomed to disappointment when Europe was won over to the conquest of world markets. Such were the bitter fruits of freedom of enterprise, which put the modern technological moment on the march less by finding its equilibrium in the direct adjustment to needs and natural resources than in the rising ambition of a market-place economy. All here is relative to a freedom of rival initiatives which had to be hastily piloted from success to success, through the pitfalls of failures guaranteed to abandon the proletariat to rags and some of the bourgeois to poverty, which no traditional respect could protect from being regarded with contempt.

After millenia of a progress so slow as to be hardly noticeable on the scale of centuries, Western humanity was suddenly enriched by the maritime exploitation whose first risks were chiefly those of adventures on the ocean, and in a few years found itself swept along by a whirlwind of machine production.

This process went through so many political revolutions in Europe that it was quite natural that a pertinent criticism should conclude that a final social revolution would restore industry to a fraternal and natural order, the neglect of which had aggravated so many wars. And yet proletarian unity had not arisen where technical progress caused it to be anticipated. If it was sketched in outline in the 20th century, it was instead in countries which had long remained attached to the old ways of production, and at the moment when they were about to renounce the old and undertake new ways.

III. If the West gave the lie to Marx at the very moment when the Third World recognized his importance, the explanation may be found in the correlations of the revolution in economics with that in the family behavior of peoples. Between the middle of the 18th century and the end of the 19th, the agrarian structures ceased to be collective and set up the right of the individual landowner. At the same time, the communal values of the country areas disappeared along with the empty pastures and the traditional customs which made the village interdependent for the survival of all. The poor and those without land were not so much attracted to the cities as thrust aside into their suburbs by the fencing of properties treated more efficiently and with less manual labor. A supply of workers was made available to industry in superabundance, but at pitiable wages. The technological innovation had its roots in the lowest strata of poverty, which a few charitable institutions could not stamp out, especially since they no longer responded to a powerful theological impulse such as had stirred them to charity in the eras of a viable Christianity. The first bourgeois industrial accumulation was then what Marx called it in *Das Kapital,* a product of pauperization.

We cannot hold this statement today to be general in the working society of the West. In the last fifty years, and at the end of a century of oppressive impoverishment of the proletariat, family education in the style of the *petit bourgeois,* plus an efficient growth of production, has raised the general level of life. But what is today called the Third World, which Russia resembled in 1917, is precisely at the stage which Europe knew at the time of its burgeoning industry. An aggravating circumstance was the following: the wretched cantons of the Europe of the last century suffered for the profit of their own capitalist industrialization; on the contrary, the colonial economy shrewdly but tragically enslaved the rural colonized zones to the advantage of nations advanced in their own transformations and hence estranged them. Since then, far from being able to set up new demographic regulations for them, even the old ones have been destroyed, whether by the unwarranted introduction of inadequate codes and manners of life, or by the destruction of traditional structures of labor and of communal security. The overpopulation resulting therefrom encouraged masked or openly acknowledged despair. This despair shows the features of the Marxist pauperization, except that bourgeois-proletariat opposition is not felt internally in the Western nations, but between them and the Third World. And this calls for the reversal of the structures by which history has been so often influenced, but by confusing conflicts of classes and nations, even of cultures, and by turning the Occident into the bourgeois city amid peoples still rural and now becoming proletariat.

Finally, if the usual convention which separates the domain of economic history from that of scientific history justifies treating industrialization as a simple given datum, that is only arbitrarily useful. Occidental societies have inspired conceptual thought whose applications have transformed them. Their dominant situation has endowed them with the technological instruments of their domination, instruments of geometrically increasing dangers.

Thus the collective regulations make sport of romantic optimisms and pious and credulous comforts. Their implacable mechanism, through chance events, ephemeral creations of the imaginative faculty, and dependent expressions, has structured the world as it is today. But also, thanks to the lessons of events, it has given rise to the imagined references, the successful expressions, the mental and material tools which, having brought humanity to where it is, draw it by the rhythm of their immanent correlations toward the future, given less as a choice than as a destination.

The success of the machine and of industry is not an effect of individual wills, since those who cooperated with it did not foresee its distant developments. Nor is that success one only of persistance or of collective regulations, since these latter were able to give satisfaction during millenia of primarily agricultural productions. It is also that of an effective meeting of cerebral labor with the disposition of things. This consideration involves the last two stages of our systematic study, the first of which is to be devoted to man the creator, the second to the order of things.

7. Determinations

To be born is to become a body subject to physical laws and predestined by genetics: it is also to be handed over without defense to a culture, a milieu, a State. From the moment a man begins to become aware of himself and to know what he wants, he is affected by the abundance, the deprivations, the certitudes and the illusions of the society in which his organism develops. Since he is molded during this same time, he does not escape from his environment except by changing in it what permits such change. And yet this same man claims on all occasions to take all on himself. No one has chosen to be born a child in Athens or in a nomad camp, nor Christian or Jew, nor even in the Germany about to be infested with Nazism. And yet each one mistrusts the other, accuses him, and on occasion exterminates him precisely because he is what he could not escape being.

Man is surely much less free than he appears to be from his behavior. Yet his pretense to being free has a certain meaning: by assuming the pride of holding himself responsible for himself and of judging his equals, he becomes involved in evolution and supports it. Now from the moment when history was thus launched, the most sublime examples of pious renunciations have not halted its progress. Thus it is that each time some tentative advantage has been wrested from Nature, she has immediately proposed one or several more to be conquered. Nature has never since ceased to feed ambition; and for centuries she has done so with increasing abundance.

What is constant here, in the realm of the certain, guarantees the collective regulations whose importance we have recognized. What is offered in the way of renewals and enrichments in the order of things will be treated in the following chapter. But we must first consider how man, a physiological agent, as will be seen below, of equilibriums whose regulative systems society makes and imposes on him, has let himself be seduced by this indefinite prospect of conquests over nature, and how, being involved in this course, it becomes impossible for him to renounce it.

I. We might trace the origin of that setting forth to the moment when man's physical constitution was finally assured. But since societies which have remained without history are composed of beings of the same species as the rest, the process is entered upon by beginning with, but not exclusively because of, these same physiological accomplishments.

Savage behaviors suggest that the spark that sprang from the long rubbing of a hard branch in a groove worn into another bit of wood was originally a ritual symbolizing love and a prayer for fecundity. It is certain that the first metallurgists did not start by seeking out minerals to smelt. Instead, it has been discovered, the first metal was smelted not with a goal in mind, but purely by virtue of a search for improvement; that is, in an effort to raise the temperature of the furnaces in which they cooked the clays previously dried by the sun alone, they may have added certain earths in order to impart an apparent brilliance to their ceramics. This success assumes that a number of chance experiments had been attempted to make probable a possible. There had to be also, as at the origin of all progress, a certain concentration of attention. Certainly the reward goes well beyond what the experiment set out to attain, and the result obtained on one first mineral much facilitated the exploitation of others. But the legends and rituals of the workshops in which China used to build its clocks, the invocations with which Adoniram accompanied the casting of his bronze basins, indicate that for a long period of time technique arose from the world of the sacred.

The evolution of the imaginative faculty, then, is that of a world larger and more confusing than that of pertinent reflections. But if the reality is encountered at the end of excursions into reflective thought, it is because the imaginative faculty has encouraged thought and led it there. On the other hand, the conquest of a certitude once achieved, the imaginative faculty is transformed by it. It expands into new dreams even before the preceding ones have been decanted into ordinary procedures. Emotion again feeds desire. Beginning with a need satisfied, it works to arouse further needs. The internal man is a process of substitutions.

This process arises from conditionings. Once one has learned how to appease one clear and precise need, symbols which excite that need may come to be attached, even though they have no direct utility. The ceremonial which precedes and accompanies a meal does not nourish, but it adorns the act of eating nevertheless, and inscribes within it a much larger cultural whole, one capable of encouraging innovations which transcend the banality of what they ornament. By thus encumbering itself with the superfluous, humanity tests and gives support to the warmth of its desires.

Now experiments made on the higher vertebrates indicate that they, too, can associate an arbitrary ornament with a satisfaction. A fairly long sequence of repetitions is needed to create such habits, though they disappear in the course of time when custom no longer maintains them. Deprived of its brain, the animal loses the means of escaping from what has thus deceived it. In man, even more, the upper brain has as its major function that of lending itself to symbolizations and of shedding them. More than any previous species, humanity adds to its needs by embellishing them. It prunes and chooses among them. Its progress begins with this manifestation of the capacity to adorn itself with rites, dreams and luxuries, to take cognizance of what has become because of them, and to judge by the result what is best suited to itself.

This double faculty of arbitrary assimilation and critical adaptation makes man's life a long sequence of choices. But these choices are by no means all voluntary. The social environment imposes the larger part of acquired habits and of lessons learned. And it is not without danger that one risks trying to escape them. The part played by truly free neurons in the brain is small in comparison to that occupied by the vegetative functions (growth, nutrition), by acquired behaviors and conditionings so rooted as to have become second nature. Thus that fraction of energy is feeble which remains available to arbitrate the conflicts that stir restlessly within us, and to impose a voluntary solution on them. It is not utilized to pertinent results except in the narrow sectors of least resistance within systems in constant modification which seize upon us from every direction. Nevertheless, it is this very feeble surplus which opens the narrow window through which man dreams of himself as outside the habits which bind him, guesses or calculates the zones of least resistance among such habits, and endeavors within his world to build that part of himself which lends itself to being builded.

It is not enough to find the courage to assert oneself. To attempt the impossible is soon to be seized by the anguish of defeat. Many of the greatest men of history have capitulated to their own inner being before being crushed by the event. Robespierre at the Hotel de Ville in Paris, resisting the faithful who urge him to act against the Convention which votes his death, invokes a legality of which only a brief time before he had thought himself the incarnation. Napoleon at Waterloo postpones for hours engaging in the combat which at Austerlitz had won the victory by swiftness of action. Poems, religions, inventions, are the expression of this kind of anxiety. Lack of this sublimation, this need to pull oneself together and to get back to the normal, may put life itself in jeopardy.

Nevertheless, though there be no happiness more assured than to remain integrated with the community, warm as in a mother's lap, this may be denied. It may be that the individual who has been abnormally reared has not learned to conform to a milieu larger than himself, one which is disclosed to him as hostile, familiar as it is to others. It may be that the milieu itself has been shattered by some effect of crisis in its affective order or in its system of representations, and so disconcerts those who may have been destined to conform to what it was, but now have nothing but violence as a remedy for their anxieties. Such was the situation of the French peasants caught in the great fear of 1789; such was the excited state of Spain disillusioned by the events and the changes of the 19th century; such again the anxious state of industrial Germany caught up in the great crisis of the 1930's. And such, finally, was the situation of colonial societies in rebellion, whom our networks of information instructed in the inequality forced upon races by the arbitrary actions of their former masters.

In all these illustrations, a reality of desires stronger than the will prevails over all else.

II. The conditions which permit of choices and yet restrict the multiplied opportunities for excess within them, are dictated by human physiology. But it is circumstances which bring them into existence. All destiny is achieved on the path which borders on desire and fear, and two madnesses, alienation and confusion. He who leaves the path and wanders does not return to it except in pain and penitence, and retraces in suffering what he had violated in recklessness. Otherwise, as a consequence of prolonging overmuch the duration of an artificial satisfaction, individuals and collectivities end in folly, unreason, or crime.

Groups, classes, peoples, become sooner or later their own victims. Society is not transparent to itself and does not clearly conceive of a humanity much greater than itself, within which it is, nevertheless, situated. Nor does society have criteria at its disposal except precisely the standards of the individuals whom it inspires by misleading them. The readjustments of society depend on exceptional persons difficult to recognize, being themselves a mixture of the exact and the inexact, and forced to use the common language to express their counsels imperfectly and inadequately. Their counsels are, in fact, controversial, and yet often the more precious by the very degree to which they give the appearance of being scandalous. The collectivity follows the event of the moment, shaped by its own wanderings, blinded by the illusions which keep it on its own course, guided only by its own partial and biased logic. In time some new event chastises it and leads it back to the point of its own equilibriums, only to send it again toward new risks. Thus each social digression in its mad stumblings and incessant gropings, dragging with it its criminals and its judges, its righteous and its fools, its malicious and its credulous, is destined to a confusion of ends that wither away and turn to blood. Yet at the same time it raises other digressions from the event, each in its own way going through its moment of pertinent innovation capable, point by point, of enriching the general system of its progress.

The individual, prisoner of collective wholes which shield him from the anguish of indecision and seduce by their representations, is nevertheless a dissatisfied person in search of differences. He tests the future which he fears and is ignorant of, yields himself to a thousand different tentatives undertaken alone or in the group, gets entangled in a number of possibles which he explores at more or less length, and out of which one or two will prevail. Thus he makes sure of a resting point only when the involutive cycle of worn-out wholes, now no longer sufficient, has been completed.

The domain of all that comes together and binds together but also dies in due time from having lasted too long, is traversed by the forces which drop off and fall without crushing the hope of regenerations. By an effect of ambiguity in the historic condition, success would not have its value if failure were not the most common of fates.

There was perhaps a time, in the first stone ages, when each group sought an alliance with most of its neighbors. Since history has interposed its violences, every collectivity aspires to withdraw into itself. We may also observe as a fact how, in the global distribution of what geographers of the last century used to call races, the constants of the genetic stock stabilize in each region the distribution of transmitted characteristics, and how the tendencies appropriate to the inhabitants are rooted in a very long past. At times, invasions superimpose imported characteristics, but at the price of fearful aggressions. But sooner or later they are rejected when they can no longer replace the people whom they have thrown into confusion, nor blend with them. This natural tendency to select specific dwelling places by solidifying the groups is correlative and compensatory to the play of heredity. Thus the influence of regional dominants prevails, yet does not abolish those of the more ancient past.

In fact, to realize all possible mixtures of peoples does not increase the feeble weight of inherited genes in a humanity which was not originally very populous. But since the human condition is more dedicated to organic increase than to genetic specification, one might possibly affirm that the physical constitution of men gains by interminglings, such as are favored by voyages and migrations.

Evolution implies change; and life introduces change much more by disturbing the collectivities than by directly affecting the genes. Thus the extreme and obvious diversification, recognized by all, must be assigned to social communications. The few wolf-children discovered on the edges of the forests of India showed no sign of having triumphed over environment; they were in no sense kings of the species amid which they had learned to live. They could only imitate the behavior of the several species found within their range. Humanity emerges from animality only by the dynamic it creates in the wholes which it forms, even when these, by spreading abroad, go astray.

Nature does not lead humanity straight to its goal, but only predisposes it to make use of its long duration to elaborate its collective systems to a higher level, as best fitted to cause individuation to flower. The wealth of the anatomic order is that of combinations rather than that of the weight of the constituting elements. Granting the gifts of heredity, if the extremely delicate processes of embryogenesis in the maternal milieu are also added to predestinations, it is still in terms of an organizing principle. The development of the impregnated cell ceases almost at once to be pure multiplication to become an organism. Structure prevails over mass. Every man, even before he is born, is destined to the unceasing transformation pursued by the social beyond the physiological. If he seems at first more dependent on his body than on the world into which he is introduced, he receives from the body the pressures which involve him in the modifications of his world. He is not merely passive, then, but is located at the junction of two systems of forces, within which, by small shocks, he may modify the equilibriums that are forever being reshaped.

The disproportion between the two immense wholes of the physiological and the social determinations which confine him and the tiny increment of energy which makes its own decision prevail, cannot fail to suggest one of the representations of chance in the field of effects and causes. Thus the will is as subject to hazard as is the event itself. This faculty of self-determination, so outstanding in its originality, is absurd in its dimensions. Action barely entered upon is determined by the mechanism of circumstances. As for man, who attempts all, he is scarcely out of infancy when he is already seized by a progressive aging process which reaches one after another of his functions before it finally binds them all together into one. Having attained this last stage, he can still produce in the area in which he moves, especially if he has an agile and well-disciplined brain, but he no longer modifies himself nor invents further. He is surrendered up to a causal system of his own conditionings. And if movement even so is not arrested, it is because the decay and death of its members allows humanity as a whole to return to its rejuvenations and regenerations.

The counterpart, for man, of this so petty and brief disposition of himself is the immense expanse of the field of human adaptations. Some have learned how to preserve their joy amid destitution and distresses, and even in the tortures of martyrdom. Those who could laugh in the *Sonder-Kommandos* were constituted like those who exhausted themselves in the search for exquisite refinements, or like those excessive Sybaritisms as capable as sorrows of passing beyond the stage of no-return, beyond which lies the atrophy of the function of accomodation and of life itself. Such diverse extremisms are ordered around an axis pointed toward satisfaction, but also capable of retrogression. They suggest a play of contrary forces set up around a center of gravity which displaces itself by withdrawal and attraction, and which is constrained by the bonds which link the emotive to the purely vegetative.

Such bonds knit the whole being, as they bind every world known to experience to the living organisms which sustain it. They are virtual, that is, in essence or effect less anatomic than functional, and force every collectivity to adjust to the physiological impulse of its members. They guarantee unity of soul, that place where the homeostasis of the organic functions is manifested in an equilibrium of a spiritual order, and where the structures, as collective as physical, are personalized. The soul, an idealized expression of historicity, is the narrow passage where the biological becomes historical, the neuroconscious pole toward which all humanity is returned when the limits beyond which destruction awaits has not been transgressed.

The inner experience forces us to become aware of, and somewhat to circumscribe, the double nature of what, in this conjunction, happens within us. Neither happy nor unhappy at will, we are at the mercy of tyrannical emotions which force us to precautions, tentative trials, and detours. Our affectivity, our sensitivity to emotional stimuli, is compounded of a heavy whole incapable of definition, weighing on us everywhere, localized nowhere.. Amid our oscillations between joys and pains, we are scarcely permitted to know anything beyond the axial point of the self, moved above by what happens to us, and below by the flood tide of moods arising from the nerve and endocrine functions. Men have long suspected that biovegetative and emotive states correspond in such a way that each determined structure of the one is the specific substratum of a distinctive structure of the other. Whatever may be the future of experiments now under way, they will not explain how the living creature can be classified as to his relations with magnitudes and quantities, nor how these relationships are transformed into feelings and ideas. Nevertheless, we shall not underestimate the importance of variations in excitability and the inrush of energy which cross over this mysterious diaphragm.

Surely these variations are of primordial importance. Without a doubt the greatest and the least of them illustrate the regulative role of the physiological unity of the self, the imperatives of its central equilibrium. The man who too completely surrenders to a passion or a plan and draws too much strength from his other areas, may lose control of himself. From one extreme he is then rudely thrown back on another. Every tendency has its opposite as a springboard, and happiness and unhappiness are relative between them. The feelings are located two by two on bipolar axes: an excessive love can become a hate, a too intense remorse can lead to a crime. Crowds, nations, are given over to acts which afterwards astound those who performed them. The greatest cultures know these vicissitudes. When the pendulum swings beyond the extreme point of their equilibriums, many men can no longer endure the disparities caused by the excessive polarization of the collective structure which they share. Then the imagination of a prophet, proposing a vision which in some one characteristic is in opposition to what prevails, reverses one of the basic axes of what has been the living experience.

We shall meet here the essential modality of historicity. Every passionate structure, individual or collective, is made up of disequilibriums mutually compensated. When sufficiently so, they make of an individual, a group, a people, or a culture, a relatively stable whole of organs, institutions, and representations, with internal but not excessive contradictions. But all may be shattered by what makes the event, and a new system of contradictions is substituted for that which has been destroyed. Historicity is a play of active dissymmetries, whose excesses are those of history itself, which stimulates innovation and progress only by destroying a previous acquisition. The historical thus prolongs the biological through passions and by the grace of inventions.

The regulations of collectivities and their successions depend on the normal play of the elementary regulations directed by the physiological homeostasis. The fact is that, even when it appears the most individual, the motive process arises also from the collective. Among the different mimetic items offered to the family by the child in its first days are the spontaneous, also spontaneously understood; and these are therefore communicative in a way just as physical as are the assimilative functions between the organism and its milieu. Others are freer, less automatic than attempted by the will, and draw meaning from the response they receive from the environment. These adjust, therefore, by imitations, successive uses, and selection for convenience. The smile of the new-born infant would already be of this type. Thus, in this way, and following the basic balancing of suffering and pleasure, society specifically identifies fear, anger or jealousy, affection, high spirits or joy. The organization of the most elementary and intimate representations becomes already that of social values, according to the summation which each culture makes of primordial experience and the customs which the immediate life-urges suggest as appropriate. What we feel in our deepest being, beyond the primordial and instinctive feeling of the variability of living, belongs to what the group learns to imagine and utilize.

Outside the tiny sector of what is available to us as undifferentiated and voluntary, all that is strictly individual is relative to the body. What is called spirit is built by assimilation and accomodation in terms of environments.

This structuring is not achieved in just any manner: it obeys the imperatives of a systematic testing by the groping and reciprocal search for adequacy in the emotive and the gesture. It is not from his inner self, by lessons far too vague, that man discovers the possibilities of his body, but by trying them out, and by putting them to the test in the external world. Each of the little events that provokes these testings or adjusts to them is to his private destiny what great deeds are to the destiny of the collectivities to which he belongs. If across this unmeasurable chasm where the physiologic becomes feeling, no specific item passes directly, but only the energy alone, there is no alternative but to catalogue the physiological functions and their operative efficiency from the outside, and by virtue of their use. It is this totality of concrete experience which society gathers from its members and joins to that of its leaders, in order to sum them up symbolically in its apprenticeships.

One may characterize as involutive the talents that permit certain persons to perform at will those vegetative functions which nature has made unconscious. Such are certain powers of fakirs, and the physiological regressions which they accomplish with great difficulty, like the excessive introversions by which men and cultures degenerate. It is not toward the visceral that consciousness expands, but in the opposite direction, that is, toward the outer and towards others, in the search for a common experience of action and a logic of expression. The progressive model for a healthy mastery of the self is the same as for the collective, whose successive testings built objective reason, and whose pertinent uses are summarized in the syllogism. The individual explores his inner self by discovering the external articulations which contain and support him. The growing child understands himself by familiarizing himself with the external world, which is the usual order of discoveries in his group, as along the stages of development traveled in his own person. All the first moments of this infantile discovery correspond naturally to those by which the original man had to grasp the rational across the flux of affectivity. The elementary processes which history permits us to distinguish in the world of the imagined, and of sign and object, have as their homologues the successive moments of individuation.

There is no reason to be surprised that psychoanalysts were able to discover in the profound and unconscious depths of adults, even within the most modern civilizations, the traces of vague, simple primordial images such as primitive religions had elevated to the rank of universal and divine symbols. The highly pleasing state of being absorbed into the all, the anxious state of having to challenge the authority of parents, or of the group, or of the existing order, to obey the compulsions of desire which consume the being to exalt it, the glorious state that rewards risks successfully incurred, all surrendered early man to the basic theophanies. And these were those of the mother and the father, of the mass of things or the breath of fire, which transcends that mass in sublime elevations and purified orders. Each in his own way thus reenacts the great historic journeys of humanity, and glimpses once again the archetypes solemnized by very ancient religions. But he does not stop here; even before he could have acquired the means or arrived at the proper age to making these a self-conscious possession, education sweeps him along through other phases of the reduction of the sacred to the rational. After this experience, he will learn by chance or by frequenting the poets something of these primitive and obscure tragedies of the inner man.

Poets have long celebrated blood and race, justifying by the restrictions of custom a seignorial and royal order dictated by its own exclusiveness. More recently, they seek in the substratum of expressions the vital elements which make logic mysteriously common to all humanity. At all times, aside from the genetic and on this side of a reason, the emotions of one generation affect the following, whether by remaining identical with them or by reverencing them. It was said of Electra that she had the native violence of Clytemnestra, but also that she had learned it from her. As for Oedipus, his suffering was not from bad heredity. If his father became his victim, it was because it was the father who had made himself the executioner of the child whom he feared more than he had wanted him. At the time of Romeo and Juliet, as in that of Pyramus and Thisbe, families bequeathed their hatreds without being able to prevent their children from falling in love.

It is from these extreme consequences, these seizures or reactions of emotions, that education seeks to protect us. Education is thus also an edulcoration, a softening process. The more education is pushed forward, the more it speeds up the evolutive order of the imaginative faculty, without destroying it, by hastening it toward representations already elaborated by the collectivity. The physiolog-

ical support or base for the primordial symbolism is already outmoded under realizations of a later order by the time a cerebral
maturation enables the modern child to express himself in a language
which has been instilled in him. There may on occasion be a
resurgence of that symbolism in its original form; for by its elementary movement, secret and underneath all, it animates all that men
accomplish, for better or for worse, according to the articulations
imposed by that fundamental and objective logic, even well before it
has been understood or expressed. It is the shuddering, underlying
support, sensitive to an evocation of the past, irritated by an inadequate present. It is appeased by action that shapes a future
according to its persistent aspirations; and finally, once it has learned
the pertinent syntax, it expresses itself in what there is of the
rational.

At the center of a fully evolved culture, there will be young people
at the age when they should be improving themselves who bring into
question the affective situation of their milieu, and who are made
restless by what the heroes of the past have accomplished. Such
uneasiness will be attributed to some ingratitude of character. Yet
the educator is under pressure to force students to assimilate the
sequence of the historic inheritance; or at least that part of it that
has been retained after the omissions and the abridgements. The
student, on occasion, will challenge the interpretation of what is
being imposed upon him and, using his own kind of logic, will
personalize what he has seen with his own eyes. Yet education seeks
at all times to strip the young promptly of such elementary affective
self-references, for they may hinder the acquisition of the most
recently and communally received explanations. Thus, even before
the young person who is being entrusted with instruction is phy-
siologically matured, education teaches him duly to profit by the
concrete and abstract regulations and operations, without granting
him the leisure to divine the mystery behind them, as their original
inventors had done. Education teaches him the use of language and
soon familiarizes him with the logic whose discovery demanded so
long and cautious a sequence of thinking over millions of years.

But it is quite evident that if education succeeds in this process, it
is because nature lends itself to it. When education asserts that there
is an age of first steps and another one of first words, that it is less
easy to divide than to add, or to grasp the notion of conservation of
volumes than of masses, it is offering the dual experience of expressive dispositions of the brain and of the order of difficulties which

human effort will encounter in history. If to clarify its knowledge, humanity had to undergo so many events which it itself stirred up, it is because the child is in its beginnings an unselfconscious but natural infinity of possibilities, which he tests by gestures of any sort whatsoever before he reflects upon them.

Every culture shares the condition of man, including that of different ages. Therefore, we must now examine with a special attention what happens when society, as well as the adolescent, arrives at the so-called age of reason. We must make note of the fact that the rational operations then mastered are all reversible. When we abstract the evidence that a subtraction or a division may be returned to the original situation before the change by the corresponding addition or multiplication, or that a first half-circle turn reverses a direction which a second one reestablishes, and that the same happens with the rest of our fundamental experiences, then we have translated into a basic logic the condition of equilibrium and compensation, the fundamental homeostasis of all physiology.

Such a result is not achieved without pain and anguish. The greatest brains have sometimes experienced the feeling of void in the new world which their discoveries have allowed them to enter. Scientific hypothesis and its rational methodology lack the warmth of the imagined inspired by emotion. He who first adventures into these spaces of infinite perspectives experiences the fright of nothingness which neither religious nor aesthetic representation will block. Pascal confessed to the same, and Darwin lost his health. Education finds itself forced, therefore, to make an alliance between the attention devoted to character and that with which it surrounds the development of reason. Throughout all history education retains this dual purpose: to master the dynamisms of passion, and to extract from them an intellectual logic. As the protector of learning, education is naturally conservative, and would have dried up the living springs of the event if it could always have been perfectly conservative. But since there are no raw facts which do not always contradict education, and no uncertainties which do not weaken it, and since also to every imposed lesson there is the response of an emotive reaction of challenge, so there is no enrichment, no experience, doubt, or acquisition which does not incite outbursts of originality. Thus evolution, habitually wasteful, still designs many more changes for man than his selective progress can authorize for realization. By opening wider the paths of invention, evolution forces into association with history the ever more numerous groups withdrawn from the immobility and the powerlessness of the peasant, to toss him finally into the disputes and rivalries of scientific and industrial competition.

The more urgent education is, the more it overrefines the organic threads linking the cultural to the natural, the more it weakens this link, and the more it multiplies the risks of challenge. By creating more destinies than it has codified lessons for, education also erects at the interior of being the articulated skeleton of rational structures. Thus it reinforces the social nature which is compensating for the unsatisfactory state of the emotive structures, which have had less time alloted to them to grow their own protective shells. Thus the so-called civilized man is more resistant to alienation than is the savage; but on the other hand, if he chance to yield to it, it is harder for him to recover. A magical ceremony is not enough; he has to reconstruct segment by segment the machinery of the destroyed acquisitions. Collectivities the closest to nature are also those which best fashion the child in their own image. Those which primarily inculcate rationally constructed systems check the source of passions the more successfully as they distribute the flood-tide by a greater number of networks whose outlets they multiply. To substitute the reasoned datum for the natural is not so much to control the living ardor as to distribute its stream the more widely, and to erode the virtual possibilities more by recognizing more of the present realities. Finally, it is to enlist history less by the model of great deeds than by the successful expressions in the unfoldings of invention.

III. Now the imagination, as a projection of desire through the channels of education, does not transfigure the inner power which animates the man of action, the artist, or the scholar, in the same way for each. The imagination, destined to find expression in some creative work, is soon snatched up by the instruments and mechanisms of meaning which will endow it with reality when in the grip of the machinery of objectification. No doubt, as far as content is concerned, and as compared to mathematics, arithmetic, or the interpretation of physics as prisoners of their data, plastic or poetic fiction appear freer in their choices. But it is a wholly relative freedom, since a thousand correspondences necessarily set themselves up between what an author invents and what he has experienced. As for the medium, which is the means of being comprehended and even the condition for esthetic realization, all depends intimately on a situation within the collectivity, and on the state of development of this last, its images, signs, and procedures of expression. Art is not a simple recomposition of former elements; it introduces new ones. But the painter does not invent his forms from nothing, nor does literature recreate language each time anew.

In the world of expression, the imagination is bound to, even restrained by, what has been already expressed. It adds to that only the feeble surplus of which the individual artist is capable. The author awakens important echoes only in the milieu which stimulated him, and plays the role of resonator. He becomes then the master of the work, the revealer of the unconscious, the prophet of the future.

In its beginnings, the action sets forth from the unforeseen, but much less so in its conclusion. No doubt challenges, conversations, excursions, all the moments that build toward a great enterprise, are so many borrowings from worlds already highly familiar in representation, word, and gesture. But the action is elementary. If we were to classify by types, a more direct manifestation of the imagination in the grip of possibles not so open to prognosis would be by reference to what has already arisen to surpass it in esthetics. Furthermore, in action, spontaneity, caught up in the temptation to risk, is at first an immediate challenge to a situation in fact. Therefore, success, having to meet the same conditions set up for any legitimacy, soon forces its hero into an ambiguity. Thus action, at the outset, is to the reality what the gesture is to emotion, that is to say, liberty running the risk of a doubtful outcome, a projection beyond the self of an inner inadequacy. It then becomes a form of submission to the aspirations of a group; that is to say, an identification of the self with a movement or a rebellion provoked. It is less a prophecy than a more explicit evocation of the past. Again, the final result being obtained, when the collective modification vaguely implied has been painfully accomplished, the work that incarnated it — whether man or dynasty— is further given over either to the mechanism of the group, or to solitude, decay, or exile. The end is alienation as regards self or another. The great moment, that of the perfect harmony of the leading character with his action, is more prompt than durable. It rewards an ambiguous attitude, that of the comedian, less in the manner of Diderot's claim in *The Paradoxes* that the actor reaching the height of his art does not identify with his role but regards it as external to himself, than in the manner of Augustus dying and content to have played his mimicry well. The chief character is at first disposable, and at the start grows more important as he remains so. But he does not become a determinant except by being determined. If with some arbitrariness he chooses among several possibilities the one of which he assumes the image, he ends like Hercules, the victim of the tunic he wore in his latest success.

Action reveals of a man less of what he intended to do than what role he is capable of playing. Action is adjusted less to a rounded personality than to one seeking his fulfillment therein. One must be capable of dwelling a long time in a state of suspense without destroying the self in order to find finally the revelation of the self in the socio-drama of the event. Thus Jehu made himself a priest of Baal in order to destroy its votaries. Alexander the Great, purporting to be the champion of Europe, smoothed the way for Islam. The young Bonaparte dreamed of being the liberator of Corsica, and Koba that of Georgia, but they became Napoleon and Stalin. Hitler was the instrument of the greatest revenge of the Eastern peoples of Europe whom as a child he had dreamed of reducing to slavery.

The most celebrated actions mark the greatest reversals of history entrusted to individualities the most capable of self-fulfillment through denial of the self, because they preferred the accidents of chance to the continuity of logic. Made sensitive by some shock undergone in childhood, these persons are the apparent heroes of an order, but actually they are the actors in the destruction of that order. Alexander incarnated Greece less than the fury of Olympus, Bonaparte less France than his father's prompt rallying to the party of the Count of Marbeuf,[1] Stalin less Russia than the slavery of Katia, Hitler less Germany than the humiliation of Clara. If the nature of the deed is like that of childhood, sharing its spontaneity along with the sudden interruptions and the exasperation of its risks, a character does not come on strong because it remains like a retarded child. It is rather that, though soon marked, it retains, and without its whole being falling into ruin, this voluntary secret and infinite gift; namely, that of the indeterminate expectation of achievement. This expectation has something of the avenger in its most brilliant episodes, but its grandiose conclusion leads it back to the first contradiction which inspired it.

1. Napoleon's father quickly accepted the French occupation of Corsica and the governorship of Count of Marbeuf, for which his reward was his son's enrolment in the military school at Brienne, France, and later at Paris, though for years the son resented his father's 'betrayal' of the cause of Corsican independence. Translator's note.

The power of the imaginative faculty required for every form of expression — and here we need to return to the light shed by what has just been said, recalling that every leading character is also the author and every author a bit of the leading character — is not less than that required by action, but sooner and at less risk it finds the opportunity to manifest itself. It also takes advantage of a social situation profoundly rent, of the kind introduced only where collective evolutions are present, and according to what their regulative mechanisms decide. Furthermore, the resources, symbols, and signs are much more prompt, diverse, subtle, and immediately graspable than deeds. Here, in the realm of the imaginative, the precocious attempt and the immediate acceptance of the self, far from harming the author's profession, strengthen it. The risk which the inventor or artist runs of spending himself on a poor moment is only that of remaining a forerunner or an epigone; but that is not the same civic exclusion or the total obscurity which lie in wait for him who is ambitious for conquest, but is denied his encounter with the opportunity. Great works have also written what their authors could not have performed. This faculty of substitution of creative work for deed, furthermore, does not belong to natural evolution; it is the characteristic of men. This faculty, the mark of man's greatness, makes civilization prevail, in the general destiny, over the event.

But nothing authorizes the claim that the most intellectual are also the most spontaneous or the most consciously aware. In the world of representation and sign, success is no more specifically individual than it is in action. We have only to refer, for example, to the inner experience admitted by those who work in the most complicated realm of discovery, that of mathematical invention. Numerous scholars of first rank have recognized in their findings less the voluntary and calculated consequence of what they were looking for than a gift of God, as Gauss said, or as Hadamard recently wrote, a sudden illumination. Invention is sometimes produced in a neighboring field or even in one apparently distant from those being explored at the moment. Such a great reward is not entirely gratuitous. It supposes aptitudes soon made manifest, a rigorous and ranging apprenticeship, a particular intense effort, related to the subject in question. But it happens as if miraculously in a time of leisure, of inattention, even of half sleep, as if the brain, properly set to work, were achieving its best by itself, by an appropriate and independent mechanism, and completing the task which had voluntarily been set for it. What the most authoritative witnesses thus describe seems to have been best summed up by Henri Poincaré when he spoke of elements consciously excited and oriented, but accomplishing beyond consciousness the final trajectory of the fortunate conjunction which a too niggling control would have prevented. Of course, the pleasure thus experienced is no sufficient guarantee of certitude; for it may happen to be illusory, and it is necessary to recapture, point by point, the steps so obscurely taken, and to submit them to sharp criticism — that is to say, to a careful control, making use of all that society has already built up of the rational and has offered as tested guides to clear meaning. Even so, it is not finally this consciousness which discovers: it merely verifies.

For the rest, all inventors, and not only in the sciences, admit that in this labor they divide into two: one part of themselves excites the possibles, tries out combinations not overmuch nor too lacking in diversity nor too few, until the other part suddenly recognizes the good in them. To sum up this process the Latin language has two words: *cogitare, intelligere* — to ponder, weigh, pursue with the mind, and to perceive, comprehend. The model thus proposed fits every phenomenon of historical evolution. The turbulence of facts sketches a thousand ephemeral structures, among which are detached and retained what best favors the equilibrium of the remodeled situation. There is no other method for progress: numerous attempts mutually refined, condensed in a flow increasingly better oriented, finally encounter the point where the collective articulations are identified with things that lend themselves to an increase of order; and this identification intelligence gives expression to and puts it to work on the road to a new halting-place. History is the objectification of cerebral labor.

The most important of physiological functions implies a vital restructuring of a limited stock of cells under the control of the rest of the neurological system which continues to be socially adapted. This stock then adjusts to the solving of the problem thrust upon it. And, because of the economy thereby realized, and the general easing of tension that results thereby, it liberates the increase of energy that reawakens attention. Thus the entire being is brought into that state of satisfaction appropriate to success.

An attentive introspection discloses that these are not merely signs which thus confront and unite, but complex realities, differing from, though intermingling with, those realities which result in expression. This final expression is collective in its morphology, neurological in its operative syntax. The economy of a system of expression is at the

confluence of two other economies: that of the society in which it is
inscribed, and that of the nervous structures in search of their best
employment. Invention, by bringing order into the brain, discovers
the order of things.

Cerebral labor is not accomplished without starting from a given
condition and impulse. Both will and a cultural setting are needed.
Obviously, the already acquired mathematical achievements supply
certain indispensible materials. In their fixed expression, they contain the stages previously covered and act as indicators of paths to be
followed. But the new paths are not inscribed therein, and that is
why no machine invents. Schemes which are taking form and
awaiting their objectification, are implicit in the structures of the
collectivity taken as a whole, which act with the power now familiar
to us on the tendencies of the individual. To sum all up, we may
write down that experience lived through, works learned, experimentations well carried out, build up obscure possibilities within the
unconscious, to which cerebral effort applies those instruments of
verification that are utilized by the clear consciousness. And since
this latter has been structured by education, it is through the social
that the axiomatic of operative dynamisms, as well as the systems of
signification, are made manifest. To extract from the implicit a
successful representation is to find a stable element within the
collective in motion, upon which the individual searching is like a
graft.

The result of this labor is expressed in a conclusion to the effort
when data inspired by the collective evolution have been restruc-
tured, and the objective conditions for a renewal of the evolution
have been assured. A demonstration reunites in one self-same conclu--
sion elements originally scattered in the hypothesis. The poetic art
does not behave differently when it brings together and recombines
images or words illuminated by this contact. When artists or poets,
Chopin or Valéry, speak of inspiration, they do so in the same way
that scientists speak of invention. The esthetic function unconsciously brings the studied gesture into association to create new
seductions. In the realm of charm, it recomposes what has been
disintegrated in the world of raw facts on the edge of the historic
event. The esthetic illustrates the progressive evolution that science
builds.

In the same way, one might say that invention, carried along by
inspiration, renews to a higher degree of coherence what action, in its
origin, had rejected in the outmoded past. As to man himself,

rejuvenated by his windfalls of invention, he is less author than agent. He is the catalyst of a process for which nature, through the intermediation of the group, furnishes the materials and the energy, as well as the laws of composition; that is to say, the basic essentials of what is inscribed in books of knowledge and in highly rated works.

But it is important also to indicate what makes the art of science different, beyond this similarity of method of working. The signs which serve art are in themselves all charged with emotivity. They are the active symbols inscribed in the sensitivity, nor is this astonishing; and they have naturally the movement of such. It suffices that the artist previously trained in his art, that is, capable of making use of the impassioned symbols, should place himself, or perhaps should have been placed by circumstances, in a situation that calls for expression; so that within him there is aroused the uneasiness, the agitation, and then the compensatory ordering which the finished work will express. The artist, properly involved by reason of his apprenticeship, his experiences and his pains, and having his creative imagination at his disposal, becomes the instrument of a revelation. The sign of the scientific, on the contrary, is that it is perfectly neutral; and that neutrality is, indeed, the condition of a pertinence implied by a reversibility of every operative reasoning. It is not enough, therefore, for the scientist merely to surrender himself to the circumstances of which he should become the interpreter. When he places his effort in the world of representations, all of them abstract, he must in the least moments of his conscious effort recharge with emotions those elements which a long collective and historic elaboration had neutralized. He must further make the appropriate effort to take what is artificial and exact to the degree that it is impartial, and reinscribe it within the dynamisms of a poetic that is voluntary in its undertaking and functional in its result.

This dual affirmation illuminates the ways by which the individual, according to his calling, behaves himself so as to enroll himself in society. As abstract as may be the nature of his activity, he would not be certain of how to bring it to fulfillment without drawing from the sources of his desire, or without building himself around, and by virtue of, this center of all, where logic is born in the passionate organicisms of the collective emotions.[2] The scientist in no less

2. That is, the collectivity is viewed as an organism with its own center of emotions shared by all, and expressed in collective representations. Translator's note.

degree draws on the results achieved by his predecessors in social representations, such as transfigures them into admirable objects, arts, music, and architecture, as well as those which the interpersonal mores and relations dedicate to the poetic experience. *A fortiori* the same is true of the artist. Nor can the man of action escape the same imperative when he has recourse to the charm of attitudes and of speech when he takes command. All that books of knowledge, works of art, and political gestures accomplish is thus social even before being a search for harmonies.

However, if all, actors and authors, are in search of the same universal seduction, each, according to his calling, is differently situated in the symbiosis of his physical nature with the world in which it moves. When the scientist has found what he is looking for, to communicate is but an easy task. The same effort at expression, which defines the nature of the artist's work, is quite the opposite. And as for the man of action, the conqueror, who has resolved on his purpose and has announced it, it remains for him to bring it about. In all three cases, the esthetic sensitivity lies at the heart of the energetic stirring of the self; but it proposes an objective for action, a reason for being to art, and a recourse to effort to the desire to know. Whatever he may be destined to, the individual sets in motion the totality of the self around the central place from which all impulses flow, but in a different disposition according to the implicit objective structures to which science is closer than action.

It is difficult for the same man to be eminent at the same time in action, art, and knowledge. Certainly, the three roles are in conjunction, but in the subordination of the others to the one. Every undertaking begins with this first and fundamental disposition of the self; and the choice is the less reversible as it becomes the more difficult to turn back after one has advanced farther into a certain excellence. This first choice does not entirely commit one, at least not before a true decision has dedicated the whole being to a subsequent determinism. The rigorous sufficiency of what one decides, with the objective conditions of what one realizes, determines the degree of excellence in the success.

IV. Thus, in the progress which, step by step, from childhood to ripe age, leads a thousand original possibles by successive sacrifices to the single achievement of his latter years, a man is free to choose himself at each fork of the road; yet he has only finite resources at his disposal to shield himself from the conditionings which create him by bestowing on him the power of things. This fusion of the individual with a totality makes for the happiness and pride of his maturity, and unites the certitude of the righteous with his last days. This is not achieved at one blow: existence traverses zones of regret or of remorse, and sometimes ends there. There are ways of making up one's mind that are too heedless or too obstinate, and many ambiguous opportunities for acting so. However feeble the will, it greatly alters the destiny of the being in the moments when the balance of contradictory characteristics, however powerful each may be, is almost perfect. Then the chosen aim, by being inscribed in the reality, bestows the feeling of responsibility on him who has made his choice. But the aim which has been refused access to the historic remains also no less alive in the being who decided on it; and he is left with the nostalgia for what he could manage no way to becoming. He may be paralyzed for a certain time, or, again, may prepare himself for it superbly by harsh conversions in the eyes of those who have not followed his obscure maturation.

These conflicts and reversals are especially frequent at the heart of societies which are being split apart by evolution in periods of the most numerous cyclic renewals. Then they impart their dramatic character to the sharp transformations of beliefs or institutions, and cause uneasiness to linger even after the changes have been apparently accomplished; or existence may be doomed to counterblows of movement whose primary origin is still located in an epoch of apparent indifference.

As for those who inconsiderately tear down the walls which enclose them and the bonds which attach them, they are soon made to feel the dizziness of the void, the suffering and despair to which those who have wandered beyond all broken habits are reduced within the infinite field of possibilities forever snatched from them. A too great anxiety to prove oneself free is to risk that social death from which instinct defends itself by the increase of violences. Indeed, these latter, whether in the accidents of daily destiny or in those of the larger history, help us to understand the color of despair, especially in its most gradiloquent accents.

The reward given to wise conformities, and the anguish which has to be the price for every recourse to freedom, demonstrate in the most common of experience undergone how man is tied to his center and contained in his periphery by the zone of equilibrium between his emotivity and the rigorously compensated structure of the collectivities whose representations change his physiological tides into emotive tides. Man cannot transgress what encloses him except by virtue of the elasticity of the inner springs of his demanding unity. He progresses only by limited sallies, enlarges his territory only by small measures, within the complicity of collective things which alone decide that on occasion a sudden leap may be attempted. The conditions of society dispose, if not of the intrinsic liberty of the individual, at least of the opportunities he has to make use of it. They determine the moments of great actions and of great works by virtue of the opportunities and vicissitudes of the general evolution and the imperatives of events. In the same way, some societies serve as a substitute for others, according to an axis, since the involution of some leaves room for the progress of others, according to an axis of development which, especially in the last two or three centuries, tends to multiply the objective availability of technical invention, produced by education in terms of the expressed economic order.

Strange condition, that of man. On the level of elementary impulses, he is in the grip of biological regulations; on the level of abstract operations, he is in the grip of the rational instrumentations which are also the laws of things. Between these two ascendencies, as exercised by a nature ever faithful to its biophysical constants, he has no liberty except at the heart of the social between the instinctive and the operative; that is, on the level where the imaginative entertains beauty with inner assurance; on the median level where historicity rejoins history; and at the heart of human experience whose true empire is that of pretexts and hypotheses, of images and the calculating arts.

But this empire and this dominion are not built in the void. Humanity has developed its certitudes as its vanities in an immense field of injustices where, concealed from itself, lie the unity of the human species and the identical quality of soul of all who compose that species. If, then, it is left to each to reflect upon himself in the inner intimacy where beauty unites with happiness and existence with logic, at the secret edge of the personality where the physiological is tied to the social, we cannot legitimately refer to humanity as an abstraction. All, outside of the point without dimension that is the soul, is historical. That is to say, it arises from laws progressively acknowledged in that testing which the imagined gives to things at whose center it is transformed.

8. The order of things

Newton, the most admired scientist of his time, had at his disposal the Galilean mechanics, the Cartesian mathematics, and, naturally, the enormous accumulation of data assembled by those who for a century, from Rome to Copenhagen and from Prague to London, had been observing the heavens from a new perspective. Still, to prove his *Principia*, whose remarkable simplicity had been denied to Copernicus, he had to delay for several years until certain measurements could be improved. Voltaire, otherwise so sensitive to the spirit of the times, should not have been satisfied to write merely that it is not often given to a man to discover a world. He should have spoken of a collectivity, a culture, a special age in the evolution of mankind. For it was an age with its own way of acting and reflecting, of expressing itself and of calculating, an age now arrived at a certain stage as notable for the art of demonstration as for the manufacture of clothing. Not only does the scientist not invent alone, but his invention is registered in history at a moment before which it would have been impossible. Every important scientific discovery comes at its hour. It is the fruit of a maturation of a milieu capable of creating it.

What each epoch is capable of inspiring in the minds of its learned depends on an order of things. The theorems of Euclid and the books by which they were given circulation are, like all others of the same sort, determined in their succession. And as cerebral labor accomplishes nothing outside of the social setting, so history is first of all and in essence nothing other than the sequence of collective adjustments, by which man masters the powers of his brain, one after another, and ranks them from the emotive to the intellectual. It is thus that he is the better able to conquer the resistances of his natural environment. A further phase will then follow, when a sufficient number of thinkers will bring order into what has been achieved in a uniformity of operative talents. Let us begin by considering the first of such, which covers the duration of time stretching from the beginnings to the great transformations of science and industry. Here we may recognize several stages signalized by the conquest of notions of number, of measurements of space, then of time, and finally of cause and probability. But before this analysis, it is important to recall certain simple verities.

Mathematicians, physicists, biologists, each according to the degree of precision demanded by the certitudes they have reached, extrapolate without reservation over the whole conceivable duration of time concerning the legitimacy of what their reason or their tools have at the moment established. That is, they assume always that what they are discovering is more durable than is the particular era which finds expression in their discoveries. They do not even absolutely dispute the former formulations, whose wholly relative and approximative character they recognize, often even long after they were discovered. Three-dimensional geometry is not held to be unique, Mariott's law to be exact,[1] Newton's astronomy to be complete, nor a rational mechanics to be exclusive. Nevertheless, they still retain pertinency in certain uses, within applications not too refined. Even if one verifies in invention how reality eludes, one is still persuaded that it does not deceive, that it does not change suddenly and arbitrarily. This conviction, without which research would be in vain, qualifies the certainty of what it finds.

Historicity and history bring us always back to the statement that man's efforts refine their own pertinency. Thus we can no longer doubt that there is a certain correspondence between the disposition of things to let themselves be comprehended with an increasing accuracy, and that of cerebral labor to perform with increasing acuteness. Every truth is of course submitted to challenge, but the legitimate claim to its being grounded more precisely is not called into question. The never-ceasing progress in precision and exactitude is but correlative to the faculty which has the supreme neurofrontal function of detaching itself from its emotive attachments, but without ever totally banning them. We note here again two conditions of

---

1. Mariott, French physicist, ca. 1620–1684, stated that 'at a constant temperature, the volume of a gaseous mass varies in inverse ratio to its pressure'. Translator's note.

intellectual progress already indicated by analysis of the processes of individuation. The upper brain is able to resist the temptations to which sensitivity submits it, to block an instinctive or habitual reaction, and to undertake within the imagined the task of reflection more clearly aimed at a still distant goal. These adjustments do not dry up the springs of emotion. They only channelize their currents in such a way that the individual, after he has undergone the first communal education, thereafter increasingly orients himself and specializes in the area which his preference, his calling, or circumstances qualify him to enter. And if the objects of truth obey the supreme necessity of belonging organically to the whole body of knowledge and science, the individual expands around a flux of unshakable certitudes, at the center of a milieu which enlarges its curiosities, its dissatisfactions, and its desires.

It has been said for a long time that man's uniqueness was that he manufactured his own tools. It must be added that he no less creates his needs. The present behavior of so-called societies of abundance sufficiently proves that. And, apart from certain savage societies whose art of living Rousseau so greatly appreciated as more attached to nature than to culture, we may say that at least since the neolithic there is neither group nor society which does not rise to the appeal of new satisfactions or take great pains to acquire the means of enjoying them. Here again, the individual, a physiological agent of these modifications and simplifications, is influenced by others, and by the rivalries of envy which give the whole process its opportunity. However disinterested, the scientist profits indirectly by whatever transforms, diversifies, and enriches the collective.

Whatever excites men, as well as what they think and express, belongs to the same web of events. Certain motives are known to a single subject only, others are obscure to all, even those who are in touch with them or drawn along in their course. Others, finally, are clear to many or all. Further, this immense and complex network is attached to all constructed objects and to every container of fixed expression as well as to every articulation of assembled mechanisms. Finally, this network is linked to the physical and the living which compose the natural environment of this immaterial whole, as real as it is compelling. Whatever a mind conceives is, before it is uttered, a modification of sensitivity involving a process of rationalization. When a result is achieved, a link is weakened between emotions and reason, but another is reinforced between things and thought. At the heart of the social world, where the physiological and the cerebral embody the conditioning factors, to understand and to know is to become aware that one is sufficiently detached from his passions to be better able to express himself, and to inject an element of objectivity into that expression. And since every invention takes on the external form of gestures and things manufactured, the milieu is thereby changed and enriched with new possibilities which in their turn will affect the passions. Liberated by the process that finds achievement, the emotive is very soon caught up in the consequences which make plain its own consequences. Man does not possess himself of things except by being entrapped in a new way by them.

The extraordinary faculty men have for creating illusions about the extent of their own freedom makes every discovery a victory. What follows proves its relativity. Thinkers as different as da Vinci, Pascal, Rousseau, Sismondi, or the physicists of today, have been disturbed, and justly so, by so much progress accomplished without humanity's ever being delivered from its ills. Whole cultures have at times been frightened and have refused this game of being duped. But nothing is halted for long thereby. The desire to be free makes men run to new chains in the creation of new needs.

It is by this difference from the rest of creation that man is thus drawn along by his unachieved transformations. Now this particularity is correlative with that which institutes all that humanity thinks and does in the immense structure of a single system. Before nature gave rise to the higher brain, it knew how to manufacture objects, tools, and weapons. The biological world of the seas, the air, or the earth has at its disposal instruments for fishing, or apparatuses for flight, methods of making signals and almost for language, means of lighting and electric contrivances. Plants even have cannons, grenades, and parachutes. There being no pure chance in nature, we calculate that these successes are not explained by accident. On the other hand, nothing is ordered, coherent, or rigorously correlative in the ensemble of animal or vegetable kingdoms. There instrumentation is, as it were, scattered about, relative only to the local and the particular. It is the biological blind-end of specific branchings obedient to the equilibriums of the whole, but not instigated by them.

When, on the contrary, one reflects on an invention as surely human as that of the wheel, it is not by observing a wheelwright at work that one will discover the secret of its invention. On this difficult subject, the philosopher errs if he does not listen to the anthropologist. For his lessons suggest that there must have preexisted in the inventor group emotive schemes at first unconscious, and substrata of notions of the circular and of radiating elements; and that these notions, fed by the needs of harmoniously organizing the collective, were expressed in ceremonies and rituals before they suggested the motions that had to be made to construct a tool which escapes from the continuity of life around it, in order to conform to the continuity of space and to utilize the friction of things so as the better to overcome it.

But since our purpose here cannot be one of treating what must or might have been the making of so many objects and tools, we shall stick to the essential, namely, the conquest of the scientific spirit by virtue of which all tools could be constructed with the utmost economy.

I. Among the realities presenting the most obvious scientific character, from which men have also drawn the greatest advantages in the disposition of their products and the development of their exchanges, there is one, the most anciently recognized and of infinite legitimacy, whose certitude no axiomatic has been able to challenge: namely, the sequence of whole numbers. Nothing is more commonplace and simple in appearance; nothing is more logically irreducible. In this primordial certitude, therefore, nature and society must be mutually implicated in their greatest common dimension.

Here we may first of all involve the principle of duality which the physicists postulate by opposing reaction to action, and which biological nature expresses in so many of its divisions, and affirms in bisexual reproduction. The same sexuality is at the origin of collective regulations, in the changes in the relationships of domination, as in the behaviors of the family, considered not as society has transformed it, but as nature has made it the social cell.

If a father or a patriarch counts his descendents and takes pride in their increase by the multiplication of generations, plus the addition of daughters-in-law and sons-in-law who came possibly from outside strains, there is no lesson in arithmetic to be easily deduced from this. Polygamy or monogamy, exogamy or endogamy, fecundity or sterility, from the fact of customs, introduce too many factors of differentiation. It even seems, at least in certain areas, that the historic vicissitudes could cause an approximative but simple relationship to be forgotten, yet one which must have been known very anciently and which modern statistics have established: namely, that which makes boys almost as numerous as girls.

If, on the contrary, it is the child who pictures to himself his ancestry then all falls into order by an obvious duplication: there are two parents who themselves had two, and so on as far back as one goes. Every social system which requires that a precise memory be kept of this past, and which attaches importance to this appeal to an amorous present or an ambitious future, conduces to a clarification of this duplication; for it remains perfect as far as the imagination can conceive of its backward progress. Now the food-gathering and hunting societies, since their populations were forced to distribute out as advantageously as possible over the territories that nourished them, were governed by conditions that no doubt played their part in prohibiting incest, as conceived in its broadest dimensions. That is, it excluded all descendents from conjugal relationships, either of the maternal or paternal line. This ruling implied well-retained memories and well-kept accounts. Thus the mind of the individual who calculated the number of members of one or several generations, whether he added himself or not, was introduced to something of the fundamental theory of arithmetic by which every number might be written to the power of two.

Obviously, a further effort must have been demanded for the abstracting of this concept from the institution in which it was still concealed. History begins to make provision for this, starting with the neolithic. Certainly the refusal of endogamy, marriage within the tribe, is not without its genetic advantages, for consanguinity increases the risk of multiplying malformations. But since this risk did not prevent other later societies from having recourse to it to defend the family patrimony, it is not what induced the primitive peoples to establish, or savages to preserve, their strict usages. These latter show a specific behavior of human society which arises from the fact that man is man; that is, a being seeking his security in terms of a collectivity into which, by so doing, he introduces a basic mathematics whose binary system is the inspiration for Egyptian multiplication. Analogous considerations, though much more difficult, clarify in some degree the importance of the number three. Naturally, a great depth of experience separates this implicit reality instinctively inscribed, as it were, in social behaviors from its clear expression and still more from its demonstration. It remains no less true, however, that even before the elucidation of these abstract principles, languages conserve the memory of the importance attached to the first three figures by causing them to be distinctly and specifically conjugated into the syntax as they are in the constitution of families,

not only as singular and plural, but also as dual and the triad. The
ancient Greek language, for example, still preserves a dual form in its
verb.

The uniting of a couple and the birth of a human being, aside from
the mysteries of fecundity, its poetry and its sacred rites, enclosed
the fundamental mathematical certitude of the genetic order of
numbers. The dual here takes its position between the singular and
the multiple, the even is placed in relation to the uneven. In the
succession of generations, marriages subtract the adult from one
fireside to double him at another; death takes away and birth adds.
At a time when numbers were still clothed in the dual nature of the
divine mystery and the everyday exchange or barter, and even before
a system had been deduced therefrom, man was in a position to
learn from all that was so often and in so many ways repeated
around him, and to make use of the most effective abstractions. In
the origins of our culture in that country of Akkad which must have
contributed much to the progress of arithmetic, we find in the
language the signs of the first three figures, at once familial and
familiar. The first is associated with all that is male, the second with
everything feminine, and the third with every multiple.

It must be added that all the necessities proper to numbers are, in
a certain way, partially rational, correlative to the guide marks to
magnitudes and spaces. Logic, by complementary experiences, orders
certain dispositions of primitive villages, and controls the derivations
of their myths and their variations in savage thinking. This logic acts
no less on the mutual dispositions of cultures neighboring on one
another, and on what orders each or transforms them by substitution. To bring these elements into play secularizes numbers.

To bring forth the abstraction from the experience lived through,
to familiarize the self with the pertinence of operative reasonings
translated into precise syntaxes of language, is the result of long
efforts. Here the function of historicity is brought into play, according to what we learn from the evolution of the imagined, and from
the pedagogical observation of the young individual in his formative
years. One must detach himself from sensations and their emotive
appeals. The event forces this. One must also think of equilibrium as
a fundamental substratum of the reversibility of arithmetic calculations. Physiology demands it. The result is achieved by attempting
many exercises, a number of them successful. The notion of number
does not emerge all by itself and alone from the collective institutions within which it is elaborated. It must be confronted along with

other notions, not directly implicated in love, birth, death, and the anxieties which they give rise to, and which must be transcended. And yet all are linked, through all the pains to be endured if one is to survive.

The immense advantages of numeration are not made progressively evident except in the light of what one learns from the pain of weights to carry and distances to cover. Among the concrete experiences which have to be met if the quality of number is to be discovered, the simplest relate to sensations of the most harsh and direct sort: those of muscular fatigue. This is attached to every motion, to whatever makes things heavy. It marks weight as the first quality of things and the first reality to overcome. To abstract this notion from experience supposes, of course, that the notion of relationships has been somewhat clarified; it is also to be confronted with a new difficulty. Very ancient, though already advanced civilizations likened the series of numbers to the families of the gods by giving a special place apart to prime numbers which engender those that follow. At the very same time, in those societies where agriculture gives rise to commerce, concrete procedures are being developed by which, as economically as possible, comparisons of quantities exchanged may be evaluated. The use of the scales, destined to be immortalized in the constellation Libra of the zodiac, alongside symbolizations of living creatures, reveals that bundles of weight are made up with the greatest economy by recourse, as when indicating ancestral lines, to successive powers of the number two — or even of the number three, when the measurer might happen by accident or necessity to be placed on the scale with the measured. Such series, perfect at least in their first terms, have been found in Africa. Their Akkadian existence precedes the pertinence of systems of measure inherited by Babylon, which drew such fortunate consequences from the density of the barley grain which served as a unit of measure, because its density was two thirds in relation to water. It was in that era that the numbers two and three emerge from being treated as divine, to be transcended by Manicheanism and Christianity.

The pertinency of the use of familial and familiar numbers, treated as witnesses of divine inspiration as well as of popular usages, finds a high dedication in the observations of the heavens and their awe-inspiring motions. The stars, the solar god thirty, the lunar god sixty, lend themselves to a relation with integral numbers defining with a sufficient approximation the division of the day, the month, the year, even the cycle of years. The convergence of numbers and

calendars in Egypt and Babylon, among the Aztecs and the Mayas, in
no way oblige us to assume that the ancient and the new worlds were
once in contact. Man will draw the same natural conclusions in each
by bringing together in his arithmetic the exchanges of earthly values
and the returning motions of the heavenly bodies.

At this stage, the elementary institutions of family relationships
are already bypassed, even though their mathematical lessons are by
no means exhausted. And if the most ancient and most certain
documents on measurements are relative to comparisons of weights,
combined with the guiding marks of volume and density, the order
of things which differentiates so as to relate weight, contained, and
space containing one to another is also a social order, proof of which
is still extant in construction discovered by archeology. Arithmetic
proves its legitimacy not only in the exchange of women or of goods,
in the distribution of seasonal labors, and the holidays which consecrate them, in the establishment of drain-ditches and the distribution of water, but also in the construction of palaces, centers of the
urban order alongside temples and observatories guarded by the magi
and priests.

When the Spanish discovered the New World, they found there
astonishing monuments, recalling those built by Egypt and Babylon.
The pyramid of Chichen Itza, called the Castle, bears witness, without the necessity of appealing to very improbable mutual influences,
to the fact that men unknown to one another had been separately
led to similar realizations. The physical laws that preside over the art
of building are not sufficient to explain all. Some internal logical
pressure is added to them, such as leads separate efforts to comparable successes. Liberated from the forest which covers it with
bushes, this immense construction still stands as a witness to a will to
unite in one single realization all that its builders knew and believed.
First came the need to summon together immense efforts into one
single result. The power of the sovereign capable of putting so many
men to work is an outstanding and inviolable counterbalance to the
resistance of a nature both imitated and overcome. Society disciplines itself as much to defend itself against the transcendental
authority of things as to render it homage. But the 'Castle' also gives
evidence of calculations. The 364 steps of four stairways to which
the final terrace is added bear witness that the year had been
discovered. This had not been easy; for another archaic and sacred
calendar exists, and research into the conjunctions of the two suggests a long cycle of years, whose number is recalled by the inter-

mediate terraces which bear witness to a past whose original date is believed to have been duly recognized.

The Babylonians, inventors of the sexigesimal system, were able to discover its advantages in large cosmological calculations. But it is hard to believe that it was with this in view that they succeeded in making sixty the base for a perfect numeration of position. Millenia had to be previously spent in occasional progresses and transliterations. In this progress, the use of the number ten is rediscovered, probably because of the convenience it offered to designate the order and quantity of things with the fingers of the hand. But the very origin of this fundamental arithmetical invention postulates a preoccupation with the use of multiplications by two and three, and with combining them, before practicing in the same way with ten.

There is no reflection on magnitudes which does not lead to further reflections as to their products. As for division, which is more complex in nature and defies the common sense of those times when the quotient is not an integer, that implies many further efforts.

It is difficult to assert that the acquisition of notions relative to weights is contemporary or only subsequent to that of numbers and their relations. The analysis of the lessons offered by the event, and of the way man has of making up his mind, suggests that the components of space were grasped as an elucidation of the effects of mass. In any case, division forced man to be no longer satisfied with integral numbers alone. Already the operation of multiplication was far from being easy, as it had appeared to be when one was satisfied to use very small numbers as multipliers, especially the number two. For example, multiplication appears to have been nowhere and in no way used among the Mayas, in spite of a culture nevertheless much advanced, yet satisfied to repeat additions as long as necessary. This illustration sets a higher value on what the Egyptians knew with their duplications and their rudimentary and incomplete fractions. The same is even more true of Babylonian arithmetic. In their case, as may be observed in young children today, the product of the first three numbers is already found linked at one time both to the notion of conservation of quantity and to a certain developed experience of space. We know that this last was indebted to civilizations with cultivated land, with property and irrigation, and to their land-surveyors and hydraulic engineers. The abstractions relating to volumes are more difficult still. Operations on the square and the root are easier than those dealing with the cube. Like the Chinese, the Babylonians made use of admirable procedures, even though they were still too much under the spell that integral numbers continued to exercise over them. They were on the fringe of becoming aware of demonstration; though the obvious clarity of that step seems to have been the privilege of the geometric spirit of their more fortunate neighbors dwelling in the rich estuaries of Ionia.

The last heir of Nebuchadnezzar had a vision: A hand wrote on the wall: *mane, thekel, phares.* A prophet of Israel, inspired by a superior ethic, declared to him that his destiny had been weighed, his days counted, and his kingdom destined to division. The legend conceals a more concrete reality: the power of things, the succession of truths which it had taught to men, wanted them not to be content with weighing, counting, dividing. Persia annexed Babylon; the axis of history, displaced toward the seacoasts, delivered the backward lands of Mesopotamia to the conquerors from the high plateaus. It was not in the regions where all had been assembled for so many centuries to prepare a new era of mental effort that this latter found expression in all its brilliance, but in a neighboring area, near enough to profit by what had thus been done, yet different enough that an operative meaning and significance still more basic could be extracted from that past.

That Arabian conquest will not modify this destiny. Many clever procedures will continue to be uncovered by the peoples who rally or are subdued by the conquest; others were imported by them from Oriental Asia. But the perfect rational precision blossoms into operative significance there where the most numerous and most sudden events make everything the more brilliant. The mathematics which opened the golden centuries of the Aegean Sea will reopen those of the Christian West.

We may suppose that coastal navigation particularly gives the eye practice in the identifying of forms. In the Greek archipelago, religion, art, authority, are exhibited less exclusively in effects of mass. Arithmetic is not exclusively the instrument of massive Cyclopean constructions. A more human standard links mathematics with proportions issuing from the demonstrable. The correspondences of art are in the image of theorems which lend precision to the speculations from which they arise. Beyond their rules we discover the joys of harmony; and, for a time, all value attaches to that. Beauty is not measured by the tonnage of stone which it has moved about, but by compensatory equilibriums. The difficulties on which the certitudes inspired by integers or fractional numbers has come to grief could not be surmounted except at the heart of a new effort of the imaginative faculty, the creator of new symbols, the explorer of a new field of certitude. In this new society images will evolve different from and almost opposed to those inspired by weight and mass, though the latter will still reign in the immense bas-reliefs sculpted by the Sassanidae on the flanks of mountains and alongside the tombs excavated by the Achemenides whose throne they have occupied.

II. But the discovery of the syllogism and its application to demonstration is more a termination than a beginning. Ionian mathematics was admirably continued in countries otherwise submitted to Oriental influences. As for the Greek city, destined to be enlarged by Rome, intelligence no longer spreads outward from it and knowledge stagnates within it. The pride of having so well mastered the highest function of reason now attempts to invoke this reason on every occasion and to refer all to it. The necessity for experiment has been forgotten. Within restricted republics the art of persuasion produces the best of laws. But the wisdom thus tested does not aid them to conceive of humanity as a whole, and this is because they do not sufficiently concern themselves with locating humanity in relation to things. Society may soften the lot of the slave, but slavery, continued in principle, foreshadows its most brutal excesses. Aristotle, indeed, returns to a more just evaluation of concrete things; but this learned teacher of the conqueror of Asia will not prevail over Plato, from whom Plotinus will relearn his lessons. The city of philosophers accomplishes in a dream of ideas what Plato and Plotinus cannot impose on material and circumstantial interests.

The preoccupations that deal with numbers are not excluded from those interests which Greece devotes to relations. But they remain on the surface of the arts. Numeration loses in Greece the high pertinency which the Mesopotamian experience had placed on it. In the Roman period, it returns to a primitivism more appropriate to the stylization of epigraphy than to a lively interest in arithmetic. Never up to that time had a republic been more powerful than this one on the hills bordering on the Tiber were plebs and patricians unite under the laws of the praetors. Yet, probably, never had the power of a conquering state been so sterile in the realm of technical ingenuity. The Romans are not duped by words, but they cease to discover the concepts which master things. All is made to return to the emotive. Structures of the imagined are reversed from abstract to concrete, and pursue in things the operative progress on which Lucretius felt that he could no longer count.

This is because, beyond the abstraction of numbers and the relations of forces and magnitudes, humanity had to confront a new difficulty, one less easy to catalogue and to condense: namely, that of the creative reality of the times. At first insidiously, minds and spirits too exclusively caught up in the logical word (*verbum*) meet with confusion. Then, at a new cost, the importance of pain and suffering is again revealed. Thus, from reflection on efforts which have things more than men as their object, philosophical nominalisms become the adequate expression. Europe, the impoverished heir of Antiquity, animated by a religion which opens the door for the restless effluvia of the Orient to blow in upon it, now measures by the abundance and the diversity of the goods which a continental commerce brings to it from China by way of Byzantium or the Arabian empires the deficiencies of its techniques and the relativity of its culture.

Christianity, sufficiently assured of its beliefs not to feel any further need to adopt new gods, is also conscious enough of its task to estimate the price of the Oriental splendors reported by its travelers, its crusaders, several of its popes, and the last of the Hohenstaufen. The Roman empire had plenty of active *negociatores,* traders, to the immense warehouses of Delos. It had, indeed, counted overmuch on the spoils and plunders whose brutal administration its proconsuls all too readily learned. When Rome purchased, it was with conquered gold. Europe itself, in order to buy, had to sell its Slavs or its produce. Thus Europe becomes concerned to appropriate all possible methods capable of bringing nature to a workable state.

The scientific spirit thus rediscovers how to quicken energy within the tedium of time, no longer indifferent and empty, like the cycle recommencing in Platonic times, but creative by a rational assimilation of the unknown.

Even mathematics is affected by the change. China had prefered an instrument with a lever to the scale on two levels, fitted only for measuring discontinuous weights. On the Chinese instrument, a runner slides along a lengthened arm, balancing the weight suspended on a short arm. The West learns to make use of this Oriental scales, called Roman because it came to Rome later by way of Byzantium. From this method the West will draw a lesson on measuring the relations of mass according to the continuity of a line. To bring the two methods together is to pose the problem which preoccupies Cartesian geometry. Arab experimentation draws incomplete lessons from Oriental pragmatism and from Occidental systematics, and transmits them to Europe after attempting their conjunction. Thus, by means of trade with Eastern luxury, Europe is furnished with a sketch of the scientific method.

Let us note, too, that the finding of guide-marks for distances such as travelers practiced on the desert, sleeping during the full sun of day to guide themselves at night by the polar star, involved the use of trigonometry. The representation which resulted, combined with maps on the orthogonal, or right-angled, and equatorial projection used by sailors navigating by the sun and drawing their barks up on beaches when night falls, prepared the geometric evidence for the roundness of the earth. Finally and especially, it was useless for Paracelsus to claim to have reconstructed several chemistries by himself, notably that of the pharmacopoeia of mineral salts. Nor had he made a collection of obscure experiments carried out in his country. Having visited the Ottoman capital, without daring to admit it, he had found there certain secrets which China had perfected centuries earlier.

This great gathering of data, the list of which could be greatly prolonged, prepares the way for the scientific renewal of the century of enlightenment. One after another, these data supply the objects and the names necessary to the experimental spirit; and gathered together, they revive the demonstrative spirit by reintroducing the irrational into it. In both cases, these data impart their value to substantive nouns, and prepare the elaboration of the indispensible nomenclatures for the imminent progresses of the physical sciences.

III. The experimentation with reasons and things developed in the course of what, from the Occidental point of view, is known as Antiquity, and the Middle Ages would not have sufficed to account for the rise of modern science had not the correlations between causality and chance been also mastered. In this area, bourgeois society turned out to be the initiator. For in it are prefigured the axioms and postulates which the mind at work feels, conceives, and expresses.

Toward the very moment when the last great trials for witchcraft are being carried on, heated battles are springing up against a judicial system long out of date. The feeling which had put up with autos-da-fé for a long time, and with preliminary and preparatory tortures, begins to refuse its consent when so many promises of abundance are beginning to be available in the daily scheme of living. Voltaire said of the battles which he led against fanaticisms that they were his best work. He was not alone in these. When victory was won in this great debate, when each case, if it was a criminal case, ceased to be treated with the cruel procedures so long reserved for them; when now they rely on civil procedures alone; when, to use the old phrase, all are civilized, the honor for this goes to Beccaria for defining the new principles of a genuine justice. Each accused, he said, must be presumed innocent; each guilty one is no less a man. The inquiry must seek with greater care the proofs for an accusation. It becomes a commonplace to think that nothing happens, even conduct which demands sentencing, which does not arise from quite human reasons which the language must explain clearly, beginning with the briefs submitted for the argument.

Furthermore, the civil as well as the criminal law will no longer be held good simply because it is the custom. An assembly will be empowered to repeal or to create by its vote, the assembly itself an issue of the suffrage. Monarchies had suffered by being of elective origin; Poland was dying of it. The Church itself had not ceased having recourse to it for the selection of its highest dignitary. Nevertheless, the procedure here was not too clear. Being an expression of an act of faith inspired by the Holy Spirit, it could not arrive at a sure decision without unanimity. If this chanced to be lacking, the least numerous party could lay claim to being the most authentic. The canons accorded authority to that part of the electoral body which they qualified not as the most numerous but as made up of the best. Many schisms resulted therefrom. In the course of one of them, a monk had inventoried all the possible ways by which a false pope could be invested. This task was a forerunner of the calculus of combinations. When the modern parliamentary state is set up, it holds to a simple majority for its common decisions; the two-thirds decision is reserved for important cases. But quantity alone enters into question; and each elector is worth any other. There is something arbitrary about this way of doing things which is challenged by the exacting demands of the theory of probabilities. Mathematicians wonder about its legitimacy, Condorcet disputes it, and Tocqueville will also speak of the tyranny of the majority. Perhaps Marx felt the justice of these critics when he referred authority to the will of the great masses. But it finally stands accepted that law, like power, must submit to the test of the ballot-box.

As chance had been banned from feudal societies where all had to be referred to custom, the prince, or even God, as in the trial by duel, so to the same degree do we accomodate ourselves to the customs of the modern era. Concerning these customs, bourgeois theoreticians will say that the common condition would be one of immobility and quietism if the appeal of profit did not intervene to keep all in motion. But the economics of competition especially, supported by the rapidly disrupting abundance of colonial commerce, does not flourish well except in a milieu of men who feel themselves equal in rights, and equally authorized to be entrepreneurs. Among them we must permit the unknowable yet rational destiny to operate its choices. Before it had expressed itself in works and institutions, the social structure had begun by itself to sketch out what science will inscribe in its postulates of its mechanistic causalities and its calculations on chance.

The evolution of active collectivities in Europe, motivated by a system hidden beneath the swarming events which had disturbed it since the conquest of the great oceans and the rise of commerce therefrom, inspired Pascal and Newton, Laplace, Lagrange and Gauss. One of them remains modest and attributes his findings to some other beside himself, or another draws boldness from the spirit of the times to defy God. But we recall the uneasiness that Pascal felt at being the interpreter, compelled by the realities which he feared. Son of an upright administrator — and there were many of such at that period — he is, as it were, drawn despite himself into the mercantile movement whose positive immorality arouses the Puritan spirit and the Jansenist predestination, after it has turned many merchants to mathematics, especially in Holland and in that England which will make Newton director of the Mint. A man of scruples, Pascal, after replying to the libertine Méré by inventing the theory of games of chance, reassures his faith by using the wager for apologetic ends.[2] The very depth of his emotion instructs us on the intensity of the power which things, by the intervention of the social, can bring to bear on the most honest conscience.

IV. Having acquired the intellectual means for its new progresses, humanity enters upon the last phase of its maturation. It presents this innovation, that the most perfect brains and the best educated have attained an unsurpassable degree of organization. History since then is no longer in essence made up of the qualitative progresses of

2. A reference to Pascal's famous 'wager' on faith, that if one believes and is wrong, he loses nothing, but if right, he gains all.

an elite, but of the quantitative increase in the number of members who comprise it and who tend to become as numerous as humanity itself. The result is a revolution in the order of invention in which the mechanistic principle prevails over that of refinement, as in the order of language where nominalism wins out over the sharpened tool of logic.

When weight, space, time, causality, theories of combinations and probability have been grasped in their abstract certitudes, man can believe that he holds dominion over his world. In fact, he was acceding to its objective conditionings, and today's reality is more grandiose and less simple than the enlightened spirits of the 17th century could imagine. Even as the scientist, however skillful at managing his concepts, remains dependent on cerebral functions acting according to natural laws, so Occidental societies which no longer fear their afflictions are subject to machines which deliver them from pain, and to words which they imagine they have transcended.

Let us return to that epoch in Europe when it so admired the products that it was receiving from elsewhere that it imitated them by intensifying their mystery. Most of these objects, even those of distant origin, are stripped of their sacred quality, but the value recognized in those most sought after remains that of a certain secret. Too long a time has passed since men first knew how to spin, weave, shape vases, and smelt metals for them not to find such tested processes quite natural. Yet the exceptional quality of the Chinese bronzes or its ceramics or those of Persia is still sometimes attributed to a strange if not suspect knowledge, a knowledge still more held in awe if the products are healing products or elixirs of long life, like spices and kohl. But only distance or scruple keeps the fable or the tale alive; and near the spots where the actual work is done, everyone knows that the admirable successes are due to some turn of the skilled hand, or thanks to some entirely natural gift, or to some incomprehensible but very human talent. Good or bad workers are judged without concern for the religious spirit. Only art, though it, too, is secularized, remains subjective.

The ancient works, the commentaries of the Arabian manuals, in the face of a perfect object, show an admiration for what it is, for what it contains, for the stages it has gone through under the guidance of the master who made it. They still do not know how to analyze the intrinsic process by which it might be realized. As we approach the century of enlightenment, the attitude shifts. Up to then, no doubt, the methods of work in the field or in the artisan's shop had profitted by small improvements, but the distaff, the profession of weaving, the potter's wheel or the smelting furnace had not changed in nature since archaic, prehistoric times. It was recognized that some products were better or more successful than others, but it was still a saying that only the bad workman blames his tools. The encyclopedists abandon this point of view. They still cover the inimitable master worker with praise, but also the inventor in his workshop; and to describe such a one, they select the best equipped shop they know or some imagined model shop where they reassemble the best borrowed instruments from the several shops visited. Interest shifts from the product to production. This modification does not affect the admiration granted the painters or sculptors, but it does a great deal affect that only recently given the weaver or the blacksmith. The words artist and artisan, up till then so often confused that Leonardo da Vinci sometimes employs one when we expect to hear the other, are now definitely distinguished. The word artist is reserved for work whose procedures escape exact analysis; but artisan is employed when thought spent on the instruments reveals that it is possible to improve them mechanically.

The inventor of the flying shuttle or the spinning frame, or of smelting with charcoal or puddling is not a scientist in the sense that he finds it necessary to resolve the diophantian equations before he can succeed.[3] This holds for all those who gave their names to the first machines. Many of these innovations occurred in Europe only, and not in Asia, which had never conceived of Greek demonstration nor of Cartesian mathematics. The first mechanics owe their advent to a closer attention directed toward the immemorial gestures of the weaver or spinner, or to what is being accomplished in the furnace or the crucible. The experimental mind finds its field of application inside the frontiers defined by mechanical theory. Nevertheless, society is soon much more changed by this than at first appeared. The direct responsibility of heads of families to relatives exclusively atomizes activity, and makes the general enrichment a function of the law of averages. The parliamentary state is a better interpreter than a king of this political dislocation brought about by groupings of multiplied interests, sometimes working together, sometimes in opposition.

3. See footnote 1, p. 54.

Scientific work is no less divided, and specialized branches venture into a thousand areas which rational mechanics will not be able to pull together again. Mathematics, whose certitudes have for so many centuries been in advance of all others, is now beginning to be forced to respond to the needs of experimentation. If the various branches of mathematics attempt to find the central ground of their legitimacy, the axiomatics fail them, or their effect is even opposed. The list of irreducibles lengthens, and incompatible geometries are side by side. True, they still reason on masses, spaces, and time, but at a depth which baffles common sense. The syllogism maintains its power, but no longer rules as master. It remains the indispensible instrument of all scientific reasoning, but with the status of a faithful servant. The ordinary public would mistrust what is held as certain by the chief thinkers of the new knowledge if it were not that impressive technological applications gave evidence of the results of its incomprehensible principles. The experimental event rules the world of certitudes. The technological products that come from the new science are sufficient to convince the public of the legitimacy of conceptual operations, whose pure description would baffle common sense, even though they are the rigorous result of an active logic.

Goethe said: 'All that is external is internal'. The world in his time seems to be turning inward, and his philosophical contemporaries went so far as to confuse the order of things with that of the mind. Nevertheless, even if the most liberal writers believed that they could affirm that there was no obstacle that reason was not prepared to conquer, reason will stumble over its own irrationals, and will surmount this hurdle only by turning to an arithmetic of experience; that is, to an experimentation too hastily despised by the idealism of Kant's successors.

The fact is, experimentation, progressively freed from the illusions of desire, becomes the more imperative as it the more often challenges common sense. The nature of number proves beyond grasp. Man had once been able to believe that in the end he would find a general law on the appearance of first numbers, factors of all the others, the smallest of which had very anciently been each one the object of particular historic inventions. But, aside from a few strong exceptions, they can scarcely be inventoried by an arithmetic of probability. And the problem is so disconcerting that neither does its opposite appear to be any more demonstrable. Furthermore, had the above law existed, it would not have elucidated the mystery: integers compose only one group among many. On each of these occasions, it is not pure deduction but a meditation on experience which gives mathematics its new, unforeseeable dimensions. Knowledge is won at the heart of the most perfect abstraction as it is in the uncertain and commonplace realm of the historic event. Nothing escapes the unknown empire of things, whose future none dares today to predict.

It is because mathematics applies only to systems of unity imposed by experience that physicists were able to turn elsewhere to such great profit. They have created a new language within the common languages, and, though it has not yet reached a perfect rationality, a language, nevertheless, whose universal usefulness is guaranteed only by its experimental reliability. It springs into birth suddenly, within a few years, toward the period when demonstration increases its rigor by identifying its proper objects. Chemistry next classifies molecules by naming them according to the atomic composition. Like chemistry, physics, returning to its original ideography which once had to be abandoned so that the syllogism might be discovered, now defines its new unities by the names of those who participated in their discovery. This new system of vocabulary opens up infinite possibilities for the formation of words, potentially more numerous than they ever were in the rudimentary languages which had not a sufficient number of vocables to permit the organization of their meaning. In this piling up of new words they do not entirely refuse to borrow from popular speech; but the number of words, especially of ordinary verbs, drawn by scientific works from all the national ways of speaking is relatively small. This number is also so rigorously reduced that only at sensitive points do the words demand a glossary as demanding as it is extensive, a syntax as imperious as it is limited. Thus all men of any culture of whatever sort are permitted to translate with increasing exactitude this experimentation with what is. No other linguistic revolution is comparable to this one in its extent.

Among these nomenclatures of multiplied possibilities we must find a special place for those of biology. In the last two or three centuries we have rediscovered Aristotle's advice. We seek for systems. The best of these are found by assuring classifications by reference to what concerns reproduction, that is to say, within the functional order whose ultimate manifestations have constituted nature's most direct incentive to man's reflection. But, beginning there, knowledge does not travel in the senses or in the prolonging of the simplifications which had led to the demonstrative syllogism, but in reverse, and toward the unfathomable depths of living realities.

In all the sciences, the importance commanded by words which arbitrarily name the thousand bonds which link the mind of the scientist to what is produced by his inventions, serves to widen the chasm which separates the ordinary man from areas of knowledge so specialized that they are incomprehensible even to each other. But this is not a sign of an evasion on the part of the common man outside of the coercion of things. Rather, it is more appropriate to speak of an increase of dependence.

Now, what is said and discovered in the laboratories is soon translated into the installation of factories, so much so that all modern society is changed, progresses, branches out, and as a consequence is interlinked with the scientific world which that society initiated. In the technological history of ancient and medieval centuries we can read a point by point correspondence between certain years, certain months and sometimes even days with what is produced in a hundred centers of research and production. Today, scientific knowledge is a distribution of brains now living a hundred times more numerous than there are in all the history of remembered names.

This science is the mother of a manufacturing industry of objects which transform all life, and it is no longer legitimate to speak of the society or a society as one could do even half a century ago. Society is constituted above and apart from a rural mass itself proportionately reduced and withdrawn from its old habits, an infinitely complex system of specific and correlative groups whose dynamics and arrangement are the same as that of the analyzed and exploited realities of our time.

Men are not more free in this society. They are wiser in it only if they are considered as a whole. For, if we judge by the most active encouragers of research, there are almost as many scientific worlds as there are great specialists. It is no longer an integrated society or a whole social class which prescribes the proper place for inspiring hypotheses or whose structures pre-present the postulates and axiomatics. Modern cerebral correlations are established in small teams, each a coherent unit, yet with a mutual understanding that their disciplines are neighbors, and that they are composed of workers belonging to not too distant generations. Finally, their dialogues and confrontations give expression to the structural realities by establishing the vocabulary, the syntax, and the principles of the discoveries, inventions, and applications which account for the enlargements and accelerations of progress. Man no longer questions oracles and sybils; he depends much less on priestly interpreters. But nature still dictates its laws, even amid the uproar of his great laboring machines and the flickering of the control boards by which advanced and specialized competencies observe what is the material of their discussion. Those who find themselves thus placed at these advanced research posts are the first to listen and comprehend. The engineers, factory workers, those who make use of the machines, are not slow to be informed in some degree on what is thus directed. Nothing entirely escapes this new submissiveness.

Throughout this violent mutation, esthetics is thrown off course. Sensitivity anticipates this immense and secret infiltration of things into the very heart of humanity. The great poets try their hand at informing us. The plastic artists warn us that now there is no time to take pleasure in what one sees, when what is being done already is acting obscurely on us and shaping us to unfathomable realities.

In this situation, all leads to, all forces, the search for an evasion: modern man wants to be mobile, ready to escape from his dwelling place and his situation. Now, toward the moment when one might have hoped that industrialization would put within the means of civilized peoples a level of life which the masses of their ancestors never dared dream of, it is no longer the level which counts but its continuous elevation. Thrust outside his myths by the reality which penetrates them, the Occidental looks his fear in the face. But he does not know its name, but only the implements, the price, and the danger.

Everyone obscurely recognizes that this uneasiness and this threat are the effect of a maladaptation of the collective structures to the body of knowledge and procedures which these structures themselves gave birth to. To believe that man has no recourse would be to admit that he is no longer man, even while his behavior and his evolution remain, if not what history makes them, at least what the constant functions of his historicity promise him they will become.

Nature, for the man of today, is not only the familiar landscapes which surround him, the rigorous demands of their seasonal horizons of toil, the seductive beginnings of their springs, with which the poets up to Mallarmé have enchanted him. It is no longer only cities whose modernity Baudelaire so violently felt. It is also an ensemble of obscure realities known only by arbitrary names, given them by the ever more numerous scientists, and the strange machines whose every detail of construction and control isolates factories and their users within the narrow frame of a rigorously demanded attention.

Innumerable new dimensions are added to the length, breadth and height of our former perspectives; and each finds himself therein in a particular situation different from that of his neighbor. The insularity to which we are thus reduced makes it the more imperative that humanity be effectively realized as a harmonious whole, according to the necessary unity on which all our happiness is founded.

PART IV

Essential history

9. Inspired societies

I. History, considered as an evolution produced by the function of historicity, may be summed up in categories or models of which the most broadly inclusive, as it relates to the genesis of intelligence, is also the simplest. This classification admits of three phases. Of the last two of these, one precedes and the other follows the mastery of the operative inductive. This second of the three, infinitely longer than the third, extends from protohistory to the scientific revolution which will substitute the technological for technique. It is also much shorter than another one, the first, which stretches from the homonoids to *homo sapiens.* Before this second phase, that is, the human adventure is entirely guided by nature, which remains the exclusive mistress of the events that are produced. In the third phase, which is only since some decennia, man finds his place in relation to the machines of his laboratories and his factories, through which he views life to find a world of skillful contrivances imposed on the landscapes of our older poetics. In the second phase — that is, during that period to which the usual name of history is most appropriately applied — humanity discovers itself in the movements, modifications, and managements of societies. It is no longer exclusively the slave of things; and it is not yet rationalized by the laws which it discovers within things. Humanity then searches itself and makes up its mind in its collective tentatives; and is inspired by what it sees. It is divided into many regional areas which do not know one another and are distrustful of others, recoil from one another, or are drawn to one another, intercommunicate, and become distinct. In this second phase, one may discover an infinity of distinctive types, out of which four are to be retained as major because they appear to amount to simple models within which all the others may be included.

Each of these four is distinguished by a certain way of uniting reason with experience under the strong or feeble pressure of events of an internal or external origin. For savages, who come under the first model, all is adjusted within a viable equilibrium for which emotion supplies the means and happiness the goal. The second model is offered by Central America, where small, rigid empires secrete an arithmetic most remarkable yet almost useless. The third model unites India and Indochina with an immense China, so often invaded, destroyed and rebuilt, a country swarming with admirable workshops which invent everything except the syllogism and demonstration. Finally, there is the Occident, the theatre of the fourth model, with many capital cities, rivals of one another, nearly all having been forced to rebuild on their ruins, yet each having also to grant to some other the primacy which finally Europe as a whole grasps — in short, the liveliest branching-off in history. Here modern science is built, endures, and unfolds.

The so-called primitive societies have covered the entire depth of their historical duration without knowing a history. Shielded by their isolated situation from the movements of the rest of the world, in territories rich enough and broad enough to prevent conflict from causing any immediate destructions, they have found varying solutions, more complementary than opposed, to the problem of their internal harmony. Their neighbors or their wars were not such as to bring about radical changes in the essential modalities of representations as inspired by the original emotivity. Prolonging in their customs certain natural regulations, they have tended to perfect their way of existing rather than to introduce the differential process of their own destruction. Their dialectic remains implicit in nature.

The activity of primitive societies is obviously quite different from that of the most socialized of the vertebrate animals, and even less resembles that of insects. Their organization is neither a rudimentary ecological one, that is, built on simple hierarchies, as among the animals; nor is it absolutely fixed in a highly organized but blind economy, as among insects. Since their skills are not innate, they must be relearned with each generation. In their world of magic, a spontaneous dynamism prolongs their elaborated harmonies, though they are sensitive to a world beyond. Their men, however, are little beyond being prisoners of instinctive determinisms; but since they have not known sufficient pressures of contradictory fortunes, they have not disentangled effects from chance. The supernatural, more perceived than conceived, is embodied in an animism which forces them to seek culprits much more than causes for the ills of mankind. The sky is a life everywhere throbbing and subject to being irritated. Their calendar is that of fauna and flora; its periodicity is that of fecundations. Its economy is that of an equilibrium found between pain, the price paid for apprenticeships that teach them how to avoid it, and pleasure, the common reference for measures of value.

Logic skims over things and finds its full unfolding in the power to imagine. The pleasure of expression, made of subtle distinctions at the heart of immediate perceptions, confers a sacred character on what must be conjoined and what must be excluded. Not knowing how to assign a rightful share to chance, the established legitimacy is admirably ordered, but its reasons are less translated into objective syntaxes than lived according to necessities intimately felt. The axiomatic of arithmetic, the relativity of mass, and the postulates of space are, like the didactic of history, implicit. Apparently absent from what is seen or done, these hide their perfection in the organic depth of what justifies customs.

These primitive societies are without doubt a kind of image of what the paleolithic and the first neolithic ones were like. They may even be the residual witnesses of such. No doubt they offer the appearance of being such because they have traveled through the millenia of human experience less rapidly, and at the cost of contingent setbacks.

In Central America and Peru, where the second type of human branching-off was still living in the pre-Columbian era, certain of the secret data which animated the savage villages might be seen objectified in the cities they built. Princes and priests suggest by the elevation of castles and temples the height of the heavens which the earth can no longer enclose. Through the openings in the stone observatories, they study the stars which define time with a precision far superior to that of the vegetative seasons, over which they now recognize the heavenly control. The protecting or menacing gods are also figures, and numbers give rise to endless calculations. Numerous votive offerings, minutely sculptured, consecrate the most remarkable among them. To combine the different calendars without error, some handed down in tradition, others deduced from new and more profound observations, commands the devotion of priests specializing in arithmetic calculations. In the service of the sacred, they have built artificial mountains, as it were, by the piling up of blocks of stones, mountains whose least proportions are the expression of rigorous calculations. The lofty steps of the rigid pyramids

are scaled by zigzag courses of plumed ceremonial processions, where
the windings on the side of the slopes evoke the plumed serpent, a
sacred monster creeping up to reach to the last level where the lower
door of the temple is opened. Here is the celestial summit of a reality
from which all abundance is awaited. Religion and arithmetic,
astronomy and esthetics, all are united in these monuments, where
the weight of things and the pertinence of numbers combine to
pledge obedience to the masters of the work, the communal image of
nature imitated in its discovered components, and the society in its
invented order.

Nevertheless, multiplication remains unknown in the Mayan
mathematics even though very large numbers are treated with accuracy, by means of tables of addition written in a numeration of
position. If the art of multiplying is a conscious expression of
implicit modalities in the system of relationships, again it is necessary
that historic shocks force their reconsideration time and again. The
Amerindian cultures were not brought to such reconsideration by the
violence of primitive invasions comparable to those which jolted the
cities situated at the crossroads of three continents in the Ancient
World, invasions which periodically thrust their highly developed
agricultural civilizations back to the elementary. The astonishing
cultures of Central America, more evolved than those of the continent around them, had not sufficiently drawn on the most common
knowledge of the villages above which they rose. The rigidity of
political structures, so stupifying in the Inca Empire, prevented their
rejuvenation, because of their return to the dominant classes from
which their logic reached its depth. The effect of history is strongly
felt, but a history confined to one meaning only, bringing to awareness the most elementary system of architectural beauty rather than
the efficiency of operative expressions. The rapture of knowing how
to count well rather than the part arithmetic can play in action on
reality is what decides the power or the humiliation of States. At the
end of the confrontation of two rival cities, the victory of Copan was
not challenged, though Palenque, the loser, was itself already on the
way to greater discoveries. For there, thanks to a genuine appreciation of the small variations within lunar behavior, they had already
learned how to write with an apparently unsurpassable simplicity,
and in terms with the heavenly movements, the very large number
which names the original date of the world.

But these advances in knowledge, however admirable they may
have been, remain sterilized by their sacred functions. The too exact

lengths of the month and the year do not allow a division of each into small whole factors nor an exact relation of the one to the other. Their study of such does not result in the totality of arithmetic operations except on the condition that they are not treated as messages from the absolute. The excess of reverence bestowed on them is a type of allomorphy, a variant on the form of mathematical progress. Societies which practice such are doomed to involution. Disoriented by the coming of the Spanish conquerors, they will be too easily destroyed by them.

The third type of evolution is that of the extreme Orient. On a territory as vast as a continent, more fertile than any other over immense surfaces, China has assembled a population with one destiny, conformed to one culture, whose density has varied greatly, though always strongest in the most habitable zones. This consolidating factor has not saved China from internal divisions, but it has allowed her to surmount them. Her mountainous frontiers guide migrations according to the whims of their geologic structure. They enclose an extent so great that the ocean attracts China less to its great crossing than to a coastal trade toward the archipelagoes. Toward the south, to which the relief and the rivers lead, the rich luxuriance of the tropics opens up zones to her influences, though not wholly surrendered to servitude. On the contrary, the northern steppes are only gateways to a long commerce by caravan with the Occident. When periods of rain revive the steppes, the inhabitants pour out invading hordes upon China, their overrich neighbor. Several such have thrown themselves upon a country so tempting, and have been able to impose their mastery upon it, but not to challenge its culture. History is harassed by events, but not to the point of excluding an astonishing fidelity to origins that are magnificent and, as if from the outset, unsurpassable.

The natural wealth of China is not the kind that enfeebles energies and makes prevision useless. A climate of fixed seasons, abundant though threatening waters, force a constant effort. There the morale, like the medicine, is made infinitely precise. An ingenuity without peer, multiplied by the size of the country, makes China a precocious paradise of techniques and of the nominalisms inspired by them. A subtle intelligence excels there in all areas of the practical; a refined agriculture which the encyclopedists and even Liebig could still admire, and workshops envied and imitated elsewhere with centuries of delay. Ingenuity succeeds there as much in the adjustment of delicate mechanisms as in the discoveries in pharmacopoeia whose elaborations command centuries of attention, or in making use of ingenious arithmetics and the measuring of time from the nocturnal skies.

And yet this great nation, object of long admiration, justifying the country's own belief that it was the center of the world's gravity, was not the place where modern science blossomed. It was not that the elements were lacking. It would have been sufficient to make small modifications of innumerable procedures, as abstract as concrete, for the Chinese to have organized all into a systematic and rigorous body of logic. But this small matter makes the difference between the highest wisdom and the demonstrative syllogism, between the usefulness of performances and an accomplished operative structure.

Arithmetic was already much too well evolved in ancient China for it to retain still the marks of its origin, but we know the importance which family relationships hold there. The veneration for antecedents, the cult of ancestors, is ruled by a ritual so elaborate that the names of branches count more than their genetic reality. They are strictly related to language, to which they provide the keys, that is, the signs which in this originally pictographic system play the role of our alphabets in the classifications of dictionaries. This extreme reference to written significance has as a corollary that it fixes not only the duration of a grief in terms of ancestry, but also the modalities for the transmission of the secrets of manufacturing and of estates. It inspires the civil laws, making each man responsible for what another of the same name does, even if he be an entire stranger. It decides the organization of the State. The wise men have uniformly placed the emphasis on these customs and rites with which society appeared to identify. Thus it cannot be said that the common origin has been forgotten here. Indeed, its persistance implies that in China events have not had that radical and transforming effect of opposing transcendence to immanence by leading each experience with historicity to its extreme limit, nor even to that point of no return beyond which a culture collapses entirely to give place to some completely new one.

The movements of social classes were not such that their structures were periodically abolished. A certain constancy of tradition, translated into the recommendations of the wise men to maintain measure in all things, treats the excessive as an evil, but imposes no change at all upon gods so tolerant that they accept any dogma provided that it accomodates itself to the piety centered around the altars of the ancestors. The encyclopedists who rejoiced at the failure of the Jesuits in the celestial empire might actually, though they did not at all suspect it, have found themselves defending an element in Christianity, also, like China, the inheritor of millenia of experience. For Christianity even then was being forced to rid itself of certain cramping structures of kinship whose arithmetic spirit could not be deduced to its perfect abstraction except by renouncing these same family structures as an institution.[1]

Though the Jesuit fathers were appreciated at Pekin as astronomers and mathematicians, they were nevertheless unable to accomodate the Chinese family order to the Roman Catholic rites. Their clearest success appears to have been to suggest the relativity of sacred truths by the introduction of Confucius to Europe. The pope, also, by sanctioning their defeat, played into the hands of the bourgeois spirit, which was soon to become infinitely corrosive by the business transactions it inspired, supported in time by gun-boats and expeditionary forces. The most anciently coherent of cultures will confront its apocalypse there, and will not be reborn to a modern science except amid its own debris.

China's elementary system of expression was preserved with its customs. It seduced foreign dynasties and prevented them from changing anything. There was nothing to force a total reconstruction of the relation of signs to what they represented; the need for the syllogism never made itself felt. This immense country, made attractive by its active wealth, and arrived at being that of a single people,

---

1. The obscurity of these last sentences demanded some assistance, and Ch. Morazé obliged with the following comment (letter of Feb. 10, 1971): 'We have noted that the orders of relationship may take the form of father, mother and children, or, instead, the totality of ancestors. This second takes into consideration the two parents, four grandparents, eight great-grandparents, etc., that is to say, indicates ancestry by a coherent numeration.

'This guide-mark reveals the importance of the formulas $N = 2n + 1$ and $N = 2n$, and instructs us in an authentic fundamental truth. At the same time, it attaches unconsciously to numbers a sentimental value, preventing their being treated as absolutely abstract entities. The Christian family, abolishing the cult of ancestors, deprives the number of all sacred character except that which theology accords to the divine identity of $1 = 3$, which is too obviously non-mathematical to hinder the development of rational reasoning. In Christianity, faith and reason thus constitute two distinct domains, and reason thus finds itself freed from all other constraint except the logical.'

In short, the encyclopedists might have seen in the defeat of the Jesuit fathers in China, confronting ancestor worship, the evidence of their own freedom from the same binding tradition.

held faithfully to what had made possible its first amazing success. The regimenting of this conservation of unity retained the value of a basic reference. It joined patience to moderation, and kept alive through all moments of experience the assurance of an unsurpassable success down to the communal foundations; a promise, as it were, in all its details of infinite refinements. The richness of Chinese nominalism is expressed in all that reflects the multiple facets of an ingenuity that nothing discourages. But there is another side to this fecundity; because time in its duration does not call this acquired experience into question, no systematic substitute for it exists.

Admirable as writings by pictograms may be as conveniences to convey meaning by drawings, through widely scattered populations, it nevertheless amounts to an obstacle to certain operational developments. Science in China diminishes with the restoration of the traditional graphics, and rediscovers its luster when oral language prevails. The historic experience here confronts us with a paradox: the spirit of geometry reaches its first perfection not at the heart of a civilization with a pictographic writing, but at the crossroads of those which make use of arbitrary letters to represent systems of sounds nevertheless irreducible. The pertinence of words is relative to images, but words did not arrive at their fullest power except by virtue of resources and complementary functional needs as served by the organs of utterance and of reception to what has been said.[2]

Phonation implies a longer elaboration of signification less immediately in general use. It best exploits the mysterious virtues of a creative time duration. Like the tragic event, it forces a reconsideration to the very foundation of the data which habit takes for granted. Again, it is not sufficient that its logical substratum be discovered. Even in India, where songs, poetry, and treatises are the object of such delicate and elaborated notations that philology selects India for its oldest area of work, there was no greater success toward arriving at that demonstration which implies that the historicity of sentences uttered be confronted with the morphology of drawing.

In India one finds, inversely oriented to the Chinese disposition of sign and sound, a method of making the concept prevail in the object, and the oral in the language. This fact suggests a com-

2. The eye explores space, the ear retains time and its rhythm, and the two in combination refer discourse to the formal components of a logic both rational and experimental. Note from Ch. Morazé, Feb. 10, 1971.

plementary situation that helps explain why at the contact of these two systems in southeast Asia, it was there that there arose the most ancient usage of our own figures for a free numeration of position. We are justified in assuming that the immense geographic whole extending from the Persian gulf to the Chinese sea might have been capable one day of knowing the miraculous hour which spelled the glory of Greece. But the dimensions of the Indian and Chinese subcontinents, where these two equally necessary and complimentary systems were elaborated, were, like the Indo-Chinese peninsula between them, too immoderate for doubt to arise and for dialectic to become so soon evident. It has been well established that in the transition from Hinduism to Buddhism something occurred similar to what happened in the Occident when the bourgeois developed at the expense of feudalism. But in India it was more by the juxtaposition of different aspirations than by the radical substitution of the one for the other. Finally, toward the era when the Khmer people of Cambodia show promise of emerging, these sea-ocracies were no longer newcomers to the point of being the theatre of this success. When Islam penetrated into India and Indonesia and reached China, it was nourished by ingenious inventions which revived the heritage it had received from Hellenism; and this it returned, enriched, to Europe.

We shall have to await the modern colonial era before Western science, having arrived at an organic corpus and having demonstrated its first technical power, will carry with it the acceptance of the Far Orient. It is the Japanese, locked as they are on their narrow archipelago, fully infused with the lessons of their great neighbor, but destined to the conditionings and the instructions of the sea and its traffic, who will undergo the most rapid conversion. The Chinese awakening will be later. But since this ancient culture has given, if not the first example in the world, at least the most impressive and most steadfast one of experimentation, and since it failed to discover demonstration only because of its faithfulness to a concrete nominalism such as has made modern experimental science so important, we may expect to be surprised by the amplitude of what it will produce in the order of knowledge and its technologies.

II. There remains now the consideration of the last of the four great types of historic evolution. This is located between the Indus and the Atlantic. It appears that it has gone through all the recognized phases of the other three branches, but without being granted the leisure to enjoy any of the others. At the crossroads of three continents and at the point of observation which gave them their names, territories considerably varied and much smaller than India or China are cut up by murderous frontiers which generate events quite capable of a total destruction. There a thousand paganisms and at least three great monotheisms have been elaborated. The profound violence of a history made up of successive uprootings reunites this region of battle fields, where so many gods and so many men have died, into an evolutive whole, in which exact knowledge might be organized and might grow. There every evolutive cycle is a total cycle; and each cultural preponderance is affirmed only to disappear. The heat of conflicts here makes maturations more prompt than in Central America, and regenerations livelier than in China. The process of relay stages is here marked by a unique efficiency; and this is pursued to the point that finally operative reasonings and the deeds of workers combine to create, in the end, the scientific society.

The great periods of historic evolution are here unrolled in violent oppositions, between Asia and Africa. Afro-Asia and Europe, Judaism and Christianity, Christendom and Islam, spread in areas confined by isthmuses and mountain ranges, peninsulas and archipelagoes. Here each overthrow of cultures takes on a total character; and it is precisely the excessive character of so many involvements that makes for the unity of this theatre. This statement is confirmed by what it has suggested to philologists. In the presence of so many and such different languages and alphabets, with each branch borrowing the elements of its innovations from the maturity of a preceding one, it was easy to believe in the existence of an original common culture. The great epochs here unfold by contrasts, each excelling in particular splendors so original in their style that each renders its ancestors or its rivals incomprehensible, until the time arrives when the universalism of syntax and of a scientific vocabulary is conceived.

Between Egypt and Babylon one finds the same types of agreements and discords as between the Aztecs and the Mayas, especially in numerical writing or the calendar; but, as in China, we observe incessant returns to elementary common traditions, returns the more easily conceived as each great illustration finds its foothold in a new place and a new people. This process, stemming from the biological, is also that of representations. Religions of Israel, Christianity, or Islam appeal to the same original prophets, syncretic figures, with traits borrowed as well as reinterpreted in the flame and blood of conflicts. Rivalries and competitions are not entered on here, as in

Mayan America, out of the frenzy imparted by the beautiful arithmetic of great numbers, but by physical destructions. The monotheism of the burning steppes exalts Abel only by cursing Cain, the man of a fruitful agriculture. And the undeserved fate which makes wealth a crime and robbery a virtue also substitutes Jacob for Esau.

So many contradictions of earthly experience can only be defended by referring the human event to a supreme and transcendent justice, a jealous God so necessary to his own that he makes fanatics of them. From these profound vicissitudes, and because of their unendurable excesses, the notion of sovereign and unique perfection is drawn. Through the violence of conflicts of interest, the aspiration for the transcendent accelerates the process of the evolution of the myth. This it does in the amazing region of confluences where experiments so often renewed by language discover the postulates of demonstration. All, then, that has since been shown to be necessary to the progress of history and science falls into place at the arrival of that period whose overall significance has been for centuries recognized under the single denomination of Antiquity.

Antiquity is not a unified and single period; it is full of contrasts and draws its meaning from them. When the sphinx or the winged bull with the human head no longer uphold the continental cultures of Africa or Asia, then on the Mediterranean shores the sacred beauty is no longer imaginary but is seen in the actual shores of the coasts, the islands, and the capes. It is then that geometry is developed. Man, his body unmasked, becomes the measure of all things. Protagoras said this much, amid the statues of perfectly proportioned gods. Furthermore, a new way of conceiving civil law, decided by popular assemblies, revaluates ancient family relationships and forces a reconsideration of responsibilities. Thus is born a rationale of causes. The power by which the syllogism finds proof in the order of ideas, gives rise to an awareness of the tragic condition of man at grips with his own history. The principles of the scientific intelligence are recorded in great philosophic systems.

But at the same time a kind of drunkenness seizes upon all thought: believing itself a reflection of an absolute universe, it turns aside from the contingent. The wisdom which defends Phryne and Alcibiades and is enchanted to discover a logic of ideas in the harmony of the body,[3] causes an absorption of the poison of

3. Alcibiades was accused of heresy for using a living model for a statue of a goddess and replied by exhibiting Phryne in her perfection of form. Translator's note.

anthropomorphic idealism, forbidden to the artisans of Africa and Asia. Thus at the foot of the Acropolis, the logistics of numbers which had been borrowed from the Aegean shores regresses. So, when the great Alexander conquers the continent of Asia as far as the Indus, is made a god there and gives a living form to Buddha,[4] the history he is now involved in is not the history of Greece. Instead, it becomes a part of that which, at the cost of centuries, will find its revenge for Troy under the banner of Mohammed, the Victorious.

In fact, it is not enough to make use of the syllogism; one must still proceed well beyond the notions of space to the inventory of words from which the syllogism constructs its pertinent combinations and articulations. Nothing explains why China did not furnish the materials for new inductions when its commerce filled the Mediterranean bazaars, unless it be that a society too blindly logical in its civil judiciary was wholly ruined beyond the possibility of an experimentation that would pierce the shell of a rationalist illusion. It is not toward the East but the West which will accomplish this encounter, after its ancient decadence and far from Ionia, and then less in Rome than on its ruins. The Latins, by introducing a too formal logic into their laws, more easily conquered men than things. Then, drunk with their own success, they become skeptics before their gods and their augurs, and mock the apotheosis of the Emperor Claudius, lover of justice, to pay court to Nero, the mountebank emperor. For a long time Roman citizens will continue to compensate for their vanity by their courage, and will draw pride from their laws to find self-assurance in contempt for what they do not understand. Nevertheless, enclosed in an empire whose breadths like its limits are defined by the resistance of the barbarians, they will not in the end prevail against either their neighbors or their slaves.

Rome had received from the heritage of Babylon and of Ionia what the Greeks had filtered from them. A too exclusive concentration on civic affairs makes their success a kind of allomorphism. The gigantism of its empire renders it less fruitful than the empire of the Chinese Han dynasties. When it flatters itself that it is mistress of Hellenism, it entrenches itself in places where its downfall is being prepared. At the heart of the proud city, in the environs which it had made its own, renewals are no longer keeping pace with the changing

4. The Buddha was not represented in human form in India until the time of Alexander. Translator's note.

world. The imagination of Asia, powerless against the Roman legions, remains more in tune with its own secret needs. Soon, even in the palaces of the Empire, will be felt the pull of emotive representations which neither war nor law nor rhetoric provide. In the city which hated the Orient where so many of its soldiers had perished, the processions of Heliogabalos announce the growing attraction of its vanquished religions. But, between the patrician class and that of the slaves, the body social is no longer renewing itself. All has already begun to decline when Diocletian tries to organize this world in the image of the City whose insidious distress finds no recourse except in a faith imported from distant Jerusalem whose walls and temples had been razed in vain. All is already turned upside down when Constantine, to bring an end to intestine quarrels, chooses as his exemplary sign the instrument of torture which the mistress of the world had reserved for the victims of its monstrous slave prisons.

The term Middle Ages has no meaning except in Europe. Also in Europe alone do we find this contrast between the before and the after, the Occident and the Orient, the South and the North. A great region of fairly rich lands, needing only to be wrested from the forests, was still in the first centuries of our era a retarded land. Hellenism had scarcely penetrated it. Nevertheless, something of the ancient heritage had been welcomed there. It retains, for example, the memory of what Rome had provided of the most fascinating lessons: the State and its law. But Christian sentiment reverses what Rome had founded in unity, its customs and its civilization of the Annona and the Circus.[5] For the rest, amid the marchings now become so frequent that Constantine establishes his capital on the Bosphorus as if to march out to meet them, Europe draws on the springs of Africa, India, and especially China.

The Arabs control these great marches by monopolizing the major centers of the Hellenistic culture. From the desert they had learned the power of a warrior god; and from Afghanistan to Spain, they restored or confirmed among peoples the belief in a single transcendence which Greek humanism had deprived of its symbolic power until the exhaustion of Roman materialism recalled the need for it. But this too exclusive transcendentalism of the Arab polarizes the imaginative faculty to an excessive degree, and puts too great a value on the realm of the deed. True, as a pretext confirmed by a great social renewal, it gives artisans courage and revives interest in scien-

5. The Annona: the yearly distribution of grain. Translator's note.

tific recipes, administers the heritage of the West, enriches itself with the discoveries of the East, and inaugurates the flowering of a dazzling culture. All in all, however, it provokes fewer discoveries among its own people than it stimulates in its rival, Christianity. In the end, it is sterilized when the potentates of invasion subordinate a too self-interested democracy, whose critical insubordination they fear to the point of forbidding the study of Euclid in the very places where the prolegomena to his works had been perfected. The culture of Islam is too much at the mercy of the immense spaces of Asia, from which it had borrowed so much. It comes later in date and is less tenacious, more brilliant in its first onset but less durable than Christian Europe. Having goaded Europe, Islam contributes to its advancement and yields to it.

From then on, the nature of Europe is such that, at the heart of a religious representation which progressively rehabilitates labor on sufficiently rich but demanding soils, it has at first much more to receive than to give. Certainly, at the start it fears what the infidels bring it from distant paganisms. It pretends to attribute Roland's sword, Durandel, to the diabolic, though it is the product of perfected iron metallurgies of the Blue river. It murmurs when Pope Sylvester makes use of numbers from India, and therefore suspect. But it cannot indefinitely resist the appeal of Oriental splendor. It solicits merchandise in exchange for its own rare minerals, for its Slavs, and, a little later, for the most easily manufactured of its textiles. It purchases objects of luxury, art, even of religious cults, wax tapers, bells and organs, elixirs of long life, pharmacopoeia, products of metallurgy and chemistry. It studies what China and Persia know, and unites it with what it recalls from its ancestors and its conquerors, and starts moving again in a procession of inventions that Rome had failed to recognize. Religious orthodoxy is fashioned in the image of what Antiquity had missed, in accord with the conditions of peoples still remote and still rustic, and more faithful than the people of Byzantium, too close to the epicenter of the older contradictions.

Greek Christianity has at first the more learned doctors and able jurists. But its capital, dazzling in its luxury, owes more to its trade than to its own artisans. By the time the workshops of the Northwest have diverted the tides of trade to their own profit, Byzantium, the illustrious heir of Alexander, the Caesars, Saint Paul, and the first councils, will have nothing left with which to resist the most recent of the Turkish feudal dynasties.

Heresies run through the Latin faith also, coming from the Orient on the currents which the Crusades carry back towards Jerusalem and Thrace, but Christian unity is steeped in the blood of the first minority sects. That unity is further shattered by their successors when wealth reveals to the peoples of the North the virtues of a liberty of conscience, a reflection of the freedom of entrepreneurial activities.

The religious system sprung from Judaism and the confines of Africa and Asia, given form by Pauline Hellenism, and consolidated by its battles against the infidels, accords with the necessities of the evolution of representations, by affirming that the Spirit proceeds from the Creator and Jesus, thus deifying both the progress and the pain. Europe once again goes back upstream to what has been abandoned by Rome and even Athens, to rediscover the meaning of Ionian logic. And, when ready to incorporate within itself the inventions of the rest of Eurasia, Europe goes into raptures over the beauty of that past in its Renaissance period, and breathes into it its own dynamism.

When the Greeks had discovered the syllogism, they had circumscribed the point where the psychological necessity for order is confronted in man by the staggering power of things, and there every resolve is rendered ambiguous. The expression of tragedy in Aeschylus, Euripides and Sophocles, after it had lost its pertinency for Rome and then for original Christianity, is rediscovered in European lands, mingled with its comic counterpart or distinct from it, as in the work of Shakespeare, or that of Pascal, Racine, and Molière, or that of Goethe, who least knows how to laugh. Thus they are reconverted from the hope of heaven to the profits of earth.

Between these two epochs there stretches a long period when the epic has taken the place of oratory. Latin eloquence had limited its beauty to the skillful articulation of the young patricians at a time when all was yielding to the Roman legions. By contrast, in the medieval period, when the belfries are already reaching to meet heaven, though still being built in the Roman style, as an effect of dream-like memories though in reaction against them, the hero of the epic is able to conquer with the arms of his loyalty and his faith alone. The forests yawned half open before him, miraculous creatures guided him within them, and the adversary broke off the combat before his marvelous weapons. Such illusory images have their usefulness, nevertheless, in troubled times when a swarming of petty events apparently devoid of reason incessantly opposes all lords and princes, compromising on every occasion the longed-for accord between emperor and pope. The holy unity itself is threatened when schismatics hurl the anathema at one another, at the very time they are vaguely experimenting with combining structures of order.

Yet amid this confusion, the epic supremacy of the transcendental myth bears witness to the fact that the abstract unity is ceaselessly being sought. The jests of popular literature and the symbolism of popular tales guarantee the counterbalance to the bold Gothic steeples. The wish is to save the unity of the robe of Christ, only too sadly torn by the soldiers. But already that longed-for and elusive unity in religion prefigures another which is biding its time, that of a terrestial world encircled by its ships, joined to a world of science hidden beneath the logic of speech.

Why, after the Renaissance, were the Europeans and they alone able to reassemble in their thought and their education all that needed to be known about weight, space and time, and to bring to their quantitative calculations and to their demonstrations of relationships that unity of style so necessary to the new and sudden expansion of scientific progress, a progress which will organize its terminology into scientific vocabularies? There is no possible answer except by admitting at the outset that so many diverse notions were finally lending themselves to a systematization that, though latent, they were destined to be successively rationalized before they could become a whole; and that that whole had itself to be handed over to operations which its elementary formation had caused to be conceived. But we must also add that of all the cultures which shine in a previous universal history, only those of Babylon, Ionia, and Europe are found on the trajectory which leads to modern science. Having a brief alphabet, they have in common a method for recording language. Otherwise, they are quite distinct. True, they are not so geographically distant as to prevent each from sharing in the inventions of the preceding. But because they have been historically separated by periods of night, it is as if each had to be drained of its own success in order to furnish a more perfect contribution to the universal synthesis. This marked discontinuity is the daughter of great events, reversing and shattering, yet bringing fecundity from the excess of their contradictions.

Every phase of the basic evolution had of necessity to be conducted to that extreme limit where significance finds its pertinency by abolishing the world of images which had sustained it; that is, language has to reduce the world of images of its origins to the abstractions which make science possible. Only this total substitution could strip expression of emotion and inscribe in neutralized signs the elementary notions of mass, space, and time, which in their ambiguity record the vicissitudes, perhaps as numerous but less radical, of the rest of the world.

For more than a thousand years, Western Asia, the crossroads of great lands, had prepared the surge of Alexandrian science, disengaged the syllabary from the pictogram, and experimented with the ideogram before inventing the alphabet, ordered like a numeration. This immense density of opposing efforts had not only the effect of establishing the identifications between sounds, and between drawings, but it also elaborated, via so many confrontations, the relationships between notions and the relations between relations reaching far back in their infinite depths. Words assumed an increase of pertinency from the image by dissecting it and by drawing apart from it, as well as by stripping spoken sounds of their affective power, reserving this latter for music. Words have thus been reduced to the arbitrariness of conventional correspondences in such a way that the sign, disengaged from the emotions of symbolism, is no more than a guide-mark of correlations as abstract as possible. Multiple and varying transfers between written or spoken morphological systems have stripped the dismembered words of emotion in order to adjust them to things by enabling them to identify concepts. It will take Europe a thousand years more to prepare for the final achievement of this task. Yet it is this labor which will enable discursive reason to rediscover the heart of the matter from its long delay over the manifestations of raw facts.[6] It is also necessary to circumscribe the element of chance, inscribe the search for causes within the material determinism which imprisons it, and arrange under the same laws the most commonplace fact of terrestial physics and the most cosmic fact of celestial astronomy.[7] Thus opens a new

6. These condensed sentences remind us that words began as substitutes for objects and emotions, and proceeded by metaphor and analogy to connotative references. But to make them useful for science, certain of them had to be abstracted from emotive uses to become wholly denotative and as neutral as numbers, either by specialized meanings or the invention of a new termonology. Translator's note.

7. Ch. Morazé suggests adding the following illustrations to the above sentence: It is also necessary to circumscribe the element of chance, as did the calculus of probabilities in the 17th century, inscribe the search for causes within the material determinism which imprisons it, as did the inventors of

era for a humanity no longer inspired solely by the obscure collective experience, but guided by the experimentation which finds names for concepts.

The scientific and technological revolution spreads with bourgeois wealth, nor is that a chance coincidence. If at any time in man's education there intervenes a moment when abstract intelligence prevails over emotive interpretations, there must also be a sufficient number of individuals prepared to take advantage of this stage, so that at the center of their collectivity these manifestations of the rational will lose their providential character and become entirely natural. This critical item of a sufficient density of such men appears to be achieved in Europe when there is a satisfactory increase in the number of men capable of devoting themselves to reflective thought. The looting of distant wealth, made possible by the great geographical discoveries, contributed not a little to building up to this situation by thrusting so many merchants, administrators, and financiers into mathematical and physical researches.

Nor is it by chance that this collective experience of the rational reversibility follows close on a conquest of the earth's roundness. The postulates of combinations, of chance, of causality, involved in the competitive system of the bourgeois, are expressed when the systematics of space places the mass within a play of forces comparable to the planet earth in the cosmic attraction.[8] When history has arrived at a stage where a fairly large group has carried historicity to the right stage in its development, a certain learned

---

modern physics after Bacon, and arrange under the same laws the most commonplace fact of terrestrial physics and the most cosmic fact of celestial astronomy, as did Newton, when he assimilated, for example, the study of surface tensions of liquids to his principle of universal gravitation. Note from Ch. Morazé, Feb. 10, 1971.

8. Ch. Morazé adds this further explication: 'Arithmetic combinations and the postulates which permit of treating the phenomena of chance rationally, are conclusions drawn little by little from experiments made by bourgeois society in which each entrepreneur takes chances on his venture, and the sum of all his efforts is translated into general economic laws. But these 'laws of chance' are not truly achieved until the moment when science has greatly refined the concepts of causality, and until, by example and a first stage, it has recognized the notion of force as a product of mass by acceleration. That is, the scientist has transformed practical mechanics into a system that takes into account the position and the movements of the planet in a world of universal attraction.' Letter to translator, May 26, 1970.

Europe, becoming transparent to itself, tears away the veils interposed between the physiology of the brain and the systematics of reality.

In the depths of the emotive disturbances of men there begins then to develop in a wholly new way the phenomenon of invention defined and directed by reflection. Europe, destined to play the first roles therein, will again permit itself to be carried along by the charm of the arbitrary event and the conflicts of blindness. Taking advantage of a freedom and a humanism of which it considers itself to be the sole depository, Europe will arrogate to itself the right to subjugate the rest of the world. A heritage of customs and imaginative systems from former times sweeps it along and encourages the illusion.

In Europe's means of finding itself, there is no detail without its importance in the internal perspective of the bloody misunderstandings by which its destiny will be accomplished. The many available languages of Europe, whether out of a local past, or imposed by invaders and more or less inspired by the Latin example, are sometimes accepted, sometimes resisted. According to what they retain or reject, they reveal their local vocation or announce the destinies of peoples. In Romania, though the Low Latin retains its Ciceronian syntax, the Vulgar Latin drops the declensions. But it has to find substitutes for their function, try out supplemental forms, and fix an order for the sentences. In a similar way, a certain French manner is settled upon as being logical, less stripped down than the English, less organic than the German. The order by which mathematical inventions appear from west to east, from Napier to Gauss, is inscribed in these distinctions which betray the differences of style, the same differences which will place Corneille and Racine between Shakespeare on the one hand, Schiller and Goethe on the other. National behavior also translates natural conditionings in the chronology of events whose movements will be stamped by Cromwell, Robespierre and Napoleon, Bismarck and Hitler.

Since men have not learned to read what lies beneath the sentences which they exchange, Europe will have to learn the relativity of its proud culture not from its grammarians, but in the events of tears and blood. This is the other side of the high privilege which endows humanity with reasons, machines, and motors whose significance they still do not comprehend. Humanity believed that it had reached political power forever, though it had but elaborated the tools capable of speeding up the physical entropy of the world after man had assured a relay stage in an exhausted biological evolution. Humanity has instigated a new process of development which is not that of its belated ambitions, but rather that of a humanity taking on the burden of the world, a process which can no longer be treated with contempt if any general future is to be anticipated.

10. Humanity considered

Since the great discoveries, the history of the planet is that of its unity. The first steps are confused: pillaging conquistadores, lords of the slave trade, business men devoid of scruples, for a long time could not be prevented by missionaries or philanthropists from bringing home a vast accumulation of undeserved riches. When competition among themselves and a certain dawning of opinion and of self-interest better understood force some improvement in fair-dealing, they still cling to the customs and imaginative values which had so well served Europe; viewing them, indeed, as a just counterbalance to the advantages extracted from the colonies, even though they were illusory and inadequate in the quite different lands to which they exported them. And yet, as a result of that dangerous injustice which an indifferent history makes a necessity, this accumulation of goods for the profit of one or another small, privileged political entity, for a time the center of everything until its turn comes to suffer from its own excesses, sets into motion a natural process of development destined to have world-wide consequences.

I. About two centuries ago, a small number of informed spirits became aware that the human condition was changing. In Paris, this thought drove the quarrel of the Ancients and Moderns out of fashion; and interest shifted to the indefinite progress of the human species. This shift would have been no more than a whim of the salons, one of those eddies of the mind and spirit to which the monarchical order accomodated itself as amounting to no more than a side-product of the pressures of factional unrest, had it not been that an influx and an unaccustomed production of provisions and objects, far more effective than another Voltaire would have been, effectively changed tastes and offered new ways of being happy. It was in vain for Montesquieu to point out that population was less numerous than in Roman times. Why believe him, when it was clear in so many places that everyone was living better?

This is the moment, too, when Diderot puts the emphasis on the family, no longer patriarchal but bourgeois, and agrees with Rousseau in narrowing the circle around the child. The father of the family now provides for the happiness and security of his own. He is also a worker, a generator of well-being, because as such he is an innovation. The physiocrats promise abundance to anyone who will learn how to treat the soil properly. Adam Smith legitimizes freedom of enterprise, as much more useful to the indefinite progress of every kind of production than were the privileges of the upper castes; and the Saintsimonians will proclaim the same even more harshly. Authority is no longer made legitimate by eminent right, nor by historic right; but by a present efficiency born of competition, pitiless, rivaling in inventions, rewarded by wealth, expressing itself in an enlightened public opinion. The massive vertical power of institutions claiming divine right is challenged. Power is now to become the expression of action on the level of the soil and the commercial horizon. Instead of being the conserver of the status quo, power must discover for itself the organs adapted to a perpetual recreation of laws adjusted to the changing needs of enterprise.

From this time on, society becomes individualized and parcelled out, just as the land is cut up into enclosures recorded in the land-survey offices that spring up all over Europe. Administrative regulations, rural estates, cities, and also factories, shops and bureaus, create a ceaselessly growing complex of related interests, the active nucleus of which is individuals coming from the common mass, and no longer affiliated with the upper classes. It is the era of a cycle, such as history has already and repeatedly known, when the commercial prevails over the feudal. But this time it is also something else. Its navigators and travelers having conquered the whole planet, Europe had the feeling that it owned it all, and that it had finally escaped from the fear of hostile neighbors and incursions from unknown and barbarous lands. In France, Sieyès makes himself the interpreter of the third world by challenging the pretensions of the aristocracy, heirs, he says, of Germanic invasions and now ridiculous since the national insecurity has lost its mystery. Everywhere the bourgeois feel themselves the unchallenged masters and guides of a civilization which was abolishing all violence, that of judicial torture as well as that of wars. And their immanent rights seem to them the more assured as the whole world becomes more mercentile.

The great cities and particularly the ocean ports show an improvement whose model is Great Britain where already the elaboration and execution of laws are subordinated to the material and moral ambitions of merchants and entrepreneurs. When a political earthquake finally shakes France and brings down the old Regime, it becomes evident that humanity is no longer moved solely by shifting vicissitudes within closed cultural spaces; but that, swept along on a new and irreversible current, it has leaped over the traditional boundaries.

But those who now agree to recognize in the word destiny the significance of a dynamism are less clear as to the motivations they give to it. Each European, according to his temperament, which is a reflection of the national situation, has his own way of viewing the relationship of the sciences, the arts, and the professions with the rights of man and the movements of peoples. The Germans, more distant from the Atlantic shores, where the bulk of the traffic still converges, are at first more witnesses than authors of the bourgeois revolutions which are materializing in the West before they are foreshadowed in their own land. Furthermore, the Kings of Prussia will soon make them captive for their own profit. The relative tranquility which for a time is theirs leaves the ancient crusading spirit of the Teuton reduced to a latent violence under an apparent amiability. It dedicates them to a metaphysic which turns into an exaltation of the State. The French, however, use eloquence to conceal the confusion left by a world rudely shattered, and attach themselves passionately to law and justice.

But everywhere and on all occasions the best informed no longer doubt that fortune has granted special privileges to the English, so efficient oh their ocean-girt and coal-bearing island. From then on, with this example before them, the ambitious everywhere strive to appropriate lands to draw profit from their improvement, and to put together ever more ingenious machines in their factories. They labor to participate in an ever more active commerce whose boldness frees men from the customary restraints of the fetishism of ancient beliefs. They invoke the laws of the marketplace and the objectivity of price, which they define in money as stable and as impersonal as a universal instrument should be when kept in line with length, volume, and weight as treated in England or as reformed in France by the adoption of a decimal system of measurements. All in all, behind the philosophic agitations, the emotional differences of opinion, and the endless variety of contradictory political statutes, a system of production is established, drawing its necessity from the commercial experience and inscribing the appropriate laws in its customs and codes. For more than a century, neither ideological disputes nor popular riotings will be able to prevail against the capitalist imperatives of material progress.

The passage from absolutisms to parliamentarianisms, as from the patriarchal family to the restricted family is an effect of a more rational occupancy of lands and of the lifting of restrictions that were hampering business. This achievement is accompanied by an exaltation of the individual. It is of minor importance that the latter do not combine their efforts. Bentham thinks it better that they do not do so. Let each follow his own interest; from this sum of risks will be born a law of the greatest number and the general welfare. Such is the conception of the family, of Providence, of activity, such also that of mathematics. Individual initiative, by causing society to slip out of its old molds, recovers a natural simplicity by preferring the original act to what has been previously done, and by exploring the greatest possible number of behaviors. Thus, relying on the rationale of conquests, appealing to naive hopes, on occasion criticising but never condemning in principle the materialist entrepreneurs who compete to supply Europe and the world with all speed, the austere theoreticians and men of good will speak of liberty, and of the general interest, and of progress. The newly privileged of Europe, swept along by the seductions of their own abundance, increase that abundance, while the philanthropists, seeing the poor driven from their transformed fields and often swelling the abject poverty of the sordid quarters of the cities, try to persuade themselves that the whole world will end by benefitting from these transformations. Poverty and wretchedness, aggravated by the too sudden destruction of old customs, are the more painful to tolerate since the compensations of a supernatural existence are problematical, and the latest pleasures spread out by the newly rich are the more to be envied. The dominant ideology teaches that the disparity of conditions in such exasperating evidence is the effect of a natural law which legitimizes the recourse to force to contain every riot or rebellion; and the civil laws are framed in the name of a good moral conscience reassured by the success of states which convert the feverish need to remain orderly into police regulations.

Between the centuries when piety was aimed at being brotherly and heavenly, even when it had recourse to violence, and the century when men abandoned themselves without remorse to the passion for earthly possessions, virtue was becoming vice and vice virtue, as Voltaire had put it when he condemned the idleness of monks, the affectation of poverty even while paying tribute to luxury. The new bourgeois were not all so bold; more often it suited them to combine, as the Puritans had done, a certain austerity of customs with material enrichment, whereas the old sanctity came close to wanting an orderly world to remain peasant. In France, a country priest, a shepherd, was canonized. In the cities, religion is treated as a recourse against revolution, before a new Saint Theresa[1] proposes to substitute for the passionate violence of her famous namesake the reign of goodness, the aspiration of the petty bourgeois.

The success of English liberalism is exactly that of the capitalism of competition. Economic competition is transposed into electoral competition, and draws a lesson from the premature revolutions of Cromwell's era to avoid their return. Thus, from the quarrels of royal dynasties it inherits a political system of two parties suited, like the drawing of lots, to making small differences determine the equilibrium of two assemblies liberally constituted. But then it turns out that the changes in the majority are not always chance and not always reversible. Certainly at first, the ambitions of property holders and of industry are easily contained within the inherited devices of contests between Tories and Whigs; and they conserve the King and his House of Lords, though stripping them of functional authority even though they continue to be clothed in the pomp and prestige of traditions. But when the cities grow, the device will be replaced and will substitute the labor party for liberalism.

As mercantile capitalism progresses from the shores of the Atlantic toward the Elbe, the model which works across the Channel becomes of interest to the continent. In France it stimulates principles the more peremptory and constitutions the more numerous as they clash the more often with survivals of the old methods of production. The absolutism of Richelieu, predominantly national though claiming to be Catholic, survived a long time before it was engulfed more dramatically in revolutions delayed for over a century after those in England. It then reappears in Bonapartism. Farther to the East, a

1. Theresa Martin, 1873–1897. Translator's note.

princely autocracy remains linked with feudal and corporative survivals. There liberal agitation in the universities is kept sporadic, and the parliamentarianism of Frankfort is illusory even before it blends into the Bismarckian state. Social democracy will not take on any large dimensions except by preferring the cooperative spirit to that of revolution; and the weight of sadly eroded traditions will contribute to the strength of Nazism. The high temperatures engendered by mechanical, technological, and capitalist activity warm the glass-houses where remains of ancient cultures vegetate, burdened with poisons.

Again, just as the appearance of new notions destined to promote the surge of science had provoked the return of the Pascalian soul, so the social mutation, at the period when it submerged the villages of a crippled peasantry, arouses a melancholy, a yearning for the past with a vague desire to defend it from a changing world. This finds expression in Romanticism, with overtones of anguish beneath its verbal lavishness. In a period when great novels offer a balance sheet of societies in the process of modification, poetry is lyric only, and returns to the epic model, an art forgotten in the century of Voltaire. Languages, legends, ancient costumes, are restored to a place of honor, and revive patriotisms and justify national passions at the very moment when the mechanicians begin to prepare their fearful weapons for their most murderous conflicts.

The poetic expression of regrets and historical enthusiasms makes their lyricism more appropriate to nations under pressure to snatch themselves from old dynastic empires than to deliver their proletariat from their new enslavements.

So brief were the periods separating the expansion of commercial capitalism from that of scientific industrialization that, while they inspire a new hope, both leave that hope encumbered still with ancient mythologies. The profits of the merchants had not sufficiently favored the people. For a time, they had even aggravated all poverty by accentuating among the plundered their feeling of frustration. The virus of romantic idealism appears at first to spare the bourgeois, who retain something of the Voltairian in the Christianity which it continues to mimic, satisfying themselves with an eclectic philosophy, humoring themselves by a composite esthetic whose mixed styles deserved to be treated by artists as philistine. Romanticism rages especially among the melancholy aristocrats who will transmit the tone to the bourgeosie when these feel threatened in their turn. But above all Romanticism reaches to the people. Their excessive enthusiasms appear in the streets with their facades in bad taste, within which the rational elite of the 18th century would never have recognized themselves. These emotions, at first patriotic, turn warlike. Between Sterne and Byron, *Rameau's Nephew* by Diderot and Victor Hugo's *The Legend of the Centuries* the epoch recovers its appeal; but also, between Kant, Hegel, and Fichte, the State is surrendered to its deification.

This longing for heroism, which contributes to the encouragement of the dissatisfactions and unrests of a daily life crippled by new modes of production, caused guileless spirits such as Michelet and the romantic socialists to believe that if the people will but appropriate to themselves the seigneurial honor, they will lift themselves to dignity. The lessons of Montesquieu are forgotten.[2] Then, and according to the stage of their advancement in social transformations, England, and France as well, export their heroic legends into the great colonial adventure, thereby furnishing honorable pretexts for the mercantile profits. Also France now and then, and especially Germany, yield to warrior princes.

Much farther to the East lies the immense empire created by Moscow out of a collection of very diverse ethnic groups; and here a revolution, the latest of those for which England provided the first incomplete model, will snatch away the dominion of merchant and autocracy, and will unite quite disparate republics into a single communism.

II. Lenin will affirm the vocation of the Russian proletariat, and at the same time will attribute the survival of Western capitalisms to their colonial imperialisms. But even if Marx did not perceive the whole importance of Russia and Asia until the end of his life, the credit no less reverts to him for having conceived the system antithetic to that which flourished at the heart of mercantile industrialism and in the moral shelter of false shows of idealism. Perhaps he also revived the defenses of these latter by too crudely assuming a materialism designed to shock the liberals who had furnished him his model, but who defended themselves the more bitterly because he ended by justifying a communist dictatorship. Yet Marx, having so early and so deeply suffered from the ambiguity

---

2. Montesquieu wrote that as honor was necessary to aristocracy, so virtue was to a republic, whereas a dictator relies on fear, having no use for virtue and regarding honor as dangerous. Translator's note.

of his time, himself offered a better critique of it than anyone else. However, a son of Europe, he waited for his proletariat to listen to him and to avenge themselves, when it was outside of Europe that they would declare him correct. His premonitions will not be realized in England where he worked most, nor in France, mother of modern revolutions, nor in Germany, whose power of thought he so much appreciated. Even less will they find realization in the United States of America, a nation born of the colonial adventure and developing as its most successful enterprise. In these different areas, Marx's influence will run up against the advantages which the workers will finally effectively extract from the exploitation of new or backward lands. Setting aside the doubtful case of Germany, where ambivalence will attract Nazism before provoking a break with it, it is in the least developed countries and those reduced to the status of tributaries that passions issuing from tradition will unite demands for independence with the demands of the oppressed classes to give Marxism the repercussions we all know about.

This great and recent success admits that Marx was right in having condemned freedom of enterprise in the name of a more general system of order and property, and in the name of a more general right to be. But humanity remains still too divided by its previous evolution for a union of the proletariat of all countries to replace the quarrels among states. States evolve each in its own rhythm, and even find themselves reinforced in those countries where, having assumed authority over the workers, they have to defend the advantages they have gained, or simply their own special character, against attacks, threats, or external rivalries. In our own time, as since the neolithic age, the localized effects of mass have as their corollaries rivalries and, on occasion, violences. Even more than the great deception of idealism would admit, death seizes on the living, and the past on the present. Like the Encyclopedists, Marx took progress for a victory, if not of the Spirit as Hegel asserted, at least of men over things, though, just as Rousseau had suspected, it is only a new way by which nature takes control over what it gave birth to.

This optical error was that of an era when the position of scientific discoveries remained minimal in the process of industrialization. The tools of the textile industry were only those of a surprising improvement, but not revolutionary of professions of custom immemorial. The smelting of iron had systematized procedures discovered by skillful adaptations of the inventions of a preceding century, already practiced in innumerable little workshops of the

China of the Han dynasty. The process of credit and banking, aside perhaps from certain actuarial operations, shared in the simplifications of arithmetic, and owed very little to post-Cartesian mathematics. The techniques of the 19th century, even though analyzed with a new spirit, amounted to little more than an amelioration of many other previous ones, before they were changed by the technologies whose efficiency will not be revealed until much later by electricity and chemistry.

At the time of Marx, commerce still dominated industry too thoroughly for the engineer not to be subordinated to businessmen and financiers, and motivated by the representations which justified them. All still depends very much on these representations, especially in the West which will attract the major part of these practices and beliefs. Science is not bourgeois; that it has proved and proves at the heart of communisms. But since it is from the collective experience of individualisms that it has drawn its new concepts, it is first found to be serving those who have served it. Science has also thrown liberal societies into immediately profitable distant imperialisms, but they were due to come to their end and find their achievement, as Lenin had foreboded, in the great graveyards of Europe.

The failure of Communism in the West and the bourgeois delusion which precipitated peoples into disastrous confrontations appear, indeed, to have the same cause: namely, the survival of an ensemble of inherited representations from the pre-scientific era, out of touch with the radical change of structures brought about by technological invention. War, therefore, will remain among peoples as the supreme recourse, that judgment of God to which ancient customs had made appeal in their trial by duel. Diverted from their future by this ill-considered reference to the past, the democratic nations of Europe equate their honor with the warlike virtues by which that feudalism which they were rejecting had prevailed. This narrowness of view and this inconsistency distorted and falsified the natural principles of economic rivalry, and imperceptibly substituted for them the synarchic or intergroup effects of mutual understandings within the States, even while continuing to transfer the ever more violent conflicts to their political frontiers. They disguise badly understood material conditionings under the old masks of heroism. The monstrous aggravation of wars is the effect of a lag in the imaginative understanding of the conquests which a still greatly restricted scientific elite is imposing on the concrete world.

Marxism could not prevent western Europe from getting involved in the colonial adventure. This European area, which owed its last successes more to the contours of its smallness than to the wealth long exploited from its own soil and subsoil, found overseas much too easily what it needed for its extraordinary expansion. Its economic system, transplanted to the immense virgin surfaces and abundant mineral beds of North America in no way limited political imperialism to that area, except to substitute for it a tendency toward a financial conquest of the world, paired with controls to guarantee its own security. In both cases, it was believed and still is believed in good faith that they enrich the countries that they endow with roads, telegraph lines, railroads, and seaports, all material equipments which nevertheless combine to empty the countries of their first raw materials, and to over-involve their elite, too soon won over to the new principles, into substituting in the labor centers products that sell well instead of products that are needed for the survival of their own peoples. There where they have been transplanted, the judicial codes and mercantile customs, the progress of Europe, too often have become the causes of troubles and degeneration. They have compromised the traditional conditions of the fragile happiness and the old regulations of these distant countries, by means of which the populations adjusted numbers to resources. Even the marvelous medical discoveries seemed to oppose their own aims as they were the more generously distributed. Though they caused many more new-born to survive, they destined them to poverty; by healing adults, they doomed them to hunger. In terms of concrete representations, nothing is more absurd than the ornamentations offered by colonization to the great cities which it has raised up overseas, the pastiche of Victorian art out of its own pseudo-classic, false Byzantine, false Gothic, and false Tuscan.

No great literary work has put in its true terms this problem of the relations between colonizers and colonized; at least, not unless one accepts as such the book by Harriet Beecher Stowe which in 1851, in the heart of the nation where colonialism was an internal phenomenon, called attention to the sad lot of Uncle Tom. The rest are mostly narratives of adventures or exotic descriptions.[3] This delay in literary understanding is doubtless an effect of the romantic tidal

---

3. It is possible that Ch. Morazé overlooks here a body of less than great literature which touched on the sad state of natives blessed by the commerce of the nineteenth century — for example, Melville's descriptions of Hawaii, anti-slavery literature in the United States, etc. Translator's note.

wave, which was such that in the France that knew 1789, one had to wait more than a century before Marcel Proust could analyze the emotive psychology of the aristocratic ritual, as it aged within the bourgeois society that corrupted it. In a world so rapidly transformed by science, society will need more sciences still, and precisely those which have as their object to reveal society to itself. Marx is a prelude to sociology, Pavlov and Freud transform psychology; and it is in this context that anthropologies are elaborated, to project positive studies of what are still called races.

Before industrialization, the most brilliant successes of art accompanied the slow social achievements without any abrupt involutions. Nor, up to the esthetic revolutions of the twentieth century, will they offer proof of anything but a breathless effort, lagging behind the machines, though ahead of the tastes of an uprooted public.

The great universal representations gradually waste away. Catholicity has lost something of its pertinency, Christianity of its unity, even before cosmopolitanism is stripped of its early, ephemeral enthusiasms. Yet the need for images had substituted particular ones for the collective ones. Material conditions have dislocated the old solidarities to set up an obvious universalism in its concrete appearances, but one which is an unknown quantity in its emotive substructures. Now comes the imaginative faculty, in its most arbitrary manner, to unite the recent technology to traditional aspirations. It creates churches, passing over the oddest, such as those of positivism in France and Brazil, of Christian Science in the United States, or again the Tai-pings in China or the god Cargo in Oceania. If religions expose their embarrassments in such heresies, the poets are no happier, even when they are suspicious of the new truth. From Baudelaire to Rimbaud, or from Verhaeren to Aragon, they go through a period of great testing. They are forced to turn within, to seek in the depths of the soul the sentiment of a common humanity no longer readily provided by the collectivity. Even the poets in Russia, who find themselves in a position to lend inspiration to a great revolution, are soon disconcerted by its consequences, or sometimes depressed to the point of despair.

For two or three centuries, man has been witness to an upsetting era. Drawn along by his own scientific achievements, he sees the fragmentation of the world his imaginative powers had created. The branches of invention, by specializing, become incomprehensible to one another. The most universal of languages in its rational foundations, that of science, is differentiated to such a degree by self-multiplication that it becomes less commonly available than the vulgate languages, which can at least be translated. This contradictory process has contrived to give modern societies an excessive feeling of their own freedom, but at the same time to subject them to a certain anxiety. For this reason, perhaps, art renounces the appearance of objects with a consequent gain in conceptual structures prompted by emotive modifications. Further, positive knowledge, working with the electronics of the brain, has lead to the discovery of the chemistry of feelings. We have still to research how nature transmits its messages of organization from one culture to another, and from parents to children, prefiguring those which assure the cohesiveness of the individual within the social. Nor does man understand existence itself any better, though he is more aware of the overturning of his situation in the world. He knows that the terrible path he has trod through total wars, and that which draws him toward strategies of annihilation, were and remain the deed of an ingenuity betrayed. He guesses that the inconsistency and thoughtlessness of the masters of his economy deliver the masses over to the hallucinatory passions of those they call to be the leaders.

The historic event has lost neither its mystery nor its power. Nevertheless, if science makes that event terrifying, the societies which it transforms simplify the event as much as they magnify it. Besides the innumerable individual and national destinies which this century's wars, and the wars still being plotted, have changed, stimulated, or shattered, the designs of the obscure disaster now take on the dimensions of the planet. Scarcely twenty-five years have passed since capitalism and communism were allied to crush Nazism and to condemn its principles and their agents, and since the disinherited peoples who had been witness to the last and worst of the dramas spawned by Europe have in their turn been sucked into the cyclone of history. With the United States and China, these are the two greatest branches of human evolution which confront each other. Heirs of the greatest successes of the Occident and the Orient, they embody the ultimate dilemma: Is it by virtue of an abundance endlessly piled up by privileged societies, or by beginning with a return to an equality of material conditions, that humanity will protect itself from the distortions imposed by things, whose laws thus far have sought progress at the price of wars? If a moral evolution is to conform to the intellectual evolution which brought us the art of demonstration, that is, that of an operative reversibility, and the condition needed for a development of the efficient nomenclatures of science, the future lies to the East, whose zones of conflict will become the Ionia of the new cultural miracle. The responsibles for the sufferings which Indo-China is going through, and which Russia surmounted, would have been the enforced, unwitting, or crippled accomplices of nature. Therefore, it is important to know how this same nature which has made conflict the first condition of existence, may grant humanity a chance to transcend the greatest conflict yet to be imagined, and may show us how to control the mutation which may enable us, in the name of a better order, to escape that extermination which would close the fate of gigantisms.

III. It is not out of pure generosity alone that Canada is feeding China. Certain interests find it to their advantage. Besides, the most powerful of industrial nations, the United States, begins to sense that it is not only the first colonial territory to have revolted against a parent state, but is also the greatest success of all colonial enterprises. However remarkable the rising level of living among the inhabitants of the United States, it does not necessarily carry everything with it in a common upward movement. More than one fourth of its inhabitants are aware of their subordinate state as a part of the painful and violent symptoms of all decolonization: for the poor of the colonizing element find themselves in sharp conflict with the colonized element in its defiance of the spirit of submission that held its ancestors in obedience.[4]

A general process confronts social classes or privileged or exploited nations, and forces the human world to take stock of its identity.

Subtle plays of attraction and repulsion, secret channels of espionage, the interdependence of schools, the paths directed away from commerce, have endowed the laboratories of Pekin with informations and materials elaborated by the Anglo-Saxons as well as with scholars and scientists trained in their country. These phenomena are small in size, as the infinitesimal and initial modifications from which the great creations of life have issued have always been. They are revealers of a tendency toward an interdependent unity among men.

4. Ch. Morazé adds this note: 'At the moment John Kennedy was summoning the economy on the path of the "great society", the social disparities became less supportable, and racial troubles the more violent; at the same time, it seems to me, the great university revolts were born.' Note, Feb. 10, 1971.

Furthermore, and above all, science no longer appears so dreaded because of its applications as because of its incompleteness. Universal in its extension, it is as yet far from being what it can be in its understanding. Its products and its lessons are well distributed everywhere, but still too attached to physics, which best lends itself to this; but it is far from having proved itself in the biological, the social, the physiological. Therefore, its technical and economic consequences have destroyed the natural regulations for which deliberately artificial ones will have to be substituted. Their success will not be the result merely of a naive good will, but a process entered upon according to the laws and the necessity of life itself. Science, fruit of a unitary religious concept which it opposed at its birth, but guided by a moral unity, is destined to reestablish that unity. Its condition is that of nature itself, from which it issued, and which it transforms without repudiating it.

Viewed in the light of the nearest aims which men propose for themselves, their labor may appear to push them farther away from that basic need for unity. Yet they are brought back to it by force, under the pressure of imperatives which they unwittingly obey. There is already no economic or political system which can dispense with studies of markets or strategic calculations. A profound tendency of a general organicism is demonstrated in short term decisions, a tendency that refers enterprises born of a purely arbitrary decision back to an era which has already run its course. Such a tendency announces new eras in which simple and complex verifications reveal the existence of what was already implicit and its impending realization.

Toward the middle of the twentieth century, the energy obtained from the combustion of coal and petroleum was already passing ten times that which mankind, up to the eighteenth century, had been satisfied to get from running water, winds, draft animals and animals of burden, or from burning wood. For millenia, humanity had been satisfied to draw on a very small portion of solar energy, such as meteorological agents, as well as vegetable and animal life, received and dispensed daily. Then humanity undertook a great increase of its stationary power by utilizing the reserves of coal, and materials of organic origin buried during geologic eras. If it had not discovered the means of breaking the atom, it would have condemned itself in a few centuries to an exhaustion of the resources whose accumulation had required an immemorial duration of time.

According to perspectives and prospectives today, the history of human labor has gone through two phases and is preparing a third, respectively characterized by the use of living energy in the first, then fossil energy, and finally artificial energy. The second phase is necessarily transitional, and capable only of assuring the passage from the natural to the technological. No doubt the way men once shared in solar energy by the intermediary of vegetative cycles was far from exhausting all resources. But a more direct utilization of the sun's daytime rays or a more judicious use of marine potentials is no longer realizable without science.

Though none of the responsible entrepreneurs had dreamed of it, mankind of the last century was defying the future by involving itself in a cumulative progress whose pursuit was dependent on unforeseeable discoveries. Those who took this gamble without suspecting it were more enthusiastic than clear-sighted. Still motivated more by unconscious inspirations than by a calculated strategy, they obey the hope that things, the accomplices to man's survival, will lend themselves no less to an indefinite acceleration of his industrial labors. The human environment is supposed to be predestined to reward man's cerebral elaborations which it has served as a guide and as a setting. Indeed, the providential alliance of nature and its creature, man, is not a novelty, hope being the oldest of the acts of faith. On the contrary, the first awareness of a progression, of its changes in reason or more especially in nature, of arithmetic and geometry, is an immense act of faith, as is also the manner by which reality will henceforth be apprehended, less by the implicit collective experience than by virtue of experimentations making use of specific tools. The world, after having manifested itself chiefly as if by itself and almost spontaneously, responds now to questions worked out by reflection. The imagination at work is less called upon to compose its representations by acting them out in natural landscapes than by elaborating them after reflection, in the heart of its manufactured environments.

This revolution in perspective is not historically, nor in its initial impetus, a direct effect of science. Laboratory work, when it first became aware of itself, still appeared more an effect than a cause of the acceleration of progress. Somewhat more than a century was needed before men grasped that the new definition of the human calling and happiness lay not only in the growth and increase by commerce through known processes, but also in the taming of a new nature to dynamisms then unsuspected.

Now, far from the moral life having to suffer from this new

symbiosis between human activity and things, it was able to find therein assurance of a flowering of every man in his irreducible reality made for grace.

The bloody battles between human groups, societies, classes, or nations, are in the nature of natural selections. It needs a delicate scalpel to recognize among the profound textures of history the fine essential network which, in its development, causes the progressive to prevail over the involutive. In all the great events on their appropriate scale, behind the thousand manifestations of the occasional, the fantasied, and the ephemeral, there hides a small but irreducible and irreversible modification of structures which build men better in their mutual relationships and in their relations to things. A reality is being built, and so slowly that only with difficulty is it noticed; but it reaches such dimensions that the data which accompany it demand all our attention.

The most significant expression of this reality is supplied by the way human labor is accomplished today. It has been estimated that in 1937 all the energy produced was the equivalent of fourteen billion tons of coal. Of this total, only a billion corresponds to what man consumes to live and to feed his muscular effort; around two billion serves to nourish draft and pack animals; all the rest is directly applied to machines. Humanity has thus increased its muscular power more than tenfold. Considering that the human body is a motor of feeble efficiency, hardly restoring efficiently more than two per cent of what it consumes, we may state that men dispose of five hundred times more calories than they furnish themselves; and we must further take into account that the number of those employed in taking from nature the power of coal, petroleum, or running waters, is very small in relation to the number of workers over the globe who remain with traditional labors. One may measure then how infinitesimal is the portion of energy issuing directly from muscular power in relation to that put to work by cerebral power in our industrial installations. The relation thus obtained suggests a comparison between what a regulator borrows and what a motor releases, whose power is controlled by a regulator.

But the comparison of the relations between the human being and the motor is not quite pertinent. The regulation of the motor comes from a fixed system, but not so that of the human being. Actually, we have but to refer to one or two centuries ago, before mines, dams, or petroleum refineries had begun to function to note that the figures present quite a different pattern. The proportion between what man was producing by muscular labor and what part he played in the total was not then in some thousandths, but a fourth or a fifth. At that time, mankind furnished with its bodies and its muscles, and by itself, the greater part of the power it utilized; and if he benefitted by a surplus, he had to put out effort in the thousands, whereas now in a few tens of efforts man puts nature to work by discovering its laws and conforming to them.

The model thus presented is obviously not precise, but it illustrates in some degree what each can comprehend if he considers the new industrial condition. It suggests comparing the connection between human labor and harnessed energy with that which exists between nervous and muscular expenditures. What the neurons consume is very little as compared with what the muscles do, but this little is organizing in function, and has infinitely multiplied the usefulness of its activities. In sum, two evolutive hierarchies are outlined, placing man in relation to things, and brain in relation to body; that is, two stages of regulation and control, or rather two domains of organization correlative to one another, whose development is not at all uniform, since, at an arbitrarily given period, efficiency increases in the one, thus suggesting that something analogous could have been produced in the other.

To make clearer the importance of this phenomenon, it must be regarded as not just any event among others, but instead as a great mutation, long and unconsciously prepared. By way of illustration, let us make use of an image, imperfect and too condensed, yet indicating a fundamental process. Anyone observing a living embryo is struck with admiration as he watches how the nerve fibre, at first independent of the muscle for which it is destined, unites with the muscle by elongating at the speed of some hundredth of a millimetre per hour. Its extremity, fed by the cell which it lengthens, seeks its path across the other tissues as if mysteriously guided by factors apparently mechanical, but which, with an effect of finality, lead it confidently to its goal. The event is completed when the linkage is consolidated between the two elements of the two systems, nerval and muscular, the one finding its pole in the brain, the other destined to place the being in its milieu.

Now, in the order of mental and technical progresses an identical process likewise takes place. That process shares in all the lessons that human labor offers and imposes on reflection; it finds its paths in the depths of cultures, across discoveries of equations and inventions of words that can be utilized to make these discoveries pertinent to physics. It is guided by social adjustments organizing the connections of productions at the heart of a new dominant class, as a consequence of enlarging needs and by virtue of the abundance assembled by commerce. Finally it reaches the point where it affects the industrial effort, and from then on it animates or rather revolutionizes it, integrates inventions into it, multiplies its power, and promises profit to a great many more men.

It is easy to specify the moment when science and labor come together in a particular way, so that the human condition is profoundly altered thereafter. In the eighteenth century, the laboratory is still relatively independent of an industry which itself is growing by perfecting procedures long known, though the artisan's ingenuity, properly speaking, borrows little from science. In the twentieth century, the great significant industrial activities are inspired by technological and economic inventions inconceivable without an immense, slow, and preliminary theoretical activity, carried on by virtue of an operative language and by systematic experimentation. In the nineteenth century, after a long period during which no one could have foreseen what human labor would become, there occurred a specific contact between the body of cerebral elaborations and the potential resources offered by nature, a contact aimed at directing action more intelligently. It would be an over-simplification not to see that previously and in a thousand instances some discovery of principle had already influenced certain effective procedures through which the discovery had been stimulated. The innovation of the nineteenth century is that not only an element of science but a great systematized whole of scientific procedures affects by its power and its organicism all economic procedures which have themselves reached the stage of development that prepares them for this subordination.

This event is also an advent. It constitutes a mutation in human evolution, though it is not such that all the past is discarded or that the new humanity erases the heritage of the old within itself. On the contrary, it is when humanity is thus transformed that it undertakes with youthful ardor to research and conserve all traces of its past, that it reexamines the value of that past, finally, as if awakened to the fact that since what had been accomplished cannot reproduce itself, it is important to preserve what is left from destruction. Since every moment assumes an appropriate meaning within a differentiated and irreversible succession, new lessons are added to the immemorial ones which they challenge in the name of what will shift the potentialities of societies by increasing the value of time already experienced. In short, at every moment man remembers older lessons, but also challenges them, and thus adds new lessons. This looking back toward past history has had disastrous consequences insofar as it has aroused feelings. But it can be an occasion for a deliverance, as biology and the sciences of man promise, and as economy forces it to be.

Nations of great industries begin to manufacture artificially something like an equivalent of what they still draw from the soil of others. They also already approach the technological progress which will force them, if they wish to maintain their active vigor, to come to the aid of peoples whom they only recently plundered. The most powerful of these nations has so heaped its productions on its citizens that it has almost reached the degree of saturation beyond which it will soon produce a reversal of the active axis of its desires. This phenomenon once affected an ancient culture, and the scene was Rome. In a moment so decisive and of so extreme a character, all remains still to be clarified, though the essential fact, if not already determined, is at least as if destined to be the reverse of what has been achieved. But today presents this new aspect, that all humanity is caught in this great see-saw movement: China is recovering its technical vigor.

Social sciences, the sciences of man, will help humanity resolve this entirely new difficulty that confronts it — will help it to rejuvenate from within, and to succeed itself, to bring home to every man the process of shift and change which up to now has guaranteed substitutions of peoples and classes. Up until now it has not been very important that an old collective body was aging; another young one was rising somewhere. Now, humanity, condemned to be one body, is its own relay, and must find within itself the new substitutes for the old. This phenomenon already permits us to suspect infinite dimensions and implications. Leaders of States, profiting by the interest in history aroused in those who are disquieted by the reversal of conditions, play a dangerous part in these fascinations with the past. The effect of this reaction is that they gain for themselves a prestige whose legitimacy, nevertheless, can only be of value now by reference to the future. They involve the peoples in dreadful involutions. If the peoples' will is lacking, the force of things will tempt the men of power to turn back to strict rules and the most commonplace morality.

Here we are, after some twenty-five years, assaulted by millions of images, transmitted to us by planetary networks of information. Each one of us becomes at once more unique and more solitary as well as more diverse and more dependent than man ever was before. The first result of the development of information is a personalization of power. There are also other effects, and of greater scope.

If peoples, the masses, who are bewitched by the leaders of State whom they themselves have elevated, still rely on them to play the part of being the great representations of the collective life, then major politics becomes every year more of a compulsory organization and an interpretation forced upon us. The conditions for the imaginative power of mankind are reversed. The spontaneity, the invention, the hazard and suspense of life, cease to be the exclusive privilege of the traditional theatres of action, the palaces of olden times with their magnificent rituals. One after another these grand palaces become museums. Authority will, of course, remain for a long time, especially at the heart of deluded nations, as an impressive bit of stage business, authorizing licences and imposing its conventions on the credulity of the masses barely detached from their past. But from now on, thanks to information and instruction, it is in each man that the new currents which converge in the general progress must find their source. Western man, accustomed to the part played by great deeds symbolizing interests taken for universals, and stimulated by the incessant challenge of a plurality of parties, still remains attached to an outmoded scenario, and that at a time when every major action takes on the dimensions of the whole globe. This means that each nation is better represented by fewer actors and a better plot. It also means that in place of that all too costly representation within the narrow confines of a nation, some other must be substituted as universal as humanity itself, such as the least of men feels within himself.

Already heads of parties, heads of States, are celebrities but conditionally; that is to say, not only by virtue of what they can break or crush, as in the days when, no matter what they did, they were the dazzling and animating figures of the world, but more importantly by what they can contribute to progress. Never has it been made easier than today to distinguish the harmful from the useful as concerns heroes, the involutive from the progressive. In former times, ringleaders in the game could be exalted, especially when they violated the most common morality; already they begin to be no longer so hailed except to the degree to which they conform to morality. The wide and rapid dissemination of what they do submits them to a universal and immediate judgment. This fact devalues what used to be called great deeds, those which once were so able to profit by an unconditional esteem precisely because a very indirect transmission of information and unreliable memories purified them of blood and filth, now become much less easily washed away.

And perhaps we shall not need to wait a lot longer before another formidable privilege of the great is lost. To the degree that religions, arts and poetry turn within, and the possibilities of invention spread out before a far greater number of men, the possibilities of action at the top of the hierarchies called on to coordinate efforts will be restricted. Decision becomes automatic. True, certain ways we have today of envisaging that prospect and of sharing in its methods are still but caricatures of what they will become. So far we have mastered but a few simplified formulas dealing with partial informations. From these errors the event will bring justice in misfortune and blood. But in the end, the networks of objectivity will bind all together again.

Just as in each brain there occurs a moment when the intellectual operation prevails over the instinctive gesture, so humanity also enters upon its maturity. Amid the blossomings of new beauties issuing from unforeseeable emenations, humanity in its turn and in its totality becomes reflective. The complaints we hear are no longer those of Hesiod.[5] The vindications we accept are no longer those of Machiavelli. Here nature comes to our aid, by developing a system of forces which, far from restraining inward thought, return it to its spontaneity by the gift of a more realizable inspiration, bearer of infinite wonders. In return, on those in positions of responsibility over great numbers she imposes the exactitude of arithmetic and its integrity.

The nature of historicity will not be changed by the above. The springs of events will not cease flowing, but the scale is already being reduced. Historic action, by acquiring the dimensions of the planet and the limit of what can be tolerated on it, reduces the initiative of princes and gives value to that of individuals of all sorts. After the appropriate duration of time shall have run its course and the last dramas of collective rivalries have been ended, every man capable of enduring in solitude his own tragedy will become a locus of history.

5. Hesiod's *Works and Days* bewails man's degeneration since a golden age. Translator's note.

As for the world assembly, it will arise from an organization less rational than logical, one that will reduce the element of chance insofar as science can do so.

Modern theoreticians of the prospects ahead assert that the historic era is but one of those traversed by humanity, and that we are even now emerging from it. They do not err in suggesting that after having submitted for so many centuries to the heavy weight of history, some solution is possible, one of those collective convulsions out of which scientific progress is born. This progress, once arrived at a certain degree of success, may be able to shield man, not from those events which at the cost of suffering and pain create a human being, a belief, or an achievement, nor from those which respond to the questions put to laboratory apparatuses, but at least, perhaps, from those events in which men rise in masses and confront one another in the blind violence of crowds. It is after all possible that we are being led toward a certain humanitarian morality, on a pattern transformed by intellect from what were the emotional equilibriums of savages of the earliest millenia of pre-history.

Nevertheless, this goal will not be reached so long as flagrant injustices left by history are not rectified, and the last and more serious disequilibriums corrected, those which today put the rich and their victims over against one another. We are on the verge of living the moments of this necessary compensation, this last peril, and this great hope.

Index

In a work so rich in topical allusions, it is difficult to Index as specifically as one might do for the ordinary historical text. The aim has been to supply a guide for reference. Translator's note.